Praise for *No Way Out of This*

T0013457

"You'll laugh at Lick's wry sense of hum
as she watches her soulmate lose his dignity, memories, and mind.
No Way Out of This is a candle in the dark for the millions of men
and women who are caring for a loved one with Alzeimer's and other
neurodegenerative diseases."

—Gail McCormick, author of *Zoya's Gift: Building a Bridge
to a Global Family*

"Sue Fagalde Lick's moving memoir is an intimate story of a journey of love.
Told with unblinking honesty, Lick takes us on the many twists and turns
and through all the textured feelings that come with caring for a loved one
as the familiar parts of them wane. Lick pulled me into caring deeply for
her, her beloved Fred, and their rambunctious dogs. They will linger with
me through the tenderness Lick conveys in her powerful writing."

—Jackie Shannon Hollis, author of
This Particular Happiness: A Childless Love Story

"Sue's personal story highlights the larger failings of American society:
undertrained and callous caregivers, inadequate facilities, and the absence
of social or financial support. Are life, growth, and transformation of the
best kind possible for a spouse after a partner's diagnosis? Lick answers
a resounding yes. This is a book for anyone who knows someone with
dementia—which, like it or not, will eventually be all of us."

—Deborah A. Lott, author of *Don't Go Crazy Without Me*

"This is an essential and beautiful memoir about the reality of loving
and caring for a partner with Alzheimer's, about the broken and confused state of both private and state-funded caring institutions, about
the loneliness of the ambiguous loss of losing your partner long before
they die, and about how even the deepest love can only do so much."

—Jody Day, psychotherapist, founder of Gateway Women,
and author of *Living the Life Unexpected: How to Find Hope,
Meaning and a Fulfilling Life Without Children*

No Way Out of This

No Way Out of This

Loving a Partner with Alzheimer's

Sue Fagalde Lick

SHE WRITES PRESS

Published 2024
Printed in the United States of America
Print ISBN: 978-1-64742-686-6
E-ISBN: 978-1-64742-687-3
Library of Congress Control Number: 2023923262

For information, address:
She Writes Press
1569 Solano Ave #546
Berkeley, CA 94707

Interior Design by Kiran Spees

She Writes Press is a division of SparkPoint Studio, LLC.

Names and identifying characteristics have been changed to protect the privacy of certain individuals.

For Fred, who showed me that
everything is possible

Contents

Preface
On the Floor

I should have seen it coming, but I didn't.

It was a Thursday in late January 2009. I had let my errands pile up. I needed to retrieve the mail, buy office supplies, and pick up three hundred copies of *Stories Grandma Never Told*, my book about Portuguese women, at the printer. My husband, Fred, waved me out the door, saying, "Go. I'll be fine."

I said I'd be back in an hour and drove north across the Yaquina Bay Bridge into Newport, our closest town on the Oregon coast.

An hour later, singing along to the stereo, the car full of office supplies and books, I rolled back onto 97th Court in South Beach and noticed a blue rope in the grass at the side of the narrow, wooded road. Odd. In the driveway, I saw Fred, bent over, limping, his pant legs bloody. My big yellow dog, Annie, ran past the car.

Engine still running, I rolled down the window to ask what was going on. Fred, fighting tears, told me Annie and her brother, Chico, had gotten out. "I ran like hell after them, and I fell." He pointed to the jagged place in the sidewalk where he tripped.

"I'm not good," he said. "I'm hurt. I lost it. I lost them." Tears streamed down his face.

I shouldn't have left him. It had been seven years since, at age sixty-five, he had started showing symptoms of Alzheimer's disease (AD), the most common form of dementia, and five years since the official diagnosis. He no longer knew what day it was, how to use a telephone, or how to turn on the television. He wandered at night, hallucinating. Paid caregivers watched him several hours a week so I could teach my writing classes at the community college and play the piano at Sacred Heart Church. But he'd seemed to be having a clear-headed day and hadn't wanted to tag along.

"I was picking up poop in the backyard, and the dogs got out," he said. "They went across the street, then ran down 97th and that other street. The big guy who lives there tried to help me. We got the black one, but the other one got away."

As I got out of the car, Annie dashed up to me. I dragged her into the house. Chico barked from the backyard.

"Where are you hurt?" I asked Fred.

He pointed to his back just above the belt and showed me a bloody scrape on his knee.

"Do you need to go to the hospital?"

"No . . . yes."

I fed the dogs, locked the house and drove us back into Newport. Fred complained at every turn and bump. Halfway there, he asked, "Where are we going?"

At the hospital, Fred couldn't undress himself. I pulled off his shoes, shirt, and pants, and tied on his hospital gown. Nurses cleaned up his knee and gave him a tetanus shot. I kept telling the hospital staff that Fred had Alzheimer's disease. I wished they'd put it on his chart in big red letters so they'd stop asking him questions he couldn't answer.

The doctor, whom the staff called "Dr. P.," said Fred had strained a muscle in his back. It would heal, but he'd need to relax and take pain-killers for a while. We came away with prescriptions and instructions.

Off to Rite Aid pharmacy, then to the Chalet restaurant for dinner while we waited for Fred's meds. Sitting across from Fred in the booth, I watched as he tore apart his pancakes with his hands, splattering maple syrup on his green flannel shirt.

"How is your back?" I asked.

"My back? Fine."

I ate my meatloaf and mashed potatoes in silence, hoping no one we knew would see the mess Fred was making.

By nine at night, we were home. Fred and the dogs fell asleep in the living room, while I watched TV in the guest room. Later, I gave him pills, helped him into his PJs, and put everybody to bed. My books were still in the car.

Fred and I no longer slept in the same room. I snored and stayed up much later than he did. He hallucinated, sometimes punching me or crawling over me to get at people or animals he saw in the dark. It was easier to each have our own beds, even if I was half-awake most nights, waiting to help him when he got lost on the way to the bathroom.

The night after he fell, he got up and used the restroom on his own.

"Are you okay?" I called.

"Fine."

I lay with my eyes open until I heard him crawl back into bed. I felt guilty. If I hadn't left him alone, the dogs still might have gotten out, but I could have helped. Annie and Chico were my dogs, my babies. Half Labrador retriever, half Staffordshire bull terrier, they totaled over a hundred pounds of wild energy, and Fred couldn't handle them. Not only were my dogs responsible for Fred's fall, but I had never gotten that jagged piece of sidewalk fixed, even though I knew it was dangerous, especially for someone whose dementia had affected his balance.

He could have fallen even if I was home. He wanted these dogs, too. He told me to go run my errands. But I should have known better.

On Friday, the day after Fred's fall, I decided that Vicodin was a miracle drug. He seemed less confused than usual, and he walked upright without pain.

But the following morning, everything changed.

At seven thirty, I awoke to Fred hollering from the bedroom floor. He had fallen and couldn't get up. When I tried to help him, he screamed. I gave him a Vicodin pill and sat with him at the foot of the bed. He didn't remember why he was in pain.

A half hour later, we were still on the floor. Fred's back hurt too much to move. I called 911, got dressed, fed the dogs, and put them outside.

Fred went off in the ambulance as the two couples who shared our street in the woods watched. I packed his clothes and drove to the hospital, where I was told to wait until Fred was settled in bed.

I paced, watching a picture of fish swimming on the TV screen in the waiting room. I suppose it was meant to be soothing.

"Mrs. Lick?" a nurse called, holding the door open for me.

Fred lay on a narrow bed, hooked to blood pressure and pulse monitors and an IV. A nurse told me the doctor would be in soon. I took my place in the plastic chair beside him.

"I'm sorry," Fred said.

I squeezed his hand. "For what?"

He shrugged.

As we waited, I overheard the drama of a miscarriage in Room 2, a woman with a rapid pulse in Room 6, and a guy with no ID brought in from a local motel.

"What are we waiting for?" Fred asked.

"You need to see the doctor to find out what's wrong with your back."

He dozed awhile, then asked again, "What are we waiting for?"

At eleven-thirty, the same doctor, Dr. P., rushed in. He ordered a CT scan and then went to help other patients. He returned at noon. The CT showed several bulging disks and spinal stenosis. He wrote orders and a prescription for stronger painkillers.

A nurse helped Fred dress while I stuffed the paperwork into my purse and went out to get the car. She rolled him to the curb in a wheelchair and I helped him in.

At the pharmacy, Fred couldn't get out of the car. He opened the door, started to put a leg out, and yelped in pain.

"Just wait. I'll be right back," I said. I literally ran into Rite Aid to get his prescription, thinking that once he had rested a while, he'd be fine.

At home, Fred still couldn't get out of the car. He put one leg out and began to shake. "No, I can't," he said.

"Yes, you can. Just ease your butt this way—wait. No."

He was over two hundred pounds of dead weight. I held him half in and half out, unable to carry him, unable to get him to move the other leg. He hollered like a dog caught in a car door. Fortunately, Joe across the street heard our struggle. He slid his arm under Fred's and half-carried him into the house, placing him on the sofa.

Fred slept while I made phone calls to tell people I wouldn't be attending our writers' meeting or going to church. No way was I leaving Fred alone again.

I called our friends Tim and Teresa to ask Teresa to play the piano for me. Tim, a former paramedic, offered to come and check on Fred. "Thank you," I said, "But I think we're okay. He just needs to rest."

A few minutes later, I would wish I had told him to come.

I was making dinner when Fred slipped to the floor with a soft *whump*. I couldn't get him up.

He was crying. He kept saying, "I'm sorry," "I want to quit," "It's all wrong."

He removed his jeans; I don't know why. He lay between the ottoman and the piano, bare-assed, shaking, and out of his head. Whenever I tried to roll him back toward the sofa, he screamed. I sat beside him, stroking his arm and his hair. His skin felt hot and damp.

"I can't, I can't," he kept saying, but he never finished the sentence. Only two words came out clear: "I'm sorry."

"Don't be sorry." I brushed at the tears trickling into his beard and down around his ears. "It's okay." I leaned against the piano he had bought me for a wedding present, now scarred and out of tune.

He needed to urinate. I handed him a plastic container from the kitchen. "Okay, you can go in this."

As I supported his limp penis between my thumb and forefinger, ripe honey-colored urine splashed into the bowl. "Ah," he said. "Thank you."

I was about to dump the urine into the toilet when he began to shiver more violently. I set the container on the hearth and tried to pull his pants back on.

"No!" he cried.

I grabbed a crocheted afghan from the back of the sofa and spread it over him.

It was getting dark outside. The dogs were whining to come in. "I'm s-s-sorry," he stuttered, teeth chattering.

A half hour after Fred went down, Tim and Teresa knocked on the door. Tim knelt down and talked to Fred, who continued to shake and talk nonsense. "He needs to go to the hospital," he said.

I dialed 911. Sirens wailed down our street again. In minutes, our living room was full of firefighters and paramedics, two of whom had sung with Fred in the Coastal-Aires barbershop chorus.

Bracing his head and neck, they eased Fred onto a gurney and carried him out to the ambulance. I fed the dogs, put them in the laundry room, and drove to the hospital.

Dr. P., still on duty in the ER, recognized us. He agreed to admit Fred to the hospital. Pen poised over a form, he looked at me and asked, "Do you feel that you can take care of your husband at home?"

I wanted to weep. I had tried. I had done everything I could to keep Fred going with the help of notes and lists, quietly taking over everything he used to do. I had hired nurses and aides. I had coerced friends and relatives to sit with him so I could continue my writing, music, and teaching at Oregon Coast Community College.

Unlike most wives of Alzheimer's patients, I was not retired. At fifty-seven, I felt like I was just getting started. I had recently earned a late-in-life master of fine arts degree in creative writing so I could teach, but that dream was fading. It was getting too hard to be away from Fred. I had already turned in my resignation, effective at the end of the winter quarter.

I didn't have grown children and grandchildren to help. I had hoped Fred's sons and daughter would fill the gap where my own children would have been. When we lived in California, they did. Now that we lived in Oregon, they seemed content to let me manage Fred's illness. They were busy with their jobs and families and the day-to-day demands of their own lives.

But now Fred couldn't walk. He couldn't stand on his own, and I couldn't lift him. We couldn't afford full-time help, and we had no family nearby.

Dr. P. asked if we had railings, a handicap-accessible shower, and a wheelchair.

"No, we don't have any of that stuff. He was walking yesterday."

"Do you feel that you can take care of him at home?" he repeated.

I shook my head. "Not like this."

We sat in that emergency room for almost three hours. A nurse had gotten Fred a sack lunch. Teresa brought me a sandwich. I spooned applesauce into Fred's mouth and gave him milk through a straw.

By the time an orderly wheeled Fred to his room upstairs at 11:20 p.m., Fred did not know my name. He said I was Ardis. That's his cousin.

At home, I had been praying for Fred to be able to get up. Now I didn't know what to ask for.

Over the next two days, I sat at Fred's hospital bedside, holding his hand, trying to make him understand why he couldn't get out of bed, covering his genitals as he repeatedly threw off his gown and his blankets. The alarm on his bed kept going off as he banged against the railings. He insisted he had to go to the bathroom, even as urine trickled steadily into his catheter bag. He also insisted that he saw a door across from his bed. He wanted me to help him leave through that door, but it was just a wall behind another bed. Meanwhile, doctors, nurses and social workers were putting together a plan to take Fred's care out of my hands.

The doctors said he couldn't stay at home. I didn't know whether they meant for a few weeks or forever.

I was stunned by how quickly it had happened. Fred was fifteen years older than me, but he had been so youthful and strong, I thought we'd be together at least another twenty years, even with Alzheimer's.

I knew things were bad. A few days before his fall, I woke at 1:30 a.m. to find Fred standing in my bedroom doorway in his underwear.

"What are you doing?" I asked.

"I need to find the agates." The shiny rocks tourists collect from Oregon's beaches.

"Oh. Well, it's hard to see in the dark. Why don't you go back to bed?"

"Okay."

But he continued down the hall. I followed him.

In the den, as he stood between the couch and the easy chair, I heard that unmistakable sound.

"Are you peeing?"

"Yes I am." It went on. And on, a hard stream pounding into the cream-colored Berber. Finally he finished, tucking his penis back into his undershorts.

After I did my best to mop up the urine with an old towel, I grabbed his hand and led him back to bed, where he promptly fell asleep.

In the morning, he remembered nothing. He was horrified when I told him what had happened. I couldn't see the stain, but the den smelled like an outhouse, and the dogs went right to it. This was the man too shy to urinate in the woods with no one around when we went hiking.

On the Monday morning after he fell, I talked to the doctor, social worker, discharge nurse, and physical therapy staff to work out a plan. Between conversations, I sat beside my husband, who thought he could escape through a wall.

Two physical therapists got Fred up in a walker. His back already much better after a day of rest, he had no problem holding himself up, but one minute he'd be making sense, the next he'd be talking about a truck in the room.

Heidi, the social worker, explained to Fred that he'd need to go to a rehab place because I couldn't lift him. He cried, but then he escaped to the crazy place in his head.

Midafternoon, our family doctor, whom I'll call Dr. H., examined Fred.

I followed him out. "What do you think?"

"His back will be okay, but he needs twenty-four-hour care." He put his arm around my shoulder. "You've done all you can."

Everybody at the hospital was saying the same thing, that I'd done enough. I didn't feel like I had. Not even close.

"Do you have any family nearby to help?" the social worker asked.

"No. Most of them are in California."

She gave me a list of adult foster care homes to look into.

Dr. H. said I had time to figure it out. "We'll keep him for a couple days, then send him to rehab so he can do physical therapy and get stronger. Go home and rest."

A few minutes after I arrived at the house, the social worker called to tell me they were moving Fred within the hour to Newport Rehab, a block east of the hospital. I needed to bring seven days' worth of clothing and $7,000.

She explained that Medicare was not covering Fred's hospital stay as "acute care," but as "observational," so everything would be charged as outpatient procedures. They would not cover the rehab place at all. You have to be in acute care for at least three days before Medicare will cover twenty days in a facility, she said.

I'd never moved so quickly. I went online and transferred money out of our savings account, then pulled clothes out of Fred's closet and stuffed them into a suitcase.

When I arrived at Newport Rehab, Fred was in a room near the nursing station, dressed and sitting in a wheelchair. The staff had put a monitor on his chair. Every time he tried to get up, an alarm went off.

Nurses and aides swarmed around him, giving him a flu shot and a TB test while trying to keep him in the wheelchair. After I'd taken care of the paperwork, they told me to go home. There was nothing for me to do. Feeling helpless, I kissed Fred good night and walked out.

At home, I called Fred's children, my father and brother, and Tim and Teresa to tell them what had happened.

Then I sat on the living room floor with the dogs, picking Christmas tree needles out of the carpet. I kept seeing Fred there, half naked, shaking and saying he was sorry. Behind me, the clock ticked away the night, and the pellet stove poured out yellow heat. Outside, the trees rocked and bent in the wind.

Fred's face looked down from a photo on the wall. In the picture, he stood upright, clear-eyed, wearing his corduroy jacket, and smiling his crooked grin.

"It's okay," I said.

But it wasn't.

1 Movie? What Movie?

From the night of our first date until Fred lost his memories, we laughed about how I seduced him.

We met in my brother Mike's kitchen during his annual Christmas party. I was supposed to be singing in Salt Lake City that night with the Billy Vogue Country Singers, but God had other plans.

I had left a steady newspaper job near San Francisco to sing with a traveling imitation of the Grand Ole Opry. Retired country guitarist Billy Vogue had hired a couple dozen young singers and pickers to tour for a year. He promised recording contracts, TV shows, fame, and buckets of money. Reporter by day, musician by night with dreams of a show business career, I quit my job, stashed my stuff at Mom and Dad's house in San Jose, got a new curly hairdo and contact lenses, and joined the Country Music Association.

We opened at the Cow Palace in South San Francisco, but the show never made it past Redding, California. The producers, counting on funding from sponsors like Buick and other big companies, had already spent all their money. Billy Vogue declared bankruptcy, and we never got paid.

Before my dive into full-time show business, my first marriage had ended in divorce with no children. At thirty-one, I was single and unemployed, living with Mom and Dad again, doing occasional gigs with an accordion-playing friend, and looking for a new job.

Things were not going well.

I had seen Fred with his ex-wife at a previous Christmas party.

They seemed like a perfectly matched pair in their his-and-her Birkenstocks.

But now he was alone, too.

"Your wife couldn't come?" I asked.

"We're uh—not together anymore."

"I'm sorry. What happened?"

He shrugged. "I don't know. One day she didn't want to be married to me."

We stood by the refrigerator talking and drinking wine for the rest of the party. I don't know what we talked about, probably my divorce, my music, his job, the weather, our plans for Christmas. It's a blur of cabernet and amazement that this handsome man was talking to me.

Suddenly it was late, and my parents, who had brought me to the party, were ready to go home.

"Can I call you?" Fred asked.

"Sure," I said. "That would be nice."

The next day, he asked me out.

On our first date, we were both nervous. My friend Sandy, who had worked with me at the *Pacifica Tribune*, warned me not to screw it up. She had seen the losers I'd dated before: the one on drugs, the abusive one, the one who happened to be married . . . Fred was a good man with a good job. He was also huggy-bear handsome with his beard and corduroy pants.

But I wondered about him. My last boyfriend drove a red 380Z; Fred picked me up in a beat-up Ford Fairmont. Our first stop was the Mirassou Winery in the eastern foothills of San Jose. He guided me into the tasting room, his hand on my back. Warmed by a fire in the dimly lit room that reminded me of a castle, I watched him taste each of the wines on display, swirling, sniffing, sipping, and smiling as a worker boxed up the hundreds of dollars' worth of wine Fred was buying for Christmas presents. I stared as he handed over his

American Express card. Practically a teetotaler, I barely knew red from rosé.

We ate dinner at a Chinese restaurant on the East Side, where we laughed about how we both liked the same foods and chatted about mutual friends we knew through the San Jose Recreation Department, where Fred and my brother had worked together before Mike went on to law school. He told me about his side job as a licensed tax preparer while I shared my history as a newspaper reporter and editor, part-time poet, and wannabe musician.

"You're so talented," he said.

I chuckled. "Yeah, and broke."

He laughed.

Over beef and broccoli and moo shu pork, I gathered more information. Fred played football in high school and college. He served in the Navy, stationed in Guam. He went to community college, then San Fernando Valley State, majoring in recreation. He married Annette in 1959.

I didn't mention that I was seven years old at the time.

They had three kids, ages seven, fifteen, and seventeen. He started working in San Jose in 1967 and had been there ever since. In the early '70s, he earned his master's degree in recreation management at San Jose State.

"Hey, I was there then, getting my bachelor's in journalism. We might have seen each other."

"No kidding!"

This date was going well.

After dinner, we stopped at a video store. *Uh-oh*, I thought. A previous date had bought me one drink, then taken me to his apartment to watch porn, smoke pot, and have sex. Bad sex. But Fred wasn't like that. "I'm still new at this dating business," he said. "I didn't know what to do after dinner, so I thought we could watch a movie. Is that okay?"

"It's fine. How about a comedy?"

He was renting a 1920s bungalow in the Willow Glen section of San Jose. It had carved moldings, secondhand furniture, and a braided oval rug by a fireplace. Through the first movie, *Prisoner of Second Avenue*, with Jack Lemmon and Anne Bancroft, we sat stiffly on the plaid sofa. As the second movie, *Flashdance*, began, I felt restless. Most of my other dates would have had me in bed by then. I really liked this guy, but the silence between us was getting awkward.

I moved closer and held Fred's hand. He smiled and bent for a gentle kiss. I kissed back and pulled him into an embrace. We started to make love, but unlike my previous lovers, he was hesitant, careful. He kept asking, "Is this okay?" The last time he was dating, nice girls didn't do it on the first date. "Yes, yes," I kept saying as the clothes came off.

Fred put down a pillow and a blanket, and we made love on that braided oval rug in front of the fire as Jennifer Beals danced on the TV screen. Fred said he was awkward at sex. He was. But he was a considerate lover, unlike my most recent boyfriend, who laughed at my requests for foreplay.

Our date ended before ten o'clock. Fred's daughter, Gretchen, was coming to spend the night, so he took me home, but not before we agreed to meet again after the holidays. He was driving to Burbank in Southern California to spend Christmas with his parents. I would be hanging out with Mom and Dad, as if I were eleven instead of thirty-one.

After Christmas, Fred, calling on his way home from Burbank, asked me to meet him in Monterey. Nervous and excited, I drove an hour from San Jose and parked behind the building that housed the arcade and merry-go-round. Dazzled by the colors, the calliope music, and the crowds, I walked around taking photos and looking for Fred. I didn't see him. Where was he? He didn't stand me up, did he?

I was about to walk out and look for his ratty red car when I saw him at the foot of the stairs looking up at me. It was like one of those movie scenes where people run into each other's arms while the music swells. He hugged me hard.

"Oh, it's so good to see you," he said.

"You too. I missed you."

We stood on the sidewalk and kissed as tourists walked around us. We ate lunch, then walked around the gift shops and the wharf holding hands. We had barely met, but we already knew we wanted to be together.

On my birthday two months later, Fred took me to the Grandview Inn on Mt. Hamilton. As we held hands and sipped vodka tonics, he all but proposed.

"I love being with you. I think we have something very special. I can see a future with you."

"I feel the same way."

He laughed softly. "Oh, you make me happy."

Over the next few months, we spent every nonworking minute together. We went wine-tasting, visited historic San Juan Bautista, walked along the Santa Cruz Boardwalk, and strolled the beach at sunset. We attended family gatherings and countless recreation department parties. We volunteered at Special Olympics, the Berryessa Art and Wine Festival, and Christmas in the Park. When I performed, Fred was always in the audience. Everyone I knew loved Fred, and his friends welcomed me as family. His older kids hadn't warmed to me yet, but the youngest was already my buddy.

In the evenings at his house, we cooked together, mostly steak or pasta, often with artichokes, usually with wine. Fred had been single less than a year, but he had furnished his home with everything a person could need, from pots and pans to condiments. I wasn't there when he moved out on his own, but I can picture him making lists on yellow legal pads. Like me, Fred was a planner.

We spent hours just kissing and touching on the bony secondhand couch we called "killer," as well as on the floor and on his waterbed.

I got a job at another newspaper and moved from my parents' house to an apartment two blocks away, but when Fred and I were together, the rest of the world disappeared.

Seven months after our first date, Fred proposed to me on that same braided rug where we first made love. It was June 22, which Fred didn't know was the tenth anniversary of my failed first marriage to a Vietnam vet who couldn't handle monogamy or sobriety.

The landlord had decided to sell the Willow Glen house, and we were packing Fred's possessions. He was moving to a friend's spare bedroom, putting most of his belongings in storage.

Between loads, we collapsed on the rug. He rolled toward me, grabbed my hand and said, "I love you so much. Will you do me the honor of becoming my wife?"

We had no diamond ring, no expensive dinner, no dressy clothes. We were dirty and sweaty, but he had finally worked up the courage to ask, and I was ready with my answer: "Yes."

He hollered, "Yes!" and grabbed me as I burst into tears. My makeup stained his green-and-white polo shirt as I cried. Not only did this wonderful man want to marry me, but I would not be poor or alone anymore.

We got out our calendars to pick a wedding date. We wanted time to plan. We didn't want to do it during the holidays. We couldn't do it during tax season, when he barely had time to sleep.

"How about May eighteenth?" I asked.

"Perfect."

He grabbed a bottle of champagne from the fridge. "Let's go tell your family."

My parents were sitting in the patio when we broke the news.

"I knew it," my mother said. "I knew that first night when he asked if he could call you."

My father cried. His little girl finally had a good man to take care of her.

2 Doing It Our Way

Shortly after our engagement, Fred took me to Hawaii for a week to share his parents' timeshare condo with them.

"Oh, taking the honeymoon before the wedding," a coworker teased.

I blushed and smiled. "Yep."

I had never met my future in-laws, and now we were sharing a one-bedroom condo in Waikiki. The day we arrived, I miscalculated the time difference so we failed to pick them up at the airport when they landed. But Helen, Fred's raspy-voiced, red-headed mom, and Al, his easygoing, jazz-loving dad, welcomed me as family. "Call me Mom," Helen said when they arrived at the condo, having rented a car at the airport.

They treated us to dinner and a show at the Royal Hawaiian, meandered with us through the International Marketplace seeking bargains, sent us off to bask in the sun and surf, and let us take the bedroom while they slept on fold-out beds in the living room.

By the time I came along, their three sons had given them six different daughters-in-law and more grandchildren than they could count, but they treated me as if I were the first.

They knew I would probably not be adding more children to the clan. I had always expected to have children. It didn't happen in my first marriage, and it wasn't likely to happen with Fred. He'd had a vasectomy after his youngest son Michael was born.

As we courted, we talked about trying to have the vasectomy

reversed, but it had been nine years; chances of success were poor. We looked into adoption, but Fred was already too old for most programs.

One night while vacationing in Yosemite, we were walking to a campfire talk when Fred blurted, "I really don't want to have any more kids."

I stared at the pine needles under my feet. "You don't?"

"No. I'm sorry."

I could have demanded to know why. I could have issued an ultimatum: Give me children or find someone else. But my throat closed up, and I said nothing. Maybe being stepmother to his three children would be enough. At that point in my life, I felt lucky just to have Fred.

Not only did we honeymoon—more than once—before we were married, but soon we were living together. Nine months before the wedding, we moved into a rented house on the next block from where my parents lived on the west side of San Jose. I could barely afford my apartment, and Fred couldn't live in a bedroom at his friends' house forever. We were getting married anyway, so why not?

We merged our pots and pans, his green-and-white-striped rocking chair, my giant crocheted beanbag pillow, his rolltop desk and my small homemade desk from my grandparents' house, his waterbed and my ordinary bed from my first marriage, and no one disapproved. We were grownups, already Fred-and-Sue, all one word.

We had both had traditional church weddings organized by our parents the first go-round. This time, we were doing it our way.

Unable to find a priest willing to marry a divorced Presbyterian and an annulled Catholic, we invited a Methodist minister friend to perform the ceremony in the amphitheater at Evergreen Community College. I wore an embroidered dress from Mexico, and Fred and his groomsmen—my brother and our friend Dave—wore Mexican wedding shirts while my friends Sandy and Sherri wore short maroon dresses. No ties, no cummerbunds, no thousand-dollar gowns. We processed down the sidewalk to a cassette recording of "Pachelbel's Canon." Ducks quacked, and kids fished in the nearby pond as we said our vows.

Afterward, we held our reception in our backyard, setting up tables and chairs borrowed from the recreation department under blue canopies rented from Mel Cotton's Sporting Goods. Our friend Pat Silva cooked a Portuguese feast in honor of my heritage, and we danced in the patio as a friend played my piano. Our wedding cake was chocolate under the white frosting.

Fred's divorce was barely final before the wedding. His ex was awarded custody of their younger son. Ted, who was eighteen, was on his own. Fred and I got custody of his daughter, Gretchen, but she didn't stay with us for long. In less than a year, we were organizing her wedding and welcoming a granddaughter. They kept it in the recreation family; her husband was the son of one of Fred's colleagues.

Fred's ex took the house in the divorce and gave up her claim to a portion of his future pension. Financially, he was starting over. With his job and his tax income, he stashed money in the bank until we had enough to buy a mobile home on Monterey Highway, down the hill from Oak Hill Cemetery where my father's side of the family was buried. After five years, we sold it and bought a house against the foothills in South San Jose. By that time, Fred's ex-wife had moved to Texas, and Michael was living with us, making me the full-time stepmom of a teenager.

My career blossomed as I moved from one newspaper to another, then "retired" to freelance for newspapers and magazines and write *The Iberian Americans* for an educational publisher. When not working, I sang in a community choir called the Valley Chorale, sang and played guitar at St. Julie's Catholic Church, and performed at festivals, sidewalk fairs, senior centers, and coffeehouses. Fred worked for the city of San Jose, did his tax business, and volunteered at Mirassou Winery.

In 1992, when the city made massive budget cuts in the recreation department, he took early retirement. He continued doing taxes and took a job at Mirassou, where he conducted wine tastings and took people on tours through the wine-making equipment. As a Mirassou spouse, I joined him for elaborate dinners with a different wine for every course, "cab nights" where the workers lined up bottles of cabernet and got soused while trying them all out (I drove), and Fourth of July where we sat among the grapevines watching fireworks.

Fred worked hard to pay for nice things and expensive vacations. Focused on his tax business from late January to mid-April, he put his files away in May, and we went somewhere special to celebrate the end of tax season as well as our wedding anniversary.

We explored the California gold country, San Juan Bautista, Hearst's Castle, Universal Studios, Solvang, and Puget Sound. We cruised the Mississippi on the Delta Queen. We walked through historic cemeteries, including the one in Damascus, Oregon, where my Fagalde ancestors were buried. We toured the Oregon Caves, the Bandon Wild Animal Park, Oregon Coast Aquarium, Yaquina Bay Lighthouse, and every other lighthouse on the Oregon coast.

Like me, Fred loved music, although he'd sooner die than sing a solo. In the car, we'd shove a cassette into the slot and sing doo-wop with the Manhattan Transfer, gospel with Elvis, or all the songs from *Paint Your Wagon*. Raised in different eras, he didn't like rock and I didn't like jazz, but we found plenty of songs in the middle. We went to Broadway musicals, small-town plays, and concerts by unknowns and well-knowns including Ella Fitzgerald, Joan Baez, the Manhattan Transfer, Pete Seeger, and Peter, Paul and Mary.

We ventured farther, too, visiting Costa Rica, British Columbia, the Grand Canyon, and the Grand Ole Opry. We explored my Portuguese roots in New England and in Portugal. We made many trips to Hawaii. It was always the same. "You want to go? Let's do it."

He became a potluck Catholic, joining me for dinners, dances and festivals but not for Mass, and a mascot for the Valley Chorale, cheering us on, carrying risers, and bringing wine to share on our bus tours.

I partied with his old friends, attended his high school reunions, and pretended it wasn't weird that before I came along, they had been friends with Fred-and-Annette.

Fred was happy to spend quiet time at home, too. He read one book after another, mostly suspense and mystery novels. He could spend all day Saturday and Sunday watching football, eating popcorn from the biggest bowl we had, and yelling at the TV screen. "Go! Go! Go!" "No!" "Come on!" "Yes!" The Rams and USC's Trojans were his teams while I quietly rooted for the 49ers. I didn't really care as long as Fred was happy.

He wanted me to be happy, too. Fred wasn't a dog person, or maybe just not a *big dog* person, but I was. Over the years of poverty and apartments where the landlords didn't allow pets, I couldn't have a dog. When we lived in the mobile home, there was no yard, but now that we had a house, why not? I dragged Fred to see the rescue dogs on display at a local PetSmart store.

We were attracted to a year-old German shepherd/Lab named Snapple. She had already been given up by two owners. She had a little trouble getting along with other dogs, they said.

Fred and I looked at each other.

"We'll keep looking," I said.

But Snapple stayed on our minds. Two weeks later, she was still on display at the pet store. Now they called her Sadie. Oh, those brown eyes. That luscious black-and-tan fur. That tail wagging as we bent over the wire cage to pet her.

"Would you like to take her out?" a volunteer asked.

We put her on a leash and walked her around the building. Ears up, she looked from one to another of us, a smile on her doggy face. We sat on a curb. She licked my face, and I hugged her to my chest.

"Is she the one?" Fred asked.

I looked into Sadie's eyes. "Do you want to be our dog?"

She wagged her tail.

"I think so."

After paying for the dog, a collar, leash, bowl, and food and signing up for "Citizen Canine" classes, we loaded her into the back seat of the Honda and took her home. She ran into the backyard as if she had been released into paradise.

Like everyone else, she adored Fred. I was the one who fed her, took her to the vet, and told her twenty times a day that I loved her, but with Fred it was true love.

At doggy school, Sadie was the most incorrigible student in the class, always going in the opposite direction of the other dogs, fighting with them, and not paying attention to us or the instructor.

At home, I pried the neighbor's cats out of her mouth and returned them soaked and terrified to their owners. When possums came down from the foothills to explore the backyard, Sadie went berserk, waking us up in the wee hours. She ran back and forth, panting and barking as if possessed by demons. Sometimes she grabbed the possum off the fence and shook it so hard we assumed it was dead. But the possums, being possums, went limp until we dragged the dog away, then went on with their business. It didn't take many nights like this to decide Sadie should sleep in the house, even when the weather was mild and she paced at the door, wanting to go outside. I can still hear Fred hollering, "No! Go to sleep!" Finally she'd slump down on the floor beside the bed, and we'd go off to dreamland.

Those years together in San Jose were blessed, but it wasn't all roses and romance. Newspapers I wrote for went belly-up. Editors didn't pay. The novel I wrote went nowhere. The city transferred Fred to a job that he hated because it was all paperwork instead of interacting with people.

Michael's girlfriend totaled my car. Thank God no one was hurt. After we forbade him to drive, Michael crashed his bike into the back of a car on the way home from his part-time recreation job, badly injuring his mouth and jaw. Gretchen's first marriage ended in divorce, leaving her on her own with two little kids.

My grandfather's confusion became apparent in 1991 after my grandmother died of stomach cancer. He could no longer live alone in their cottage at Seacliff Beach, near Santa Cruz. My parents moved him into a nursing home, where we watched him descend into dementia. I visited often, but soon he didn't know who I was.

There was trouble in Fred's family, too. In 1993, we were sitting in our living room watching TV when Fred's father called. He and Helen had moved to Las Vegas a few years earlier to share a home with Fred's brother Don and his daughter Ashley. I answered the phone.

"Is Fred there?"

I recognized Al's deep voice. "Hi, Dad. It's Sue. How are you?"

"Don's dead," he said. Or at least that's what it sounded like. The TV was loud, and his voice was faint.

I clicked the TV off. "Honey, it's your dad. I think he said, 'Don's dead.'"

Fred took the phone. I watched as his face crumpled and tears filled his eyes. Don, a burly forty-eight-year-old Vietnam veteran, owned a trucking business in Las Vegas. He had been working underneath his truck when the jack slipped and the truck fell, crushing him. Their father watched it happen.

Within the hour, Fred left for Las Vegas while I stayed home with Michael and worked at the *Saratoga News*, where I had just taken a job as editor.

Fred never spoke much about the time he spent in Las Vegas with his parents. When I called to see how things were going, expecting tears and sadness, Fred's dad said he was "fine, never better." That didn't make sense. Helen suspected Al had had a small stroke the night Don died. He was beginning to show early signs of vascular dementia, which, thanks to my grandfather, was becoming much too familiar.

Through it all, Fred and I held each other up, still on a never-ending honeymoon.

3 Let's Move to Oregon

Santa Clara Valley had morphed from the "Valley of Heart's Delight," a land of orchards and blue skies, into "Silicon Valley," home of the computer industry, smog, and bumper-to-bumper traffic. After working all day at the *Saratoga News*, I'd spend ten minutes idling on Saratoga Avenue, waiting to merge onto Highway 85. It could take an hour to travel the fifteen miles back to South San Jose. The six lanes of traffic moved so slowly that some days, I propped a book on the steering wheel and read, just to keep from going crazy.

San Jose, with nearly a million residents and still growing, had gotten too crowded and too expensive. Our older relatives were dying, and the younger ones were moving to other parts of California.

I had grown up playing at Seacliff Beach a few blocks from my grandfather's retirement home in Aptos, and I yearned to live by the ocean, but California's beaches were far too expensive. On the Oregon coast, the beaches were colder and more rugged, but the cities had a small-town charm one could not find in San Jose anymore. Plus ordinary people could afford to live there.

By summer 1996, my grandfather had died, and Michael had graduated from high school. Even with income from my job, Fred's tax business, his job at Mirassou, and his pension, we were struggling financially. An extra-large "balloon payment" coming up on the house would clean out our savings.

One morning when Fred sat at his desk paying bills, I pulled up a chair beside him. "Is it time to move to Oregon?"

He smiled and set down his pen. "Yes. Let's do it."

My family was shocked. Fred's family, spread across the West, were fine with it. They were used to long-distance visits. But my family didn't do that. For generations, everyone had clustered around San Jose and neighboring Santa Clara. With few exceptions, our people didn't move to other states. It was bad enough my brother had moved to Merced two hours away to take a job as an attorney in the Public Defender's office. My mother grieved, saying she never thought her children would be so far away. My father insisted it would never work out.

Our house sold the day it went on the market. As we said good-bye to family, church, friends, and jobs, reality hit me. Things were moving too quickly. Did I really want to leave everything I knew?

That Fourth of July, I took the dog up to a spot in the foothills where people from the neighborhood gathered to watch fireworks happening down in the valley. As families chattered around us and fireworks flashed below us from the displays in Morgan Hill, San Jose, and Santa Clara, I clutched my dog and wept into her soft fur. I didn't want to go, but it was too late. The house had been sold. We had quit our jobs, and we were going.

We invited Michael to come with us, but at eighteen, he was ready to live on his own, sharing an apartment in San Jose with friends.

I wept for everything I was leaving, but I never imagined that trouble was coming, and that because we lived so far away, Fred and I would have to face it alone.

We rented a house a block from the ocean in Lincoln City while we decided exactly where we wanted to settle. The beach was across the street and down a flight of stairs. We had an ocean view, three bed-rooms, a fireplace, and a fenced yard for the dog, all for under $1,000 a month. You couldn't rent a doghouse for that in San Jose.

We envisioned a life at the beach where I could do my music and writing, and Fred could volunteer at the Oregon Coast Aquarium and continue his tax practice, going to California in February and March, doing the rest long-distance. We would walk on the sand, go to movies at the Bijou Theatre, eat lunches at Maxwell's on the corner, and spend the rainy days reading by the fire. And we did.

But winter came. Fred left for California. I was alone with Sadie. The weather was horrible, with months of sideways rain and wind and black ice on the roads. I missed my family. I missed my job. I wanted to go home. Fred said we couldn't afford to go back. Plus, he loved Oregon.

I sniffled, walked on the beach, wrote poetry, and sang and played at the senior center, Maxwell's open mic night, and our front porch. Fred came home, and spring eventually arrived.

Fred took a desk clerk job at the motel across the street, but it lasted only a few months. He couldn't master the computer program they used. Looking back, I see this as a harbinger of things to come, but we blamed the "damned computer" at the time. This was early in the computer age when we connected to the internet with modems plugged into the phone jack and printed on continuous sheets of paper with dot matrix printers. There was no Google, no Facebook, no Zoom.

Gradually, we became Oregonians. We learned to shrug off the weather. So it rains a little. At least it keeps our towns from getting too crowded. I joined the Lincoln Community Chorus and the Sacred Heart Church choir. I received a contract for my next book, *Stories Grandma Never Told: Portuguese Women in California*. That book required trips back to California to interview fascinating Portuguese women who had settled a lot farther from home than I had. After I turned in the completed manuscript, I answered an ad in the *News-Times*, the newspaper that covered Newport and Lincoln City, and was hired to write features. Meanwhile, Fred got a part-time job at the Flying Dutchman Winery tasting room on the Newport Bayfront.

Like so many retirees who brought their California pensions to the Oregon coast, we dove into all the things we loved. I even started a low-residency MFA program to get my master's degree in creative writing.

All we needed now was a permanent home. Armed with a VA loan and a minimal down payment, we went house-hunting in the Central Coast area around Newport.

I grew up in the suburbs of San Jose, accustomed to street after street of lookalike houses with front lawns and fenced yards that backed up to other lookalike houses. My grandparents were horrified that their grown children had moved so far out into the country, where the orchards had just been torn down to make post-WWII housing tracts. But my parents' neighborhood was soon surrounded by shopping centers, car dealerships, and freeways.

When I saw the house for sale at the end of 97th Court in South Beach, four miles south of Newport, I felt the same way my grandparents did about my parents' house on Fenley Avenue. It was in the middle of nowhere. It wasn't within walking distance of anything but trees. We could hear the ocean, but we couldn't see it. The street was barely wide enough for one car, and it felt like we had driven forever before we came to this house hidden by an eight-foot-tall hedge at the end of the road.

A long, tan, one-story rectangle on one-third acre, the house had four bedrooms, a garage-turned-family room, and a massive backyard surrounded by alders, spruce, pines, and blackberry vines. The kitchen had recently been remodeled and a deck and hot tub added. But it also had a green living room, purple kitchen, one turquoise bathroom and one pink one. Instead of the gas and electric heaters we were used to, a pellet stove provided heat.

As we toured the backyard, a garter snake slithered past.

Oh, hell no!

We had looked at nicer places in Newport and nearby Toledo. But they all cost more than this house, priced at $148,000. In the end, it was all we could afford. It had rooms for our offices and a yard for the dog. We could buy lots of white paint.

An older couple lived in a double-wide modular home across the street. We had no neighbors immediately west, north or east, just trees and blackberries and salal so thick only rabbits, raccoons and newts could squeeze through. Also the occasional bear or bobcat.

We put up a chain link fence to keep the dog in and wild critters out. It didn't keep Sadie from barking for hours at squirrels in the shed, rats in the woodpile, and raccoons raiding the feeders we put up for the robins, jays, and juncos.

We learned that winter lasted from Halloween to Memorial Day. When it wasn't raining sideways with gale-force winds, it snowed on the beach, and the frozen roads became too slick to drive. At the height of winter, we only had eight hours of daylight. We could not count on electricity or cell service. The pellet stove would not work when the power went out.

But we had a real home at the beach, a home where I could sing and play music at all hours. We could soak naked in the hot tub under the stars or lie on the deck watching the Canada geese fly in *V* formation on their north–south commute.

Technically, we lived in South Beach. "Town" was Newport, four miles north, at ten thousand people the biggest city in Lincoln County. Soon the restaurant servers greeted us by name. We got to know the checkers at the grocery store. We made new friends through church, writing groups, singing groups, the aquarium, the winery, and the gym in South Beach where I started taking yoga classes on Tuesdays and Thursdays.

When we walked the dog, the neighbors waved, even the ones who didn't know who we were. Unlike San Jose, where you could stand in line so close to other people you could feel their breath and not say a word, people talked to each other on the street, from table to table at restaurants, or in line at the J.C. Market.

In spite of the rain, in spite of missing my family, life was good, so good that Fred's parents decided to join us. A year after we moved to Oregon, they rented a house in Newport.

Both in their eighties, they had expected to spend their senior years with Fred's brother, but now he was gone, and Fred's dad was showing signs of dementia. He was often confused and had caused several minor car accidents. He joked that he could read books over and over because he forgot what they were about, but Fred's mom was scared. Although she hated the rainy weather on the Oregon coast, she didn't want to be alone if anything happened.

Years later, Helen's fears became my reality, but for now our focus was on Fred's parents.

They sold the house in Las Vegas and rented a three-bedroom house in Newport for $895 a month. As we helped them unpack, Fred's dad sat on a chair, apologizing for not having any "get up and go." Always rosy-cheeked and cheerful, he now seemed gray and tired. His new doctor in Newport diagnosed him with congestive heart failure.

"I'm gonna beat this thing," he vowed.

But he lost the fight. A month after they moved in, Fred's dad died of a massive stroke. Fred's kids came to offer their support, but we didn't have a funeral. Al and Helen didn't know anyone in Oregon yet.

We invited Fred's mom to live with us, but she insisted on staying in her yellow corner house behind the Fred Meyer store. She kept me company during tax season, and we three went to shows, ate out, and watched TV together at home, like family.

Aside from missing Fred's father, life was still darned good.

4 No, That Can't Be It

Fred's mom was tough. Widowed in an unfamiliar place with barely enough money to scrape by, knowing only us and her neighbor across the street, she fought her way through grief and poverty while giving us the kind of parental support I had never experienced before. She saved everything I published and came to all of my concerts. We got together often and were constantly on the phone with each other.

But she couldn't beat lung cancer, diagnosed in April 2001, three and a half years after Al died. As Christmas approached, her condition worsened. She was enrolled in hospice care. Fred spent most of his time at her house.

I was in the midst of my low-residency MFA program and was scheduled to fly to Los Angeles for the ten-day winter residency. But I didn't know if I should go.

Helen sat at the table in her green bathrobe, coughing blood into a tissue.

"I don't want to leave you like this," I said.

"Nonsense. You'll flunk if you don't go."

"No, I'd just have to redo the semester."

"What, because of me? You go and have a good time." She reached into her purse and pulled out a telephone calling card. "Call me when you can."

I still remember our last hug. Her skin was hot, her robe soft. I didn't want to go, but I had my orders.

On the second to last day of the residency, Fred called to tell me his mother was dying. I turned in my assignments and flew home as quickly as I could, but she was already gone when I arrived, an empty hospital bed in the living room where she had died.

That night, we were sitting at a restaurant on the Newport Bayfront. We had spent the afternoon organizing Helen's papers and making phone calls.

Fred fiddled with a packet of crackers as we waited for our food. "I can't remember things," he said.

"It's okay. You're stressed out. Your mother just died. Of course your mind is not working normally. I'll remember stuff for you."

We clasped hands across the table until the waitress arrived with our plates of chicken fried steak and mashed potatoes. I tried to push my worries out of my mind and enjoy the Christmas music playing through overhead speakers, but I was not in the mood for the holidays.

I had been remembering things for Fred since we got together. Everyone knew he was "absent-minded." If he forgot to take his calendar to work, he didn't know what he was supposed to do that day. If we ran into someone who recognized him, he'd look to me to supply their name. Nothing had changed, right?

If his memory was worse, it would explain why we kept arguing, why I kept saying, "But I told you that. Don't you remember?"

I knew too much about dementia, the blanket term for malfunctions of the brain marked by memory loss, personality changes, and impaired reasoning. My grandfather and Fred's father both had vascular dementia caused by strokes. But the type of dementia that gets the most attention is Alzheimer's disease. In my last California job, as editor of the *Saratoga News*, I had published several articles on the subject. I had spent many hours in nursing homes visiting my grandfather, interviewing the staff at other facilities for newspaper articles, and singing for the residents. Fred's problems were starting to sound too familiar.

I insisted he make an appointment with Dr. H.

The doctor blamed Fred's memory problems on his drinking.

"He doesn't drink that much," I protested. "It's something else."

"Alcohol does kill brain cells."

"I just have one glass of wine a day," Fred said.

"I don't see any other explanation. You're healthy as can be."

Fred did like his wine, as well as his gin, vodka and rum, but I had rarely seen him drunk. Neither one of us believed he had pickled his brain with booze.

Could Fred have dementia?

Grandpa was in his nineties, my father-in-law in his eighties. Fred was only sixty-five, and so healthy I accused him of being "bionic," like TV's *Six Million Dollar Man*. He rarely got sick. Injuries healed overnight. This could not be happening.

Things were going so well.

Maybe it was just a superstition I inherited from my Portuguese ancestors or from parents who lived through the Great Depression and World War II, but I knew better than to declare that we were completely happy.

One by one, the dominos fell.

During Fred's third summer at the winery, he had trouble counting the money in the cash drawer and filling out the simple accounting forms. They didn't hire him back for the next season.

His tax clients started getting letters from the IRS about mistakes on their returns.

At the gas station, I watched him hit the door lock, the ashtray, and the light switches before he figured out which button opened the window of the car we had been driving for two years.

He spent hours puzzling over the bills. Finally he gave up. "You do it," he said. That was becoming our new theme song: *You do it.*

I was in Los Angeles for my third ten-day residency with my MFA program when Fred was arrested for drunk driving on his way home from a friend's house. Handcuffed, fingerprinted, photographed, and put in a jail cell, he had to call his friend to drive him home at four in the morning. He walked four miles the next day to reclaim the truck.

Maybe Dr. H. was right about him drinking too much. But his blood test had shown a .04 alcohol level. Although he and his friend had been drinking wine, he was not legally drunk. It was dark and confusing out where Reggie lived, and Fred got lost. The officer saw him make an illegal U-turn. When she pulled him over, she smelled alcohol on his breath, and he flunked the roadside sobriety test.

It wasn't booze; we both knew what it was. I ached, thinking about Fred's shame and fear. If I had been there, I would have been driving and sober, as usual.

When the area underneath the pellet stove that heated our house caught fire, Fred didn't smell the smoke or react with concern. If I hadn't been home to unplug the stove and put out the fire, the house might have burned down. Loss of smell is a common symptom of Alzheimer's disease.

At my MFA graduation in Los Angeles, Fred was the only family member who attended. I was the class speaker, and I entrusted him with the camera and tape recorder (this was before we could do it all with our phones). He couldn't operate either one, so I have no record of the event. I spent my entire graduation watching out for Fred, wondering if my plans to use my degree to teach were doomed.

Our sex life ended. Fred couldn't do the deed anymore. Viagra didn't help because the problem was not in the plumbing.

Once my technical coach, Fred kept asking me for help with simple tasks, like turning the computer off and on.

A docent supervisor at the Oregon Coast Aquarium, Fred couldn't remember the names of the sea creatures and was having trouble organizing the schedule. He tearfully accepted demotions to regular docent and then to "greeter."

Fred went to an aquarium conference in Roseburg, Oregon. On

the Saturday night he was supposed to come home, he neither came nor called. Late that night, when I didn't know whether to go to bed or call the police, the phone rang. He didn't know what town he was in or whether he had a room for the night. Unable to work the cell phone, he had had someone dial for him. Thank God he had his aquarium friends to watch out for him.

He came home on Sunday, happy and unable to understand why I was upset. On Monday, I called Dr. H. for a referral to a neurologist.

We knew in our hearts what was coming. As Fred's Nov. 4 appointment with the specialist, "Dr. Mac," approached, we read books and articles about AD, alternately nodding in recognition and shuddering in dread. One always hopes for a different answer. Perhaps it might be a chemical imbalance that could be corrected with a pill. Or a minor problem that would progress this far and no further.

For two years, we didn't have a name for it, not officially. But we knew.

5 Naming It

November 2004. Sun sparkled on the ocean as we drove north through Lincoln City and then east toward McMinnville through the yellow- and red-leaved autumn trees, singing along to a Ray Charles tape. We didn't talk about the upcoming doctor's appointment. First, we were headed to the Evergreen Aviation Museum, which Fred had always wanted to visit. We told ourselves this was an adventure.

We emerged from trees into farmland and wine country, fields of grapes and grass, farms and sheep, and comfortable old houses. We passed fruit stands, diners, and a man and woman in a cow pasture taking down election signs, piling them into the back of a pickup.

Passing through downtown McMinnville, we saw the three-story hospital on the right, noted its location and went on to the museum.

The nose of Howard Hughes' Spruce Goose, the world's only wooden flying boat, looked as if it were about to fly straight at us through the glass wall of the building.

Fred gloried in all those airplanes, P-38s, B-17s, Messerschmitts, and a Ford airplane that looked like a flying car. Helicopters and little planes hung from the ceiling. Videos played on TV monitors surrounded by authentic airplane seats. A kids' area with a school-age volunteer offered little ones a chance to pretend to fly.

The best part was climbing into the Spruce Goose, which spread its massive wings over everything else in the building. You could see all the way to the nose and the tail, the wooden structure exposed, doors open to view the fuel tanks and pilots' seats. I found myself surrounded by men Fred's age and older, most of them pot-bellied with baseball caps. Like Fred, who had served in the Navy, they shared a veterans' brotherhood that I could never join. I wondered how many of them could not have found their way there without their wives' help.

From the museum, we drove into town for lunch at the Golden Valley brewpub, all dark wood and designer food. We cherished our lunch this last time together before we faced the doctor. We didn't speak much of *it*, but I held Fred's hands across the table.

"I love you. Whatever the doctor says, we'll deal with it together."

"I know. Thank you."

We pulled apart as the waitress brought the bill and Fred took thirty dollars out of his wallet to cover our meal and a generous tip.

Then, like a football team heading out after halftime, we gathered our courage and charged onto the field.

Inside Willamette Valley Medical Center, much larger than our small-town hospital, we went straight to the third floor. In the neurology waiting room, we handed over Fred's MRI films and health history forms. I noted an Alzheimer's support group flyer and another for Parkinson's disease. Old couples came and went. A young woman who seemed to be drunk rushed to the inner door when a name was called, but it wasn't hers and the nurse sent her back to her seat. Meanwhile, Fred read *Sports Illustrated*, and I stared at *Ladies' Home Journal* until the nurse called us in.

We went into the examining room together and waited. When Dr. Mac entered, looking just like Major Charles Winchester on the old M*A*S*H TV series, he asked Fred if he knew why he was there.

He grinned. "Uh, I can't remember."

The doctor didn't laugh. He turned to me. "Why are you here?"

"Fred's having trouble remembering things. He gets confused."

"I see."

The doctor turned to Fred. "Is this a problem in your life?"

"No."

"Do you drink?"

"Not much."

"You wrote on your form that you were a tax preparer but you retired this year. Did this memory problem have anything to do with it?"

"No."

But none of that was true. "That *is* why he quit," I said. "It *is* getting to be a problem." I felt like I was betraying my husband, but the doctor needed the facts.

Dr. Mac talked to me over my husband's head after that. I kept trying to direct him back to Fred, and he kept coming back to me. I suppose I was the reliable witness while the patient was no longer considered reliable, but Fred was not a babbling idiot, just a scared man who got confused sometimes. He was more normal than not.

In the end, what we said didn't matter. The tests told the tale. With Dr. Mac's assistant, "Sunshine," smiling at me every time I looked her way, he administered the standard Alzheimer's disease questionnaire, known as the "mini-mental" exam. What is the date? Where are you? What city is this? Who won the election? Fred did surprisingly well on these questions. He also did well at copying a geometrical shape and writing a sentence. He wrote that he had been to the aviation museum. He could name the planes he had seen. But he couldn't spell "world" backward or count back from one hundred by sevens, and he couldn't remember the four words the doctor had shown him at the beginning of the test. Potato, green, Mars, horse.

The doctor had Fred touch his nose, stick out his tongue, raise a leg and the opposite arm, and walk normally, then on his toes, and on his heels. He did fine. Maybe he was okay.

Maybe not.

"I think there is a problem," Dr. Mac concluded. "A man of Fred's age should score higher on the memory test. Seeing no physical problems, he is most likely in the early stages of Alzheimer's disease."

Fred stared at his hands, picking at a hangnail.

"He's only sixty-seven," I said. "Isn't that a little young?"

"Yes and no. Most people are diagnosed later in life, but it happens."

Dr. Mac said he would start him on a drug called Namenda, then add another drug, Aricept, in a month. The pills would not cure him, but they might slow the progression of the disease.

He ordered Fred not to drink hard liquor anymore and to cut back to just one glass of wine a day.

"He can't seem to smell anything," I said. "Is that related?"

"Yes, that is significant," he said, without going into detail.

That was it. I had expected a long sit-down talk about AD and its implications, but no. He handed us a prescription slip and sent us out to the desk to set up an appointment to return in three months.

In the elevator, we hugged.

"What now?" Fred asked.

"I don't know. We go home."

In the parking lot, Fred remembered where the car was; I didn't.

We silently slid into our accustomed places, me in the passenger seat, Fred behind the steering wheel. Dr. Mac didn't say anything about Fred giving up driving. At that point, I didn't see any reason why he should. He was still a better driver than I was, as long as he knew where he was going.

We didn't say much or sing on the two-hour drive back. Fred had no interest in stopping at the antique stores, bookstores, or coffee shops we passed in McMinnville. I squeezed his shoulder, he touched my leg. I stroked his beard, and we said we loved each other, but mostly we were quiet—not unlike when we had driven home from the hospital after Fred's father died.

That night, we ate pizza and toasted with beer. We agreed not to tell the family yet and retired to the den to watch television. It was practice night for the barbershop chorus where Fred sang bass, but he decided to stay home.

In a way, I was glad for the diagnosis because now I could join a support group, take steps to deal with the problems, and understand what was going on.

I wanted to toss my own life out the window and replace it with my new obsession, Alzheimer's disease, but I knew I must not lose myself. I needed to build a life for when this was over. The one thing every website, book, and support group emphasized was that the caregiver had to take care of herself. I could not stop writing, teaching, or singing, could not devote every minute of my life to Fred or I'd fall apart.

The next morning, while I wrote in my journal, Fred was in the other room catching up on email. When we met in the kitchen for lunch, he would need me to help him pick out his food, and he would take forever to eat it. If I asked him later what he had eaten, he would not remember.

He was no different than he was the day before, except that now we knew. The problem had a name: Alzheimer's disease.

6 Our Secret

A few weeks after our visit to Dr. Mac, we were packing for our annual Thanksgiving trip to California. The family hadn't seen Fred in nearly a year. One of the disappointments of our move to Oregon was that the visits seemed all one-way. We visited them, but they didn't visit us. Too far. Too busy. Work. School. They only had one vacation, and they'd been to Oregon before.

As we stood on opposite sides of the bed packing our suitcases, mine as always an overstuffed mess while Fred's was neat and had room to spare, I asked, "Should we tell them?"

"Tell them what?"

"About the, um, Alzheimer's."

He didn't look up from the shirt he was folding. "No."

"Okay." I pictured my brother's dining room, two long tables crowded with our family, his wife and kids, and his in-laws. Not a good time for depressing news. They probably wouldn't notice anything anyway.

"Can I put my slippers in your suitcase?"

We celebrated the holiday at Mike's house in Merced, a farm town in California's Central Valley. I sat between Fred and my dad. We were elbow to elbow, passing turkey, stuffing, sweet potatoes, salad, and rolls. Fred had brought wine as usual, but this time he wasn't drinking.

"Is the wine bad or something?" my sister-in-law Sharon asked.

"It's fine. I'm just trying to cut back," Fred said. "Do you have any coffee made?"

"I'll make some." As Sharon hurried to the kitchen, my nephew asked for more turkey, and the conversation turned to other subjects. Fred, normally a quiet guy anyway, didn't talk much. Nor did I. This Thanksgiving, we were all very much aware of the ones who were missing, including our mother, my sister-in-law's father, and Uncle Bob, who had died a few months earlier. As the wine flowed and we stuffed ourselves with good food, the chatter got louder, swirling around us while Fred and I kept our problems to ourselves.

After dinner, some of the women started washing dishes while the men settled in the family room to watch football. Aunt Suzanne, who had been married to Uncle Bob, invited Fred and me for a walk. Mike and Sharon's home was at the end of a cul-de-sac, surrounded by upper-middle-class, ranch-style houses with big yards and well-kept gardens. As we circled the neighborhood, I was dying to tell my aunt what was going on, but Fred was right there, so we talked about other things.

It was that way all weekend. Over turkey sandwiches in the evening, we talked about traffic, weather, jobs, and kids. We didn't mention Alzheimer's.

The next day, we stopped in Livermore on our way home to have brunch with Fred's son Ted and his partner Shelly. They had just remodeled their home. We followed them around, admiring the woodwork and new furniture, then sat in the kitchen watching Ted, a professional chef, prepare the food. The kids did most of the talking. They had no idea Fred was not his usual self. If he forgot a word or said something that didn't make sense, they probably blamed the champagne we drank with our quiche and croissants.

Soon we were on the road back to Oregon.

We thought we had gotten away with it, but the day after we arrived home, the phone rang.

"What's going on with Fred?" my brother asked. "How come he's not drinking?"

It was Fred's afternoon at the aquarium, so I was free to talk. I told

Mike about Fred's Alzheimer's. I heard him grow quiet on the other end of the line as the news sank in. Fred and Mike had been friends since Mike, now an attorney, was a teenage recreation aide. Fred had run the community center in East San Jose where he worked. I hated to lay this on him.

"We haven't told Dad. We haven't told anybody yet," I said. "Please don't say anything."

"Sheesh," he said, clearing his throat. "Well, keep me informed."

When we hung up, I reached for my dog. "Oh, Sadie," I said, holding her as tightly as I could. Things were getting too real.

Shortly after the diagnosis, longtime friends from San Jose came to visit. They brought the husband's recently widowed mother, Madge. She told us what had happened to her husband, who suffered from dementia.

For five years, she said, Bill called her "Hello." That was after the stroke that transformed him overnight from a normal adult into a two-year-old boy. He no longer knew her name, and she never knew what he would do next. "For five years, I slept with one eye open," said the feisty octogenarian.

Finally, she had to let go, placing Bill in the nursing home where he died. She had already buried her first husband when her sons were small, and she had lost her younger son to AIDS.

Sitting around our table eating seafood lasagna, Madge and our friends told "Bill stories," completely unaware that Fred and I were entering that same dark tunnel through which Madge and Bill had struggled. This was Alzheimer's, not a stroke, and our progress was slower. We could still see the light at the entry, but we were definitely inside, with no turning back.

Bill sometimes poured coffee on his corn flakes. He tried to fix a burned-out light bulb with a hammer and screwdriver. He repaired a leaky hose by sawing it into pieces. He cut off the plug end of a lamp cord, then didn't understand why it didn't work.

With each story, the three visitors laughed harder.

Fred and I were not laughing as they foretold our future. My husband sat red-faced and silent at the end of the table, playing with his napkin. I jumped up frequently to refill coffee cups or remove empty plates. If they had only known, they would have shut up. *Tell them, tell them,* my mind screamed, but of course we didn't. These were our friends. They would be devastated when they found out. They would also feel guilty forever.

Why hadn't they guessed yet? I already had a collection of "Fred stories"—the time he called an ice cube an apple at a restaurant, the time he called the dog by his son's name, the time he sat watching a blank screen because he couldn't work the TV controls. But I was not ready to tell these stories out loud. Besides, Fred should be the one to decide whether or not to tell.

We moved into the living room, our friends on the couch, Madge on the loveseat, Fred in the big chair. I sat on the floor beside him, close, protective. The conversation changed to other topics.

Now Madge was quiet, twisting two diamond-laden rings on her gnarled finger. Was she missing the powerful man who had given them to her on bended knee, promising to love and care for her, or the ghost who called "Hello" in the dark? Or was she just tired?

I looked down at the gold band on my own ring finger and at the bearded man beside me and reached for his hand, holding tight.

When our company rose to leave, I hugged Madge hard, although I barely knew her.

"Did it bother you?" I asked Fred later in the hot tub.

"No," he said, sliding into the steamy water and staring up at the stars.

A week later, Fred looked handsome in his red vest and white shirt, ready to sing with the Coastal-Aires at the aquarium's "Sea of Lights" Christmas party. The aquarium glittered with colored lights. We were not thinking about AD.

Then this volunteer, Polly, was suddenly in my face, jingle bells on her fuzzy Christmas vest. "Don't wait too long," she said. "Put him in a nursing home. Move back to the Bay Area. You're too young and talented. Don't wait until it's too late."

We hadn't told her about Fred's illness, but she had figured it out. She said she was planning an aquarium party to honor Fred, as if he had finished volunteering, even though he had no plans to quit.

She talked on and on while I kept watching to make sure Fred wasn't close enough to hear us. All I could get out was, "Please don't say anything about it. Please."

Fred had no idea. Later, when Polly was helping the children get their pictures taken with Santa, Fred sought her out, arms open for a big hug. She talked to him as if he were a child. *Don't. Don't knock him off his post-concert high. People keep thanking him and praising him for his music. Let him bask in it. Don't mention AD. Don't you dare.*

If she did say anything, Fred didn't catch it. I watched him grab a candy cane from the basket behind her and move on.

Once people know you have Alzheimer's, they treat you differently. They talk down to you and don't trust you to do things on your own. They see every verbal stumble as a symptom. In the early days, he was still a functional adult human being. He had quit his tax practice, but I still kissed him goodbye every Tuesday afternoon with no doubt about his ability to drive to the aquarium and entertain visitors with his knowledge about the animals there. Even on his days off, he couldn't help sharing. As we walked through the exhibits, he would ask the children clustered at the windows, "Did you see the way the otter sleeps with his paws on his chest?" Or "Did you know that some sea birds can fly in the water?"

He still ordered the "two two two" (eggs, bacon, pancakes) breakfast at the Big Guy's Diner and sang with the tunes as we shopped at Pirate's Plunder.

He still kept the pellet stove filled and changed the chemicals in the spa.

He was changing, but for now, it was between us and Dr. Mac.

7 This is My Brain on Prozac

As Fred's memory problems increased, I began to have trouble sleeping. Having heard that I had been treated for depression back in California, Dr. H. had been trying to put me on drugs for years. Tranquilizers, antidepressants, hormones, whatever it would take to "even me out."

What a chauvinist, I thought. Yes, I went a little nuts for ten days every month with PMS, and now I was premenopausal. Yes, I got depressed sitting in our house in the woods while it rained for months and the sun never appeared. Yes, I grieved when a dozen loved ones died in the same year. Now my husband had Alzheimer's disease. Yes, I was depressed. Who in their right mind wouldn't be?

I was also anxious and prone to panic attacks. They had started the year before we moved to Oregon when I came down with Graves' disease, a hyperthyroid disorder that sends everything into overdrive. I couldn't drive on the freeway, ran off the risers during choir concerts because my heart was beating too fast, and felt the room spinning while I talked to people at work. There were other symptoms, including weight loss, blurry vision, rapid heartbeat, and hot flashes, but the panic attacks were the most debilitating.

Before the Graves' was diagnosed, I saw a therapist, took an occasional Xanax pill, read self-help books, and worked through the twelve steps in a codependency group at church trying to get a grip on my emotions.

Finally my ophthalmologist took one look at my protruding eyes and sent me to the lab for a thyroid test.

After drugs and radioactive iodine treatment subdued my thyroid, most of the symptoms subsided, but the panic attacks lingered. Having a husband with Alzheimer's didn't help.

I can't sleep, I told Dr. H. Was I willing to take something? Maybe. Hormones? No thanks. I hated the way I skipped a period, then made up for it with a double. I wanted my ovaries to work menopause out on their own.

Dr. H. suggested Prozac.

I would take a small dose, ten milligrams, just enough to let me sleep and relax. I decided to try it.

Soon after I started taking the pills, I experienced panic attacks two days in a row, one at the library and one at choir practice. After that, I just felt numb and a little crazy. I heard myself saying things I wouldn't usually say and saw myself doing things I wouldn't usually do. Playing the piano at church, I was completely free of stage fright. I still made mistakes, but I didn't care. I was the all-powerful maestro.

Then the nausea started. After a few days of that, I sat in the doctor's office staring at the barf basins, wondering if I should put one in my lap just in case. I breathed shallowly, trying not to move.

Dr. H. suggested taking three days' worth of Prozac on Mondays and nothing the rest of the week. That sounded dangerous, but he was the doctor.

I took my mega-dose of Prozac on Monday morning and went out to lunch. I was so tired by the time I got home, I crawled into bed at three in the afternoon. I slept till almost dark, waking up tired and achy. The next day at the grocery store, still so nauseated I couldn't look at the meat, I got dizzy. The world revolved around me in such big circles I had to cling to the shopping cart to stay upright. I really didn't want an ambulance to come roaring up to the J.C. Market for me.

I thought about calling Fred, but he was at the aquarium and probably wouldn't be able to help me anyway.

I made it home, threw myself onto the couch and called the doctor amid the nonstop hula hoop going around my face. "I'm @#$% dizzy!"

"Oh, I'm sorry," he said. "It's such a tiny dose. How about taking the three pills on Mondays, Wednesdays and Fridays?"

All right. I bought a purple days-of-the-week pill box to help me remember what day to take my pills. I swallowed them obediently. I felt less stoned, more normal, and slept like a squashed raccoon on the highway on Tuesday, Thursday and Saturday mornings.

But I wasn't getting any work done. I was too busy sleeping, watching TV, playing solitaire, and telling myself I'd get around to it sooner or later. Besides, I had already written too many things that nobody was reading.

Depression turned everything dark. Unable to work, I spent days crying and eating all the chocolate in the house. Fred didn't seem to realize I was having trouble. I still got out of bed every day. I cooked his meals and kept track of his schedule. I played my church music, and I sat at my desk every morning while he played solitaire on his computer and volunteered at the aquarium. But I felt horrible.

I went back to the doctor and told him my story.

"I don't like the sound of this," he said. "Let's take you off Prozac. Don't take any more. It will stay in your system for a couple of weeks. Call me in three weeks, and I'll start you on another drug called Lexapro. People usually tolerate it better."

I strutted out of that office feeling triumphant. No more Prozac. I laughed, I smiled, I looked around at my work and my world and said, "This is good." It was the week between Christmas and New Year's. Time for a fresh start.

I didn't sleep much. I had too much to do. I reorganized my office, practiced the piano for three hours, cleaned the house, and went through my financial records and manuscript submission files.

Everything looked as if I had been gone for months. I was back in my right mind, and things were going to shape up now. While Fred was in bed by eight o'clock, I stayed up late and woke up early. I engaged my friends in long babbling phone conversations, which must have made them wonder about me.

When I played the piano, the keys felt like magic under my fingers. My hot flashes were back, but so what?

And then, and then, and then. Eight thirty Tuesday night, Fred was reading in bed while I read the newspaper on the couch under one of his mother's pink afghans.

Suddenly the world started spinning. I had been dizzy before. It passed. Not this time. Dizzy grew to *dizzy* to *OhMyGodDizzy* as in I-can't-stand-up, think-I-might-faint dizzy. I staggered to bed, the room swooping now, not just gentle turns but hard, fast, blurry ones.

"I'm really dizzy," I said.

"Do you need to go to the hospital?"

"I don't know."

As I lay next to Fred, the circles spun faster. I picked up a book. Instant nausea. Shallow breathing. Sweating. Gonna vomit. No I'm not. Yes I am. I ran to the toilet, but nothing came out.

I pulled out the guidebook from my old HMO and struggled to read the dizziness section, especially the part where it says *if this happens, go to the hospital.* I gathered my clothes from the couch, slipped back into my jeans, tee shirt, and pink fleece vest, and staggered back to the bedroom. "I need to go to the hospital."

Thank God Fred could still drive. We left Sadie sleeping at the foot of the bed. As we drove up the highway, I saw everything in a blur: a neighbor's Christmas lights still on, a sign promoting *Fiddler on the Roof* at the local theater, a patch of fog.

I breathed shallowly, clutching my purse. Cold. I had thrown the coat I got for Christmas in the back seat for fear I would vomit on it.

The hospital. Parking lot. Holding onto Fred through the

emergency door. A friend, Lorrie, was working the desk, wearing a flowered top and white pants. I gasped out my plight, presented my insurance card, told her my birth date, doctor's name, and that yes, I was still having periods. Breathing shallowly, nauseated, trembling, scared, angry.

Private room. A short balding doctor in green scrubs checked my breathing and tested me for stroke symptoms. No stroke.

He looked at his chart. "You were taking Prozac for depression, correct?"

I nodded. "Yes."

"I have to ask. Have you had any suicidal thoughts?"

"No. I'm just dizzy."

"And how long ago did you stop the Prozac?"

"Three days."

"Well, this is not unusual. I'm pretty sure you're having a panic attack caused by withdrawal from Prozac," said the doctor. "We'll give you Ativan to calm you down."

I was calm, just dizzy.

The doctor and nurses went away. I sat on the bed staring at boxes of purple plastic gloves and *Sports Illustrated* in a rack on the wall. Fred offered me a magazine. Too dizzy to read. People talking and laughing outside. Where's my pill that will make this stop?

Finally. The nurse. A small paper cup with icy water. A tiny yellow pill. More pills for the next three nights. An information sheet on panic attacks. See your doctor within two days.

Feeling shaky, I let Fred lead me through the waiting room and out to the car.

Back through the quiet streets of Newport. I leaned against the car door and wept. So much. Too much. Fred was sick, and I was falling apart, needing him to take care of me. Stuck in a vicious cycle of drugs administered by a doctor who didn't know what he was doing, I was now officially on the books as depressed and anxious.

My post-Prozac high was gone. The Ativan made me sleepy. That week I bought a book of piano music, couldn't wait to play it, but ran out of energy on the second song. I let Fred go to an aquarium potluck empty-handed. I lost two days of work and wondered if I could pull myself together in time to teach my next class at the community college.

Prozac, you bastard. I wanted to take the rest of those white-and-green-striped capsules and stomp them into dust.

8 Alzheimer's Nights

One night, just as I was falling into a delicious sleep, dreaming about a banquet filled with fruit and autumn colors, Fred made a grumbling noise and slid out of bed. He poked around at the mattress. Suddenly he was on top of the bed on his hands and knees, starting to crawl over me.

"What are you doing?" I mumbled.

"I have to go to the bathroom."

"You're going the wrong way. It's over there."

He kept going across my knees toward the window. I slipped out of bed, grabbed his limp hand, and pulled him toward the hallway.

"Ow," he said as I bumped him into the light switch.

"Sorry. But now you're awake, right?"

He wasn't. I led him into the hall. When I let go, he sleep-walked into his office and stood there, his white T-shirt shining in the green lights on the photocopier and fax machine.

"No. Come on." I pulled him the rest of the way to the bathroom and nudged him in. I wanted to shout, "Wake up! Come back! Be normal!"

I thought about Phil in the weekly Alzheimer's support group I had joined after the diagnosis. One night at a hotel, he had found his wife out in the hall in her nightgown, thinking she was in the bathroom. More recently, back in Lincoln City, she had gone outside and gotten into the car, where she had sat waiting for him to drive her "home." So far, Fred had only wandered as far as his office.

* * *

In a few days, we would fly to Burbank, California, for Fred's fifty-year high school reunion. Early flights both ways, minimal sleep time. Please God, I prayed, let him keep it together in front of his classmates and don't let me weep through it all.

The ninety-minute flight to Burbank went fine. Fred's best friends from high school, Barry and Irene, picked us up at the airport. We checked into our room, then joined the party downstairs for dinner, sharing one of the big round tables in the hotel ballroom with Fred's classmates. As the band played music from the 1950s, we danced, Fred in his blue suit, me in my long black skirt and glittery top. His cheek close to mine, we sang "Old Black Magic," "My Funny Valentine," and "Can't Help Falling in Love."

It was beautiful, but I kept fighting tears. This might be the last time we ever got dressed up and danced together. If I thought about that, if I thought about how Alzheimer's was taking everything away from us, it would ruin the moment. So I held my man and sang with him, surrounded by other couples from the John Burroughs High School class of 1955.

All weekend, people came up to Fred, shouting his name, reconnecting with the popular football player Fred had been. Fred might not have remembered their names, but he was in his glory.

I ached to share my worries with Barry and Irene. I imagined the motherly Irene would grab me up in her arms and let me cry.

But no. We kept our talk to the meals we ate and the memories of their years at Burroughs, memories I couldn't share because I was three years old when Fred and his friends graduated.

Barry and Irene drove us around all weekend as we joined other classmates touring the school, visiting the old neighborhood, and eating at their favorite Mexican restaurant.

Fred tried to pay for lunch with his room key, but no one noticed.

* * *

Fred had slept well that weekend in Burbank, but at home, he was often up at night, his state somewhere between waking and sleeping. In the dark, under the influence of his illness and his Aricept pills, he turned into someone I didn't know. It usually began around midnight.

I felt a trembling in the bed. Fred started thrashing around as if his skin were on fire. Suddenly he slipped half off the bed toward the floor, taking the covers with him.

I held my breath. Sadie, sleeping at the foot of the bed, stopped snoring.

Pulling himself back up, Fred lay on his back laughing.

"Are you all right?" I asked, rubbing his shoulder, hoping he was awake.

"Get a load of those hats," he said.

"What hats?"

He pointed toward the blank wall. "There. That one's pink."

"Oh. Pink's good. I like pink."

I rolled over and tried to go back to sleep. Just when the fog of dreams began to thicken, I felt the trembling again. Once more, Fred did battle.

Meanwhile, wherever I looked, the room was slowly spinning, as if I had had too much to drink. Anxiety. Gritting my teeth, I turned my back to my husband and tried to sleep.

At one forty-five, I got out of bed, grabbed my slippers, robe, and glasses, and retreated to the guest room. As soon as I got settled, the dog appeared in the doorway, needing to go out. I stood in the kitchen doorway, looking at the deep gray night, hearing the mist-muffled ocean and the dog's tags tinkling in the dark, until she came bounding back across the deck. I gave her a Milk-Bone and we both went to bed.

The next night, I stuck it out until four o'clock before the trembling, thrashing, and crazy talk got to me.

"It's dark," he complained.

"It's nighttime."

He got up, walked to the bathroom door, and stood there, then turned around and came back to bed.

Another night, he turned toward me and asked, "Who are you?"

A week later, I woke to find him scrabbling toward the wall behind the bed, almost as if he were swimming.

"What are you doing?"

"There's someone there. I have to get them."

Another night, he slugged me in the shoulder.

He wrestled with the covers as if they were demons.

One night, he chased dogs gathered at the head of the bed. He went after them with his pillow, banging it near my face.

"There are no dogs," I said. But he kept going. I guess he won the battle because he put down his pillow and went back to sleep.

Usually he didn't remember anything about his wild nights. Standing at the kitchen sink, sipping his orange juice and reading the paper, he would greet me with a hearty "Good morning!" I'd tell him what he had said and done. He'd widen his eyes in surprise. "I did? No!"

One morning, he did remember. "Oh yeah, there was a giant lady beside the bed. She was just huge. She had this pink hat on. It was pointed at the front and back. I didn't want to tell her she was fat, but she was! And there were giant football players . . . You were there!"

"Yes, I was." I sighed.

I was losing my husband to Alzheimer's disease. Someday soon, he would move permanently into that halfway state between waking and sleeping. For now, he plunged into a sea of nightmares, hallucinations, and confusions at night but got a day pass to reality between dawn and bedtime. Not that there weren't daytime problems, too.

"Where are you going?" he asked on a Monday evening when I went into the den to kiss him goodbye.

"It's Monday. I have to teach my class."

"Where?"

"Oregon Coast Community College."

"Oh yeah." He waved the remote control at the blank TV screen. "I can't work this thing."

"Football?" I pushed buttons and got the Channel 2 news. "The game doesn't start for another twenty minutes. You just have to wait. Don't touch anything."

"Okay. Thank you."

Dinner hanging like a rock in my stomach, I kissed him goodbye and went out the door.

Fred was in bed when I got home, the TV still on.

I missed talking with him, rehashing our days. His conversation, once a colander with tiny holes, had deteriorated into a fishing net with more holes than string. Often we sat through an entire meal without saying anything. It took all of his concentration to eat. But the nights, God help us, the nights, were eternal.

Most nights, Fred retired around eight, and I found my way to bed with a flashlight after the eleven o'clock news. We no longer made love, but sometimes he rolled toward me in bed and I slid into his arms, feeling his warmth, stroking his soft hair and his strong hands. He'd kiss me and rub my back, shoulders, and belly. Then we'd move to our separate sides of the bed. A minute later, I'd hear his breathing slow as he fell asleep.

I missed being touched. Some nights, tears filled my eyes and rolled down the sides of my face. I wanted to sob. The books I'd been reading about caregiving preached that I needed to present a positive, optimistic, reassuring attitude. Fred was the one with the fatal disease.

So I rubbed the tears away with my hands and forced myself to think about the shows I had watched on TV that night. From there, my mind wandered to my departed mother, to long-ago days at music camp, to past jobs, past lives, to what I might make for dinner the next day. I began to feel sleepy, began to descend into my dreams.

Then the trembling beside me began.

9 "Your Dad Has Alzheimer's"

My first Oregon shrink looked alarmingly similar to Fred's ex-wife. Same long hair, narrow face, little mouth. I had joined her grief group when my mother died of cancer a few months after we lost Fred's mom. This had been the first major loss in my life, and I hadn't known how to deal with it. Several other family members and friends had also died that year. I needed to talk about it. But I soon discovered that listening to other people talk about their grief didn't help me with mine, and now I needed to talk about what was happening with Fred.

So I didn't object when Dr. H. referred me to a psychiatrist after the Prozac fiasco.

It wasn't my first foray into therapy. That started back in 1983 after I was dumped by my boyfriend, who bounced between telling me he loved me and wanted to father my children and telling me I was a selfish, worthless bitch only good for sex. I hadn't completely processed my divorce before going into that relationship, and when that went south, I became so depressed I couldn't function. I needed help. It was during those weekly therapy sessions that I decided to dump my life to sing with the show that went bust.

If the show hadn't gone bankrupt, I wouldn't have been at my brother's Christmas party, and I would not have met Fred. I'm sure God planned it that way.

I headed back into therapy in the late '80s as I struggled to deal with childlessness and again in the '90s when I started having panic attacks sparked by Graves' disease.

My family had always called me the "nervous" kid. I suffered frequent stress-induced stomachaches and headaches, but my parents believed in pushing through minor discomforts and getting things done. So I might have a migraine or screaming menstrual cramps, but I still got straight A's. In Mom and Dad's view, only crazy people needed counseling or medication for mental health. I wonder how my life might have been different if I had learned ways to calm myself when I was young.

In my adulthood, sometimes depression sucked all the color out of my life. But I kept going, writing, playing my music, getting my MFA. During grad school graduation week, where I was the class speaker, I popped Imodium pills every day to keep the nervous diarrhea at bay. I knew I couldn't keep doing that forever. I had to deal with my stress.

So I made an appointment with Dr. Smith, the psychiatrist Dr. H. recommended. His office was located in a beach cottage full of art, leather furniture and kids' toys. Dr. Smith was young, probably late thirties, with a Dutch-boy hairdo. His massive dog named Gus greeted me with a sloppy kiss.

Dr. Smith's mother had early onset AD when he was just a teenager, so he knew about living with dementia.

"What brings you here?" he asked.

I told him about Fred. I shared my Prozac story and my experience with Graves' disease.

"Which is worse, the depression or the anxiety?" he asked.

"Depends on the day."

"Are you open to trying a different medication?"

"I don't know. I'd rather do things naturally."

"I understand, and we'll work on that, but you've got a lot on your plate. You said you took Xanax before. Would you be willing to try a little of that? A low dose might iron out the free-floating anxiety and occasional panic attacks."

"Okay." It sounded better than the evil Prozac.

And it was. My first night on Xanax, I had a long, wonderful sleep. Would it keep me asleep on nights when Fred woke up hallucinating?

Apparently not.

On the second night, before I even turned off my light, Fred told me he saw men in blackface, as in Al Jolson singing "Mammy."

"There's nobody there. Go to sleep."

At one o'clock, I woke to find him walking around the bed to my side.

"What are you doing?

"I can't get out. I need to go to the bathroom."

"Turn around and go the other way."

He stood there, confused. I got up and led him by the hand into the bathroom. After he found his way back to bed, he told me he hadn't been able to get out because there were "too many people" on his side of the bed, people dressed in white. They looked like kitchen workers to him.

The rest of the night, he seemed to move constantly, battling more demons. Despite the Xanax, I was awake.

In the morning, he remembered it all. He kept shaking his head, horrified at the thought that I'd had to lead him to the bathroom because he couldn't find it on his own.

"I used to walk in my sleep when I was a kid," he said.

"You did?"

"One night, I walked down the street in my pajamas to the neighbor's house and knocked on the door. They let me sleep on the couch the rest of the night. I was sure surprised when I woke up there in the morning."

"I'll bet. Do you think this is related?"

"I don't know. That was a long time ago."

While Fred wandered through his nights, I wandered through my days, sleep-deprived and Xanax-numbed. Alzheimer's pills and tranquilizers, mail, and books on AD piled up on the kitchen table. Dirty dishes grew mold in the sink. I had articles to write and classes to teach. Fred needed my help every five minutes. At noon, I was still in my bathrobe. I really didn't care.

After driving for two hours through hard rain and wind, we saw Dr. Mac again for all of six minutes. At this three-month follow-up visit, he changed Fred's meds, stopping the Aricept and adding Razadyne, hoping to end the hallucinations.

The doctor was already halfway out the door, but I asked him for an estimate of how long Fred had. He said, "I'm not God, but I'd guess about ten years. There are always new drugs and new research offering some hope."

Yes, I thought, but when?

That night, during our weekly phone call, I told my father about Fred. He was surprisingly calm. Not happy, of course, but he had seen plenty of dementia and lived through it with his own father. Over the years that followed, we would trade stories about doctors, hospitals, nursing homes and dying spouses. Who would have guessed we'd wind up with so much in common?

Fred's adult kids still didn't know. Busy with their own lives, they didn't visit and rarely called. Fred being a hands-off kind of father, he contacted them maybe once or twice a year. I was the one who remembered their birthdays and sent them Christmas presents. But they were his children, and the people in the Alzheimer's support group insisted it was time we tell them.

Their reactions varied.

Ted, the oldest, was the first to return Fred's call. Fred told me his son sounded calm but concerned. He asked how I was doing.

A while later, he called back and suggested that we all go to Hawaii.

The next day, Ted sent me an email. He wanted more information. I gave him the Alzheimer's Association website address and a general overview of his dad's condition. I cried as I typed. Maybe the kids were really going to help me with this.

By the time we talked on the telephone, Ted had done a lot of reading. He had good questions about long-term care insurance and other financial matters. He also needed reassurance that I would stay with his father. I promised I would not abandon Fred.

Gretchen, who was thirty-five and lived in Newark, California, was a different story. She returned our call from a noisy birthday party for her husband. By the time I got on the other phone, Fred had given her the news.

She shouted, cried, told us she loved us, and scolded us for not telling her sooner. She put us on the speaker to sing "Happy Birthday" and to say hi to everyone. She ordered me to set up a family reunion or bring her father down to visit. Would he like to join them for a season-opener football game in San Francisco?

I told her she just needed to call more often, that it was hard for us to travel, that she needed to come here. I knew she wasn't listening. She insisted her father would beat this thing, and he wouldn't forget her.

Fred's ex-wife, Annette, was at the party. She had been married to him for twenty-four years before their divorce. She was stunned.

When we got off the phone with Gretchen, I pulled out the mint chocolate chip ice cream. "You want a bowl or a cone?" I asked Fred.

"Bowl."

"Me too."

When child number three, Michael, twenty-seven, called from Portland, Fred was at the aquarium. Michael sounded like he was in a blue mood already, but there was no putting it off.

I asked if he had spoken with his sister, his brother or his mom. I hoped they had already told him. No. So I did it. "I'm so sorry to have to tell you this, but your father has Alzheimer's disease. It's not too bad now, but the future is pretty scary."

"Oh," he said. Then silence.

"You should try to spend time with him and call him as much as possible."

"Yeah."

We went on to Michael's troubles. Just like the singer in a country song, his girl had dumped him, he had no money, his debts were growing, and he felt bad.

"I'm sorry," I said.

He had a new job that paid more than the last one, so there was hope. But I could tell he didn't feel it just then. In fact, his misery was already so complete that I didn't know whether he could really absorb what I had told him about his father. But the deed was done.

I guess I was hoping the kids would say, "What can I do to help? I'll come once a month to give you a break. We'll figure this out as a family." Or . . . something.

But they lived far away and weren't free to run back and forth to South Beach. They had never seen dementia up close the way I had with my grandfather. And they had already had a hard couple of years. Their mother, who had not remarried, had been fighting cancer. Their maternal grandparents were nearing death, and their paternal grandparents were gone.

Ted was running a business and getting married soon. Gretchen had work and kids to take care of. Michael was busy working, although he did visit occasionally.

I understand their reactions better now than I did at the time. When my mother was dying, I visited a lot, but I always knew that my father was there to handle most of her care. It was painful to watch, and I tried to help, but the biggest burden wasn't on me. It was the same for Fred's kids. I was the wife, and they were the kids. To them, his care was my job.

Why did we stay in Oregon when nearly all of our family lived in California? Fred loved it here, plus we couldn't afford to go back.

Costs had skyrocketed in Silicon Valley. A $200,000 home in Oregon cost over a million dollars there.

At one point a few years into his diagnosis, I decided we had to find a way to go home to California. Maybe we could rent something cheap. Maybe we could borrow money. Sitting in the flickering candlelight on a rainy night when the power had gone out, I told Fred what I was thinking.

He nodded. "It's because of me, isn't it?"

"Yes."

"Damn."

I looked at houses online and started talking to a realtor. But when I added up the numbers, we just couldn't do it. We could barely afford this house in Oregon. Besides, we had established our lives here. Though I yearned to be near my family, and I knew there were more options for Alzheimer's patients in San Jose—things like daycare, support groups for patients, and neurologists we didn't have to drive two hours to visit—I didn't see how we could move. Even if we had the money, relocating would be too much upheaval for Fred and hard on me because he wouldn't be able to help.

But my relatives pushed for us to come home. They sent me real estate ads and information about Alzheimer's facilities in California. Some implied that we wouldn't be in this fix if we hadn't moved all the way to Oregon.

Should we have gone back to California? I don't know.

10 Giving Up the Keys

A year went by. When Fred said he was going somewhere off Highway 34 to buy fuel for the pellet stove, my immediate thought was that I needed to go along. He couldn't tell me exactly where the store was, just somewhere east of Waldport. I wasn't sure he would be able to find the place or drive there safely. But I wasn't dressed, and I couldn't come up with a convincing reason for him to wait while I got ready.

When he wanted to take Sadie with him, I hesitated. I knew how much of a distraction she could be, jumping around, panting in your ear as you turn or park the car. But I didn't say anything, just got the leash and handed it to Fred.

"At least take the cell phone in case you get in trouble."

"I won't. Besides, I can't work that thing."

Off they went. I tried to write, glancing at the clock every few minutes.

An hour later, I heard the door open and the dog's tags jingling.

"You made it," I said as the dog dashed past me to the bathroom to drink out of the toilet.

"Of course."

I squelched a comment that two years after his Alzheimer's diagnosis, there was no "of course" anymore. "What do you want for lunch?"

"Ham and eggs."

"Fine."

As I ate, matching a piece of ham with a forkful of scrambled eggs,

I remembered why the date, December 7, had been tickling my brain all morning. "It's your dad's birthday. Want to go to the cemetery?"

"Okay."

He drove. We stopped first at the post office. He nearly hit a truck on my side.

At the cemetery, he almost hit the wall by the mausoleum. With no room to get out of the truck on the passenger side, I slid over the brake and out the other door before joining Fred in the small room lined with full-sized creches and glass-fronted niches for urns. It smelled of dust and rotting artificial flowers.

Fred's mother's, father's and brother's ashes were lined up in a double niche halfway up the far wall next to the window. "Hi, guys," I said, pulling plastic flowers out of the bag I had brought, switching out the daffodils and daisies for poinsettias and pine cones.

Fred stared at the urns, sniffing back tears. "I miss them."

I hugged him. "I know. I do, too."

I meditated on the urns with him for a minute.

"The flowers look good," Fred said. "Ready to go?"

Coming home, I could feel him nudging the truck closer and closer to the edge of the road.

"Honey, get over."

"I'm fine. Let me drive."

Just a week and a half earlier, we had taken turns driving on our long trip home from California after Thanksgiving. But suddenly, he seemed to drive in uncontrolled jerks and couldn't judge the distance between the car and objects on the right.

During a talk our support group attended, an Alzheimer's Association spokeswoman told us that a good way to decide whether you should let a loved one keep driving is to ask ourselves if we would let our children ride with them. I didn't have children, but I was afraid for my dog.

* * *

One of the dangers of attending an Alzheimer's support group is that you hear about the loved ones who are ahead of you on the downward trail.

On this day in early 2007, our group was small, just Phil, whose wife, Fran, had AD, and Bob and Carol, who had been helping their friend Joe. Carol had brought cookies. It was their last time coming to the meeting. Joe had been hospitalized in Portland and would not be coming home. His daughter was making arrangements for long-term care in a skilled nursing facility.

While in the hospital, Joe was so crazed and belligerent that the hospital staff kept him drugged and sometimes tied him down. When Bob and Carol visited, he acted calm, and he seemed overjoyed to see them, but his daughter reported later that he did not remember who had come to visit.

Phil's wife, Fran, was a step ahead of Fred, so her stories were the most alarming. Phil told us how she had wandered away while he was watching *Jeopardy* on TV. He couldn't find her in the house or the yard. He searched the neighborhood with no luck. No one had seen her. He called the police and the sheriff's department. Finally a nurse who encountered a confused Fran at the post office and saw her Safe Return bracelet, called him. Phil met the nurse, police, and sheriff at the woman's house, and took Fran home.

Phil had just bought the bracelets. Fran's had her name, her diagnosis, and a toll-free number to call. His own bracelet said he took care of an AD patient. A manly man, he said he didn't relish wearing a bracelet, but he was glad he had bought them.

"I've been looking at nursing homes in the Portland area near the kids. I'll keep the place on Devil's Lake, but I'll get an apartment or something so I can be close to her. We've been married for fifty years." His voice broke.

We had further to go on this road. Fred forgot things. He wandered at night. He needed help with the TV and the computer. But these were minor frustrations compared to having your wife wander so far you can only hope a kind stranger finds her. They were nothing compared to Joe throwing screaming, arm-flailing, leg-kicking fits at the hospital.

We were all rowing on the same river, where the current was too strong to fight and ultimately would send us over the rapids. Two by two we went in; one by one we came out, battered and broken-hearted, searching for what was left.

After two and a half years of Dr. Mac's too-busy-for-us attitude, we started seeing a different neurologist, Dr. L, whose office was in Corvallis, a college town about fifty miles east of Newport. Most of the people in the support group were taking their loved ones to him.

Dr. L was tall and slim, with graying hair, a beard, and glasses. He arrived softly, not the tsunami that Dr. Mac was, but a soft lake lapping the sand. He shook our hands and greeted us as friends. Although he was running behind schedule, he seemed in no hurry to leave. He talked to both of us, instead of just to me. For the first time, we felt cared for.

On the advice of the support group, I had previously emailed him a list of my concerns.

Dr. L:

You are seeing my husband, Fred Lick, today. Because you are very busy and it's difficult to talk about Fred with him right there, I'd like to mention a few things about his condition:

- *His verbal ability has decreased considerably in the last six months. He has trouble finding the words to finish a sentence. You may notice this when you talk to him.*

- *He has good days and bad days, but more of the bad.*

- *He has had a few incidences of bowel and urinary incontinence.*

- *He has no sense of time.*

- *If not reminded, he forgets to eat and stays in his pajamas most of the day.*

- *His lack of ability to smell has recently caused him to miss muffins burning in the toaster oven, fish rotting in the trash, and bromine powder he unthinkingly emptied into the wastebasket.*

- *He complains that he can't see very well.*

- *He continues to have occasional restless nights and gets lost on the way to the bathroom.*

- *On the plus side, he is still driving during the day in familiar territory, still volunteering at the aquarium, and still singing with the local barbershop chorus. He reads one book after another, although I wonder how much he comprehends.*

- *Although he is not as cheerful as he used to be, I am grateful that he is not violent or paranoid. He is usually agreeable and easygoing and lets me handle the things he can't do anymore.*

    Perhaps this is all typical of his illness, but I thought you should know.

    I would really appreciate it if you gave him the mini-mental test again to reassess whether his medications are still doing the job.

    Thank you.
    Sue Lick

Spurred by my note, Dr. L administered the mini-mental exam. Fred earned sixteen points out of thirty. He could not say the day or the month, and he got the year wrong. He did not know what city we were in or what county we lived in. He could read and write, and he could draw a clock, but he couldn't draw the hands to indicate the time. In three attempts, he could not read the correct time off the gold watch I had bought him for his birthday years ago. Given three words to remember, he retained one (ball). Asked to count backward by sevens, he couldn't begin to do it.

Listening to him miss one thing after another, I felt like I was watching the man I loved be bludgeoned, each blow breaking more bones that would never heal properly.

"It's time to increase your medication," the doctor said, checking his records. "Oops, you're already taking the maximum dose of both Alzheimer's pills. Well, new pills will be coming out in a year or two."

"Fred's decline is faster than expected," he said to me. He encouraged Fred to do whatever he could to stimulate his mind. "Orient yourself every morning as to the day, date, and activities for the day. Perhaps write it down and carry a memory journal so you will know what you have done and what is to be done. Buy a digital watch with big numbers."

Fred admitted to being worried and frightened about not being able to remember things. He tried to tell the doctor about the exhibit being featured at the aquarium that year. I made claw-like gestures with my fingers, but it didn't help. "Crabs," he finally said, which was close. They called it "Claws."

Dr. L. was kind and sympathetic. He went right down the list in my letter, addressing all my concerns.

The doctor looked at Fred. "I'm sorry, you really shouldn't drive anymore."

"He just drives during the day to familiar places on the coast," I said.

"No, he should not be driving at all. In fact, the coast is one of the most dangerous places around, with all the beach-loving tourists who don't know where they're going."

I couldn't argue about that. From May to September, our streets were full of vehicles with out-of-state license plates.

Fred and I both had tears in our eyes. This was the end of Fred's independence.

Fred had driven us to the doctor while I napped. There were moments, especially at first, when he didn't seem to be quite in control of the car, but it had smoothed out.

"Shit," he said when we got to the parking lot.

"I'm sorry." I pulled out my keys and got into the driver's seat.

"Do you want to go anywhere around here or just go straight home?"

"Home."

Driving west on a sunny spring day, Fred's big band music playing on the stereo, my mind raced. Where did Fred drive that he would need rides for now? Would his blue pickup just sit in the driveway and rot? How could I get him to the aquarium without missing my yoga class at noon? Dared we just cheat? It was only three miles, all daylight.

What about the trip to California we were planning for June? Would I have to drive the whole 1,400 miles with Fred just sitting there?

I remembered the first time he drove up to my parents' house to take me out in his beat-up red Ford Fairmont. I remembered all those car trips with him at the wheel, the goodnight kisses, the feeling that with him driving, I would always be safe.

That Friday when I arrived for the AD support group, I stood in the parking lot staring across the street. This would be the first time Fred wouldn't meet me for lunch at the Big Guy's Diner afterward. It was surprising how happy I felt simply parking my Honda next to his truck and meeting him inside, where he'd say, "Well, hello there," as if we hadn't planned this. Maybe we'd read the paper or just talk while we ate, but it felt good, especially after the painful meeting.

When we had met here last time, we didn't know. Thank God. It would have spoiled it.

* * *

In May, after a month of going along with the driving ban, Fred announced that he was driving to the spa shop to get the water tested. "It's not very far," he said.

"It's not the distance; it's your brain."

He scowled.

I was tempted to let him go, but if he drove once, he'd want to do it all the time. I grabbed my purse and drove Fred to town.

While we were in Newport, we closed his business account at Bank of the West—or tried to. He had an outstanding debt from giving his debit card number over the phone for a magazine subscription. He didn't know what magazine it was.

My name was not on the Bank of the West account. Luckily, the teller honored our request. I told Fred what to say: "It was a business account, and I don't have a business anymore." But when she asked for his ID, he handed her the debit card.

"No, your driver's license," she said.

Soon he had cards all over the counter trying to figure out which was his driver's license. This was not a man who should be driving.

11 Zombie Days

I sat on the guest room bed surrounded by books and postcards. Here it was, *Stories Grandma Never Told*, the new edition from my own fledgling publishing company, Blue Hydrangea Productions. The original publisher had sold out and decided not to print any more. They had returned the rights to me, and I wanted to keep it going. I picked up a copy and inhaled the fresh paper-and-ink scent.

I had copyright forms to complete, orders to fill, and arrangements to make with booksellers. Another book, *Freelancing for Newspapers*, was about to launch from another publisher. They were setting up book signings and talks. I also had article assignments for *Oregon Coast Today* and *Northwest Senior News*.

No one in my professional world knew what was going on at home.

I was tempted to burn all my books and folders stuffed with notes and articles about selling one's writing, even though I was in the thick of marketing my own book on the subject. Couldn't I just tell people, "Here, I put it all in this book, and now my husband has Alzheimer's, so I quit"?

I could not. God forbid they think I couldn't do the job. In fact, if you read the newsletters I emailed to friends, family, and fans, you'd think we were living the dream. Our days were full of writing, music, wine, and walks on the beach.

But they weren't. Now the dog had cancer. After weeks of chemotherapy that seemed to help, she took a turn for the worse, and we agreed to stop the treatments. She spent most of her time lying on the bathroom floor, barely looking up as I straddled her to brush my teeth. Watching Sadie losing weight and fighting to breathe hurt me to my bones.

Dr. Smith prescribed a beta blocker to help with my anxiety, but it made me depressed and sleepy.

I felt like a zombie. Nothing seemed worth doing. I pondered what it would be like to die. I didn't actually want to commit suicide, just curl up in a ball in front of the TV forever.

I stopped taking the beta blockers and hung on.

Fred needed help every few minutes. I could no longer leave him alone and saw nothing ahead but constant caregiving.

I lived for Tuesday afternoons, when a fellow volunteer drove Fred to the aquarium, and Thursday evenings, when Fred rehearsed with the Coastal-Aires. Friends drove him to rehearsal now and helped him keep track of his sheet music and where he was supposed to stand. Grateful for their kindness, I comforted myself with my own music. I played piano and guitar and sang until my fingers hurt and my throat felt raw. Then I held onto my dying dog and wept.

One morning in November, three years after Fred's AD diagnosis, we heard Sadie gasping for breath. As we bent over her, she looked at me, her eyes clouded with pain. It was time to let her go. Fred lifted her into the car for her last trip to the vet. On the floor of the examining room, I knelt by my dog, saying, "I love you. You're the best dog ever," as Dr. Fineman gave her the shots that ended her pain. Fred and I held each other and sobbed.

I skipped the AD support group the next day. I didn't want to talk about Fred. I wanted to talk about Sadie. I kept looking for her in patches of sunlight on the carpet or in the bathroom seeking coolness on the linoleum.

As I tried to work, Fred came into my office, tears streaming, arms out to be held. I let him cry and knew I was right to stay home. Later, the loss hit me again, and I went to his office. "It's my turn," I sobbed.

At least I had the relief of writing, music, prayer, and friends. Fred just had this big emptiness.

To cheer us up, Gretchen and Michael met us for a weekend in Portland. Driving in the big city with its many bridges and one-way streets, I got lost for over an hour while Fred became more and more agitated.

At least it wasn't raining. The sun lit up the old stone and glass buildings downtown and sparkled on the Willamette River that divides the city into east and west.

The kids met us at the hotel, and we went exploring. Our first stop was Powell's Bookstore. When the men went to look for a book Michael wanted, I found myself alone with Gretchen.

"He looks so different," she said, her eyes full of tears.

He did. He looked old, small, and pale.

"Sometimes it's like a switch is flipped off," I said. "One minute he's there, and the next minute, he's gone."

"You're right; he's not there," she said.

I felt so sorry for her. I saw her father every day, so it wasn't as shocking to me.

All weekend, Fred followed us around, confused. He couldn't read a menu, and he kept repeating himself. At OMSI, the Oregon Museum of Science and Industry, we lost track of him until I looked out the window and saw him outside wandering along the river. We hurried out to grab him before he got lost.

That night, when we stopped at a coffee shop for dessert, he went to the restroom. When he didn't come back, we panicked. Michael went down the hall to the men's room and discovered a door leading outside. We grabbed our things and went looking. Michael found his father on the street about a block away.

"He didn't know who I was," he whispered to me. "I said, 'Dad, it's me, Michael.' Maybe he thought I was some homeless guy or something. I-I didn't know it was this bad."

"I know. It's hard to believe. Thank God you found him."

I turned to Fred. "You ready to go back to the hotel to sleep?"

He nodded. We hugged the kids goodnight, not sure when we would see them again. In the morning, Gretchen would fly back to California while I drove Fred home to South Beach.

Later that month, after spending Thanksgiving with the family and hearing again that we needed to move back to California, we checked into a Best Western motel in Eureka on our way home. Fred went out to get a newspaper from the car. But it was taking too long.

I stood on the balcony outside our third-floor room, hoping to see him in the parking lot or on the stairs. No Fred.

It had been a long drive, with rain so hard we couldn't see as we took the long way along narrow roads through the wine country because it was snowing on I-5. Fred wanted to drive, and I kept telling him he couldn't. He insisted I was going the wrong way until I started doubting myself.

We stopped in the redwoods for a bathroom break. Queasy and half blind with a migraine, I breathed in the rain-freshened air and stared up at the giant trees until I began to relax. The redwoods always made me and my problems seem small. But this road seemed endless, and I was grateful to reach Eureka.

I loved this motel. Cookies in the lobby, full breakfast, beautiful indoor swimming pool, a silky comforter on a soft bed that hugged you, real coffee mugs, and chocolates by the phone.

But where the heck was Fred?

Ten minutes. Twenty minutes. I waited in the doorway, hoping he would see me outside Room 303. What if he had wandered off? He didn't even know what city this was.

After twenty-five minutes, he came up the stairs. He had forgotten what room we were in. A maid had called the office and directed him to our room.

That's it, I thought.

A week later at lunchtime, I brought out the Safe Return kit that had just arrived in the mail. Fred seemed clear-headed and in a good mood.

"I've done something that might make you mad," I began. I took a deep breath, explained the program, and showed him the medallions, wallet cards, refrigerator magnets, and key chain. "I know you won't get lost around here, but you did have trouble at the motel the other night."

To my surprise and relief, he was not upset. He put on the medallion, which hung on a long chain he could hide under his shirt, tucked the card into his wallet and let me shift his keys to the Safe Return key chain. People seeing it would know about his illness. But he didn't object. In fact, he thanked me. Later, he rubbed his chest where the medallion touched and said, "It feels funny. I guess I'll get used to it."

My own medallion was stuffed in my pocket. We didn't need it if we were together, did we? It felt funny to me too, that cold circle of metal dangling between my breasts.

A while after the Safe Return kit arrived, I realized these medallions were just like the name tag we'd had made for our dog. *My name is Sadie. I belong to Fred and Sue Lick.*

What a lovely drug. Dr. Smith and I agreed in mid-December to switch from Xanax to Klonopin, also known as clonazepam. The morning after I started Klonopin, I woke up happy, despite a storm pounding the windows with rain and wind. In my dream, I had introduced Sadie to the joys of bubble baths. I could see her doggy chin on top of the bubbles, almost hear her sigh with pleasure.

Fred was active, but I stayed in dreamland, a good place to be as we moved closer to Christmas. Fred had always been Mr. Christmas. He loved everything about it, especially cutting down the tree and decorating it. This year's tree came from a parking lot. I decorated it while Fred watched listlessly from his chair.

Every ornament sparked memories that hurt. I counted the days until Christmas was over, grateful for my new drug to cushion my sorrow.

Other years on December 17, the anniversary of our first date, we'd dress up, gorge on steak, lobster, and chocolate by candlelight, get tipsy, and have long, deep conversations, interlaced with I love yous and hand-holding.

Not this time.

We sat by the window at Georgie's Bistro. If I hooded my eyes with my hand, I could make out white surf and the lights of crab boats on the horizon.

When our food arrived, we ate in painful silence. I couldn't think of anything to say that Fred could respond to. If this were a date, it was a bad one. No conversation. I had to drive, would have to pay, and would not get any sex.

I searched for topics. Long-term memory is supposed to stick around. "How did you and Annette (his first wife) meet?"

He couldn't remember. He needed prodding as to when he graduated from high school and the name of his high school sweetheart (1955, Lynn Alice). I, the relative newcomer, was in charge of the story of his life because he had lost it.

He frowned. "What happened to Annette?"

He didn't know what happened to the woman who'd divorced him after twenty-four years? Then he remembered. "Oh yeah, she kicked me out."

I prayed he still remembered the beginning of our story. The winery, the Chinese dinner, the video store, making love by the fireplace.

"Can you believe it has been twenty-four years since our first date?"

"I was so nervous," he said.

"Me too."

He was wearing the same corduroy jacket he'd worn that night. The coat was the same, but not the man. Once we got started that first night, we couldn't keep our hands off each other. Twenty-four years later, we rarely touched at all.

I watched a baby boy gnawing on French bread at the next table. The tot was probably about eight months old, with a full head of dark hair, pudgy cheeks, and a killer smile. He saw me and grinned.

All those Christmas card pictures of my friends with their kids and their grandchildren were getting to me. My cards just said Merry Christmas and Happy New Year.

It came out of my mouth: "I should have had one of those. I should have a family picture with more than two people and a dog."

Fred looked right at me with those green-flecked brown eyes. "Did you want children?"

He didn't know? He didn't remember all those years of angst, the misery of every Mother's Day, the conversations about how he just didn't want to have another baby?

"Yes," I said.

"Then I was a fool."

"But you have made it clear all these years that you didn't want more children."

Silence.

I felt tears welling up. I hated this anniversary.

When our waiter arrived, asking if we'd like to see the dessert tray, I said no. My stomach was too full of disappointment.

I paid the check with my credit card.

He forgot about his first wife. How long would it be before he forgot me?

12 I Need a Little Help Here

When our neighbor Wayne got hit by a car while crossing the street next to Starbucks, his partner, Carol, hired a local care agency to help him until his broken leg healed. That way, she could still work, and they didn't drive each other crazy.

"You should call them to help with Fred," she said.

"Maybe I will."

I waited a week before I found the courage to mention it at dinner.

"Wayne has those people from Aging Wisely helping him," I said. "You remember I wrote a story about them for *Northwest Senior News*?"

Struggling with the lid on the salad dressing, he shrugged. "No."

"Well, they're really great. We should talk to them about helping us."

"Oh no. I don't need that," he said as the lid broke free and honey mustard dressing spilled on the white tablecloth.

"I need it," I said.

He ran his finger through the spilled dressing and licked it off. "No."

Sadie had been gone three months when I saw a flyer at the post office advertising puppies. I rushed home and grabbed Fred. The family who lived at the top of the hill up 98th Street had a dozen puppies, half Lab and half Staffordshire bull terrier, from two different mother dogs. Most of the pups were black, but there were three tan and one white pup. Fred picked up puppies and laughed as they licked his face.

I squatted in the midst of them, petting left and right. A tan one with a cute brown squiggle above her nose climbed onto my knees.

"You want to come live with me?" I asked.

She wagged her tiny tail.

Fred brought a black male puppy over. "Can we get two?"

So we did. Six and eight pounds of puppy love.

With Fred deep into Alzheimer's, we should never have taken them on, but our home was not the same without a dog. I had no children and would never have grandchildren. Fred's kids were grown and far away. We needed something young and healthy to cuddle.

The early months were a blur of urine and feces, barking, chewing, and constant need. Fred was not able to help. They just added to his confusion. He'd let them in when they were covered with mud. He'd watch helplessly as they peed on the carpet or chewed on the ottoman. Mostly he hid in his office.

Despite Fred's misgivings, I signed up with the caregiving agency after Christmas.

Fred was calm as co-owners Doris and Kathleen talked with us at the kitchen table. Tactful, they never mentioned his illness or his shortcomings. It was all about helping us, especially me.

A man named Dave was supposed to come from two to five on Monday afternoons. For $20 an hour, he'd do grocery shopping, cleaning, and dinner. He would feed the dogs. He'd also entertain Fred while I prepared for my class and went to the college to teach it.

But the next day, Fred woke up anxious and angry. "What am I going to do with this guy? Why is he coming? When is he coming? How is this going to work?"

Fred would not go quietly into these caregivers' care, no matter how nice they were or how carefully everyone said they were helping *me*.

He knew it was a big step in the AD journey. He didn't want

any part of it. Who would? Imagine your spouse hiring someone to babysit you because you can't take care of yourself.

Like balloons about to burst, Fred and I inhaled tension all day that first Monday, waiting for our $60 session with Dave. I had made a list of possible things to do besides cooking and cleaning, guy things like setting mole traps and fixing the torn hot tub cover. When he arrived, I planned to say hello, give a brief overview of what needed to be done, and leave.

Fred was dressed and ready by nine thirty. I found him cleaning the bathroom. "Don't clean before the cleaner comes," I said.

"Why not!" he snapped.

He read the paper. We ate lunch. I boiled macaroni for macaroni salad. By two o'clock, we were both more than ready. It was like waiting for a blind date.

I tried to relax by playing the piano. Two o'clock came and went. At two fifteen, I started pacing. At two twenty, I called Kathleen. She said *Doris* was coming at two thirty. Did I want to change that? Um, no.

The doorbell rang.

Shooing the puppies into the backyard, I opened the door to Doris, whom I had met at the kitchen table the week before. She was dark-haired, plump, smiling, and awfully dressed up for house-cleaning.

"Oh! It's you," I said, letting her in.

"I'm here. What do you need me to do?"

Things moved quickly after that. I mentioned macaroni salad. "I love making macaroni salad," she said. She started pulling stuff out of my fridge. She glanced over the list of chores. No problem. Feeling as if I were in the way, I grabbed my papers and said goodbye.

It's a weird feeling letting a stranger take over your house.

Once I had amassed my stack of collated handouts in the faculty room at the college, I headed for the beach. I didn't have a plan. Maybe I would sit somewhere and write poetry. But I wasn't feeling poetic. I

sat in the gazebo overlooking Nye Beach and admired the view of the
lighthouse, the blue water, and the green hills. I walked down the path
to the beach, the first time I had walked on the sand in months.

It was a warm day, with a breeze that felt like a massage. I took off
my shoes and touched my toes to the icy water, then walked across
quilted sand to a dry spot near the Sylvia Beach Hotel and sat. I had
been so busy planning Fred's activities I hadn't considered what I
would do with my free time. I didn't have to do anything.

I stared at my sandy toes and wondered what made the sand here
so dark. I took notes in my journal about the people I saw.

After a while, it occurred to me that the art galleries nearby might
be open and I could wander through them. Unfortunately, they were
closed on Mondays.

It was getting late anyway. I had to teach in an hour. I went home.

Doris and Fred weren't there. I walked through the house, amazed.
Not only had Doris made macaroni salad, but she had also made dev-
iled eggs. The bird feeder had been cleaned out and filled. The vacuum
cleaner sat in the hallway, its cord stretched from the living room to
the bathroom, and everything looked dusted.

They returned at five fifteen. They had been to the town's hardware stores, seeking mole traps. All sold out.

With fifteen minutes left, Doris slapped a burger into a frying pan,
heated the corn she had found in the refrigerator, and prepared Fred's
dinner.

"Do you want lettuce and tomato on your burger?" she asked Fred.

I made frantic gestures. We didn't have any lettuce or tomato. I
felt like a loser for not having a fully stocked refrigerator.

"Do you want celery on it?"

Fred had gone to the bathroom. Taking advantage of his absence,
Doris said, "He did really well." She told me someone else would be
coming the next week. Not Dave, who didn't work for the agency
anymore.

Days later, we were still eating macaroni salad, and the jays and juncos were back at the feeder. Doris didn't do things exactly as I would have, but she did so much in three hours while I was free to do . . . nothing.

Then came Boni.

Boni was late, very late. Doris filled in, cleaning a little while she waited. Go, she told me. I went off to copy my handouts, filled the car with gas, visited a couple music stores, and walked along the Bayfront. I sat for a few minutes on a bench near tourists fishing for crab and drafted a new poem.

Home at four forty, I discovered Boni had not yet arrived. Fred had done a beautiful job of removing years-old cobwebs from the laundry room, and Doris was mid-vacuum in the living room. She had already cooked Fred's corned beef hash, leaving a tiny bowl of fruit salad and a corn muffin on a plate on the table.

The phone rang. Boni. I handed her over to Doris. She slowly repeated the directions to our house.

Doris covered the phone. "Am I telling her the right thing?"

"Yes. That's right."

Boni arrived around five o'clock. Doris gave her a quick overview, then left.

I was hoping to watch a little TV while I changed my clothes, but Boni, fortyish, her ponytail half undone, stood between me and the television.

"What should I do?"

"Clean." I pointed her to the vacuum cleaner and left to get dressed.

Not hearing any vacuuming, I went to check.

"I don't know how to work it," Boni said. "Whether you take that thing off."

"What thing? Never mind. Just dust a little."

She waved the rag around my piano a bit, like a kid who's

pretending to do chores. I gritted my teeth as she shuffled my sheet music. I caught a glimpse of butt crack above her jeans and retreated to the bedroom.

I took off my sweatpants and slipped on my black slacks. The most important thing I needed Boni to do was finish Fred's dinner, which at this point was just to fry a couple eggs. But that was a problem, too.

"Where's a frying pan? How should I cook the eggs? What should I cook them in? Butter, oil?"

I stood there barefoot, buttoning my blouse. "Boni, the idea is that for these three hours, I'm not responsible for everything."

"Oh, but I just got here. . . ."

"Butter. Use butter."

She put a big glob in; we were running short. "You won't need that much," I said. She put half back and cracked the eggs into the pan.

I hurried to the bedroom to put on my shoes and came back.

"Is that done enough?"

"No."

"Is that enough?"

"No. Give it one more minute," I said.

I found Fred in the laundry room. "Good job on the cobwebs!" I hugged him hard and whispered, "She's an idiot."

He grinned.

I knew Boni was tired from working as a hotel maid earlier in the day. I could see that in her eyes I was rich and had a house full of expensive things. I was sorry for her troubles, but Boni needed more direction than Fred did. While she fussed with the eggs, I got the TV going so Fred could watch *Monday Night Football*.

I'm not sure Boni understood that she was supposed to be taking care of a man with Alzheimer's disease, that this wasn't just a house-keeping job. I didn't trust her to make decisions for him, to take him shopping or anywhere else. How was this supposed to work?

That night at school, I welcomed the chaotic classroom and the chattering students.

It was delightful to come home three hours later to a house with no strangers in it and eat leftovers while Fred watched TV. For a whole hour, nobody asked me what they should do.

I called the agency ladies and explained that I didn't need another person to take care of. I needed someone like Doris who would take care of me and Fred. If I couldn't have that, Fred and I would handle things ourselves.

Compared to Boni, there was nothing wrong with Fred.

Next came Judy. After her second week, I sat her down for a talk. The first week, she hadn't finished making dinner or cleaned the kitchen, leaving me with last-minute chores that almost made me late to class. Her response: "I had something on my mind; in fact, I went to see a counselor. The kitchen looked clean enough to me."

Still chatting while I changed into my teaching clothes, I reminded her that we'd talked about her starting to come in the mornings when the fall quarter ended in December. She replied, "I don't remember anything about that."

The worst part was that she ignored Fred. He hid in his office. When I telephoned from the college, he was eating the same thing for dinner that he had had for lunch. He had forgotten about *Monday Night Football*. When my students arrived, I was talking him through turning on the TV.

I was all set to complain about Judy's shortcomings, but Doris told me Judy had to leave on a family emergency. Would it be okay if Jim came instead?

I had heard about Jim, heart of gold, male. Sure.

Fred liked him right away. Jim, whose face was badly scarred on the right side, seemed friendly and competent.

I went into my office to work, but I couldn't resist coming out to check on them. They were standing in the kitchen, brewing coffee, chatting as Jim washed the dishes I had left in the sink. He would work out fine.

And he did for a while. One afternoon when Fred and Jim returned from the grocery store, Fred was in a tizzy. The checkbook was missing. Fred had no idea what happened to it. I called the credit union, and they put a hold on our account.

Fred couldn't trace what happened, but Jim's story made me wonder if we were ever going to get a caregiver we could trust. While Fred was picking up my prescription at Rite Aid, Jim had gone off to check his blood pressure. While Fred was choosing lightbulbs at Fred Meyer, Jim had left him to get cash from the bank. At the grocery store, while Fred was at the checkout counter discovering he had no checkbook, Jim was at the service center buying lottery tickets.

I scolded Jim, telling him he needed to watch Fred, that Fred couldn't handle money, couldn't keep track of a bunch of things in his hands at once, couldn't run errands alone. That's why he needed a caregiver.

To his credit, our young, scar-faced caregiver seemed to feel awful about it. But a few minutes later, he left early to meet his wife for lunch.

"Tell the company you left early, so I don't have to pay for the time," I said.

"I'll write it in the journal."

He didn't.

Meanwhile, Fred was in tears over the missing checkbook. "I'm worthless," he said.

"No. It could happen to anyone."

Later that day, I got a call from a South Beach resident who had found the checkbook at the grocery store. Thank God for small towns. I called the credit union to tell them to forget the whole thing.

The next week, Brian was assigned to us, but Brian didn't show up. We waited. I dashed to the post office and back. I telephoned the agency, but got no answer. Around five o'clock, the agency called. Brian was going back to school; he had forgotten about us. So sorry.

Yeah, sorry didn't do us any good.

The caregivers weren't all bad. We fell in love with Janey, the small, scratchy-voiced powerhouse who could clean, cook, shop, and have time left over to sit around laughing with Fred. We mourned when she and her husband moved to Costa Rica.

But the agency sent us Nancy, a middle-aged woman who soon felt like the sister I had never had. Cheerful, loving, and totally trustworthy, she listened to my troubles and hugged me when I couldn't stop the tears. She wrangled the puppies and treated Fred like a human being instead of a patient. Instead of rolling his eyes when I told him a caregiver was coming, he'd say, "Nancy's coming? Good."

Alas, Nancy was not on duty the weekend Fred fell and everything changed.

13 Back at the Piano

One day, Fred was hauling in stove pellets and helping with the dishes, going out to lunch with me, and pushing the cart as he and Nancy shopped for groceries. He was still greeting visitors at the aquarium. The next day, he was on the floor, shaking and speaking gibberish until paramedics took him away in an ambulance. At the hospital, doctors and social workers told me he needed twenty-four-hour care. We had both thought it would be years before it came to that.

His laundry was still in the hamper. I hadn't washed the dregs of his coffee out of the pot yet. But now he was at Newport Rehab. Although his speech was back to what it had been before he fell, and he could walk if the staff would let him, he didn't live with me and the dogs anymore. Instead, I visited a few hours a day.

Aides started bringing people into the dining hall at four for the five o'clock supper. Fred and I joined the parade. He propelled his wheelchair with his feet. As we looked for a table, I noticed there were no chairs. Everybody had a wheelchair. I dragged a chair in from the hallway for me.

The residents looked old and unhappy, sitting there staring at the pink and green tablecloths as workers passed out tiny plastic glasses of milk and cranberry or apple juice. What happened to grownup drinks like coffee and tea?

I think Fred felt as conspicuous as I did at dinner that night because we were so much younger than the other people. Once we were seated, we heard someone yelling, "Where's Mr. and Mrs. Lick?"

They brought a hamburger for Fred and a grilled cheese sandwich for me. I hadn't asked for dinner, but I was hungry.

"Oh boy, looks good," Fred said, grabbing his burger, dripping ketchup on his khaki pants.

As I ate my sandwich and sipped my apple juice, I considered all the things I had been doing behind Fred's back. I had spent $7,000 and signed forms specifying what funeral home they should call if Fred died. I had talked about him with the staff and the AD support group. I had made plans to tour adult foster care homes with Nancy, who insisted on helping me even though she wasn't getting paid for it anymore.

I didn't tell him about any of this. I just watched him enjoy his hamburger and listened to a guy named Jerry rant about how he "wouldn't eat this crap."

My grandfather used to complain about the meals at the nursing home where he lived with his dementia. They put him in a wheelchair, too. A Filipino family ran the place. Most of the food was Asian while Grandpa was a steak-and-potatoes man. Whatever he ate wound up all over his clothes. He had lived with Grandma Rachel until just before she died. None of us had any idea what she was dealing with. Now, a little over seven years after Fred first said he had trouble remembering things, I knew.

I saw our lives separating, going down two different roads. Fred and I could still hold hands across the divider for a while, but ultimately we'd have to let go.

While we were having lunch on the third day, an aide came to tell us Fred's son Michael was in the lounge. I rolled Fred out to meet him.

"Hey, Dad," he said, bending way over to hug him. "I'm sorry. I saw all those old people in the dining room, and I just—sorry, it freaked me out." He sank into an easy chair where he wouldn't tower over his father. "You look good."

"I'm glad to see you."

Michael looked around the room, which was furnished with upholstered chairs, a TV, a bookshelf, and a table with a half-finished jigsaw puzzle.

Silence.

"Has it been raining a lot in Portland?" I asked.

"Oh, yeah."

Fred stared at Michael. "You live in Portland?"

"Yeah. So, uh, how do you like it here?"

"It's pretty good. I'll be glad when I get to go home."

Michael looked at me. I picked up a blue puzzle piece and studied the sky portion of the picture.

I knew how hard these visits could be. There's not much to say. That's why I played the piano when I visited my grandfather in his nursing home. I also remember the shock I felt the first time I saw him in a wheelchair.

Michael didn't stay long, but it was good not to be alone in this situation. As I walked him to the door, he told me he had been thinking about moving to the coast to help us, but he would have to give up so much and wasn't sure he could provide the right kind of care.

"You'd be as good as anyone, but I understand."

"Your son is so nice," the nurses said after Michael left.

"He is," I said.

The next day, the persistent winter rain had stopped, and the sun was shining. Fred, parked in his wheelchair in the lounge, smiled. "I'm having so much fun here."

He missed me, but people were entertaining him and taking care of him 24/7 while at home I was always busy.

When I visited, away from home and office, we could hold hands and cuddle. I could put all my attention on Fred and be romantic instead of divided in ten different directions. I began to think this was not such a bad thing, that God had stepped in and tripped my husband, saying, "You've both had enough."

I went home at lunchtime, feeling more relaxed than I had felt in months.

When I returned to Newport Rehab at four fifteen, Fred was in the office with Kim, the manager. She had given him the mini-mental test. She showed me his score. He got an eight. Out of 30. I wondered if the score was accurate, but Fred had clearly slipped into a new phase.

"He definitely needs full-time care," she said. "We can keep him here as long as needed."

I wondered later if nursing home personnel always said that to sell more rooms.

I sat with Fred during dinner, canned raviolis and green beans with a slice of slightly buttered white bread and a two-inch square of yellow cake. Plus the ubiquitous apple juice and milk.

"I didn't know where you were," Fred said.

"Oh, just running errands, working, walking the dogs."

He told me he had lunch and physical therapy, went to a cooking demonstration, spent some time by the nurse's station, and talked to Kim.

I pushed the raviolis around on my plate and vowed to eat something better later.

I left after dinner, telling Fred it was church choir night, but I knew I wasn't going to choir practice. I went to Café Mundo instead, where friends were playing bluegrass music.

Café Mundo, in Newport's Nye Beach neighborhood, was like a giant tree house. Customers entered through a garden full of mismatched tables and quirky sculptures, passed a small counter and stage area, and went upstairs to the dining room, where fabric art and fishing nets hung off the ceiling, and white girls with dreadlocks served beer on tap.

Finding an open seat on a high chair at a long wooden counter, I spotted Tony, a friend from church. We sat together, got buzzed on beer, and talked about our childhoods, our parents, school, booze, and Fred. It felt weird but wonderful to be conversing with this handsome man who didn't have Alzheimer's. He was younger than I was and engaged to be married, but people might have wondered. I didn't care. I was still in shock from the way my life had just turned upside down.

I wanted to stay in that drunk, happy place. I had been putting so much effort into Fred's care, but I thought I would have to go much further down this road, that I'd be wiping his bottom and helping him shower, waiting until he didn't know anybody or anything. I didn't think it would be over like this. So, it felt good to be a little drunk, talking to Tony, pretending we were on a date.

Visiting the nursing home began to feel like my new job. I went there every morning and evening, eating dinner with Fred and the other residents.

When I came in about ten o'clock a week after Fred went to the hospital, he was sitting in his wheelchair by his tray table. He had a toothbrush in one hand, toothpaste in the other. He didn't know what to do. I talked him through the process of brushing his teeth.

He dropped his toothbrush into the spitty water. He had to go to the bathroom. He couldn't get out of his wheelchair without the alarm sounding. I pushed the call button, but no one came. He had to go *now*. I helped him up. The alarm shrieked. In a minute, we had two aides watching him pee.

After lunch, I raced home to check on the dogs and do some laundry. Folding Fred's shirts and underwear, I thought about him not coming home, about not washing his clothes anymore. How could that be possible?

It hit me like a bomb: I'm alone.

Fred no longer thought it was fun being there. "They put me in this thing (wheelchair) and let me sit here for hours," he complained one

Sunday when I visited after church. I knew it was not exactly true because he had had visitors from the aquarium, lunch, and physical therapy, but it had probably seemed like forever to him. Grandpa had said the same thing before his dementia completely took over. It's hard for people who worked all their lives to sit and do nothing.

"I want to go home," Fred said.

"But I can't give you the care you need."

"I know."

At dinner, Fred sat in his wheelchair at the pink-clothed table, fumbling with the silverware. I perched on a rolling green stool.

Paul and Vivian came in. Vivian was one of the few allowed to walk. Fragile and nearly deaf, she ate very little. I wondered if they were a couple, the way Paul barked at her and hollered at the aides to speak into her good ear. His gnarled hand slid across the table. She slid her fingers toward his, and they clasped their old worn hands together. They smiled at each other.

I was undone. Fred wouldn't live long enough for us to grow old together.

Brushing away tears, I went to the piano. By the time my grandfather moved into a nursing home, he didn't know who I was, and we couldn't really talk, but he loved music. He would sing along as I played pop songs from before World War II. It made us both feel better.

At Newport Rehab, I played "Five Foot Two" and "Good Night, Irene" over the clatter of plastic cups, the blare of the TV, and the incessant shouting from the guy who kept complaining about the food. Tonight, he said, "These are my waning years, and I'll do what I want."

Nearby sat Dorothy, always wrapped in layers of afghans and shawls, always bent over the table. Whatever the aides told her she was getting to eat, she would say, "Oh, that will be good."

There was Joanna, who slept all day, except for meals; Ruthie, who dozed between bites; the lady yelling, "Can somebody help me?" And

Juanita, mouth always wide open. She spilled her drink twice that night. The second time, nobody cleaned it up. The woman sitting next to her called for help so softly none of the staff heard her.

And so many more, men who could have been my father staring at their plates of overcooked, mushy meat and canned fruits and vegetables. One delightful little man with suspenders seemed tickled just to have someone cooking for him.

I thought about Grandpa and all those Japanese and Filipino people he lived with. I would sit at the old upright with the broken D next to middle C and bang out "You Are My Sunshine" and "Battle Hymn of the Republic" while Grandpa sang along if he was awake.

Behind me, dinner at Newport Rehab went on. A woman with a hairnet slapped stuff on trays, and aides delivered them to the residents. The better meals were served on weekends, perhaps to impress visiting family members. Other days, they served tuna salad, chicken salad, or ham salad sandwiches, which all tasted the same.

A spiky-haired blonde gave out meds and punctured fingers for blood sugar tests.

Aides tapped on a computer screen, charting what the residents ate and drank. The staff tracked everything they did, every bathroom trip, drink, or tantrum.

As I played old tunes on the piano, Jerry talked, and Vivian applauded after every number.

"They like it," she told me when I returned to our table.

All day, I had smelled the beef cooking for the stew, but it turned out to be a disappointment. It was watery, with one and a half chunks of beef and a little bit of potato. The cornbread squares were tiny and cold, the salad just lettuce with bad ranch dressing, the dessert canned fruit salad.

It wasn't great food, but the staff was kind, cutting up meat for big men in wheelchairs, encouraging Dorothy and Vivian to eat a few bites, quietly wiping faces and hands or rubbing shoulders.

Family members could eat there for three dollars. It beat eating alone at home.

After dinner, we sat in Fred's room, a generic hospital-type two-bed room. He didn't have a roommate. Sometimes I used the other bed as a sofa or I lay on Fred's bed while he sat in his wheelchair.

I had been there since two o'clock. It felt like forty hours, not four. Playing the piano gave me something to do and an excuse to look away from the sadness behind me.

Every day, Fred thought this was the day he was going home. He kept saying, "Put me in that car and take me home."

"No," I answered. "I'm going, but you have to stay here."

It sounded like what I told my dogs, but at least they got Milk-Bones to chew on as I drove away.

14 You Live Here Now

Fred couldn't stay at Newport Rehab forever. The original plan had been to give him a few weeks of physical therapy so he could get out of the wheelchair. But the staff didn't seem to be doing any actual "rehab," so what was the point of him being there? We both felt like prisoners. After days of being the squeaky wheel, I met with the administrators and learned that Fred could be discharged any time we wanted as long as we had a plan for what to do next. So, I made a plan.

Su Casa, a new adult foster care home, was a big ranch house in Toledo, Oregon, a mill town a few miles east of Newport. Nancy and I went there one afternoon to see if it would be suitable for Fred.

The house, once headquarters for a cattle ranch, sat in the middle of several acres of open space, nothing but trees, meadows and a branch of the Yaquina River that trickled through. The owners, a middle-aged couple named Elena and Max, welcomed us at the door and beckoned us in. Elena, short and wide, had a strong Mexican accent while Max was a cowboy down to his boots. He'd been a logger, a rancher, and a building contractor, but now he was dedicated to helping his wife realize her dream of opening a care home. She had been a nurse in Mexico, but was not certified here.

As I tell you about Su Casa, I must tell you that this is not the real name or location, and these are not the real people's names. I am certain the real people would sue me for libel if I told the truth. But what happened with Fred and me is real.

Nancy and I walked around the big house, admiring the fireplace, the soft green sofas, and the pastoral paintings on the walls. The five bedrooms were cozy, already furnished with beds, dressers, televisions and curtained-off bathroom areas. The residents would eat around a dining room table family-style.

"We have many activities planned," Elena said.

"And if he's up to it, there are always chores Fred can help us with," Max added.

"Sounds great." A border collie nudged my leg. "Oh, hey, hi," I said, bending to pet its soft fur.

Elena smiled. "That's Boomer. We love dogs. Do you have dogs?"

"Yes. Two."

"Well, they can come visit. We want to be just one happy family. You'll meet our daughter, Cristina, too. She goes to Toledo High."

That was all fine, but I had to ask, "Do you know how to handle people with Alzheimer's?"

"Oh, sure. My papa had it, and I have taken care of many other people with dementia at hospitals and nursing homes. Don't worry. Your husband will be okay. We're hiring a couple guys to help with meals and the night shift."

Elena was charging $5,000 a month. People would snap up the rooms, she said.

I had one more question. "We're going to run out of money in a few months and will need to go on Medicaid. Do you accept Medicaid payments?"

"Sure. We'll work it out."

I looked at Nancy. She nodded. This was a huge step, but it was better than where Fred was now.

"Okay. We'll do it."

When I told Fred about Su Casa, he wept, mostly because he was so glad to get out of the rehab place. I don't think he understood he would be living there, and I would not.

I had to figure out what to take from the house to furnish his room. When we had moved in together in 1984, we had merged our belongings. It was crowded and wonderful. Now, after twenty-five years, I'd be taking everything apart.

I missed my husband. When I came home, he wasn't there waiting with a smile, a hug, and a kiss. And I was filled with doubts. Was he really as bad off as they said? He didn't seem any worse than he had been before he fell. He was stuck in the wheelchair because the rehab folks were afraid he'd fall again. Doctors, nurses, and social workers told me it was the right thing to do, that he had to have twenty-four-hour care, but still, was I doing a horrible thing?

On February 9, Fred was waiting in his wheelchair at nine o'clock when I arrived at Newport Rehab, my nose running, my head hurting so bad I wanted to amputate my right temple. The stress of the past two weeks had finally overcome my immune system. It didn't help that it was twenty-five degrees out and snowing.

"Is it time to leave?" Fred asked, starting to stand up. The wheelchair alarm squealed. "I hate this thing."

"Me too. In fact. . . ." I reached behind Fred and disconnected the alarm from his shirt. "There. We're leaving as soon as we can."

Fred's underwear, socks, and toothbrush lay on the bed. Newport Rehab didn't seem like such a bad place to me, but I could walk, amuse myself with puzzles, books, and the piano, and leave whenever I wanted to. I didn't have to call an aide every time I wanted to go to the bathroom. I could snub the bland canned meals and take myself to a restaurant for real food.

As I packed Fred's suitcase, glancing out the window at the snow coming down harder by the minute, workers hurried in with pills and forms to sign. I barely read them, but I got the impression that if they didn't approve of where I was taking my husband, they'd sic the Department of Human Services on me. In their eyes, I was no longer capable of caring for my husband.

Now I realize I had more choices, including taking Fred home and resuming life as it had been just before he fell, but at that point, I felt trapped. The homecare workers were undependable and more expensive per hour than the nursing homes. I couldn't leave Fred alone, and I couldn't stay awake twenty-four hours a day.

Nurses and aides showered Fred with hugs and goodbyes. Then he rolled out the door to freedom and stood up. I was ready to grab him if he fell, but he was steady on his feet.

"Look at you," I said.

"Ah, it's great to get out of there."

Max had come from Su Casa to help us. He slung the suitcase into his truck, helped Fred into our car, and off we went, my windshield wipers pushing clumps of snow back and forth.

The road to Su Casa was narrow and tightly curved, and I had yet to learn its ups and downs. The farther east we went, the thicker the snow got, until everything was white—pavement, grass, trees, and houses. Even a tabby cat beside the road wore a snow hat and mustache.

Driving in first gear, holding my breath, I made it to the big house where Elena was waiting at the door. Fred's new Medicare-financed wheelchair had not arrived, so he walked across the snow, Elena and I each holding one of his hands. I doubt that he heard the soft alarm activated by the open door. Soon he was settled on the sofa next to Cristina, who was enjoying a snow day off from school. As they watched a *Jurassic Park* movie, I organized Fred's new bedroom, plugging in his clock, arranging photographs on the dresser, and hanging his clothes in the closet. When we brought him in, he smiled. "Looks good."

Elena showed him the view from his bedroom window, the vast open space where a family of deer often came to graze, a faded red barn, trees, the river. The snow fell hard and thick, like a picture on a Christmas card.

Next came the paperwork. Dozens of multiple-choice questions along the lines of: Eating: Is he independent, needs assistance, or totally dependent? Over and over. Then the contract and the writing of the big check. Fred joined us at the table, snacking from a bowl of orange wedges and sipping coffee as I signed my name repeatedly. At one point, Max offered Fred a chance to sign, but he got stuck on the letter F.

If I had felt better and weren't so worried about the drive home, I would have loved to stick around, take pictures, and play with the dog. But over an inch of snow had already piled on top of my car. I gave Fred a hug. "I have to go."

He seemed surprisingly calm as I went off to what used to be the home we shared and left him at his new home. Perhaps it was okay. During a moment when we were alone, he whispered tearfully, "You have done so much."

Back in the snow, I let out my breath as I drove onto Highway 20 and west into Newport. It was snowing hard there, too, the roads mushy and slick, crisscrossed with tire tracks. But the snow turned to rain as I crossed the Yaquina Bridge into South Beach.

Greeting my muddy dogs at home, I looked for signs of snow and saw none. In fact, as I settled in at my desk, amazed to have a whole afternoon and evening to myself, the sun came out.

If I pretended Fred was at the aquarium or running an errand, I could forget for a second everything that had happened since Fred fell. But it didn't get rid of the weight in the pit of my stomach.

15 When Can I Go Home?

On Valentine's Day, five days after Fred moved to Su Casa, I arrived with a bag of shoes for him to try on. He hated the sneakers I had grabbed in a hurry when he transferred from the hospital to Newport Rehab, and he hated the next pair I brought on one of my daily visits, so now I was determined to have him try them all on and figure out once and for all which shoes he liked and which should go to Goodwill.

He did not recognize any of the shoes as his own. I pointed out the ones I had tied and untied in the ER after he fell. He looked at me, eyes looking sea green in the late-afternoon sun pouring through his window. "I fell?"

Once he settled on a pair of shoes that felt good, Fred and I went for a walk along a driveway between the house and the barn. It was cold but clear and dry, a soft wind rustling the grass. I matched my pace to Fred's slow steps. Boomer ran ahead.

When we reached the barn, its boards faded and leaning away from the wind, we turned back. I wanted to step off the pavement and run across the pastures, but Fred was afraid to go too far.

Back in his room, holding hands, Fred asked, "When can I go home?"

"I don't know, honey." I stroked his beard. "I'm so sorry, but I have to go."

As he was walking me to the door, Elena stopped us.

"He seems depressed," she said. "I am worried. I saw him with tears in his eyes."

"Well, it's a big change. It's to be expected."

"Oh Fred," she said, turning to him. "I don't want you to cry." She turned back to me. "Susan, do you think we could get the doctor to order an antidepressant?"

"Let's wait a bit and see how it goes."

I had made it to the front porch when Elena stopped me again. "Just a second. I have something for you." She hurried back through the house, returning with a card and a white vase with three plastic red roses. I opened the card, a cartoony one designed for children, and read "Happy Valentine's Day." At the bottom was Fred's desperate attempt to write his name. My throat flooded with tears as I kissed Fred one more time. "Thank you."

As I drove away, Elena and Boomer stood outside with Fred. I headed toward the ocean, winter sun too bright in my eyes.

At Su Casa a few days later, I found Fred and Elena down the road in the vegetable garden. Fred looked old as she held him by the elbow, leading him along.

Elena and Max didn't restrict him to a wheelchair, but they never let him go out alone, and they guided him through every move. I wondered if they made him more helpless that way.

As soon as he saw me, Fred said, "Let's get out of here."

I took him for a ride on a narrow road lined with pines and wild berry vines. I thought there was a lake down there, but the road just went on and on. It didn't matter. I parked. We kissed. I joked about how the Honda Element, with its bony parking brake between the seats, was not designed for making out.

We kissed hard, melting into each other as always. But instead of the thrill we used to feel, I opened my eyes and saw that Fred was crying.

"Oh, babe. What happened to us is rotten," I said. "We have to enjoy each moment."

"Yes," he said through his tears. "That's exactly what we need to do."

I kissed him some more. "You're still a good kisser."

He sniffled.

After a few minutes parked on the country road, I decided to head to Newport's Bayfront for a change of scenery. I had imagined we'd sit at a coffee shop, look at the water, and relax. But tourist season was over. The only things open were the taverns and the fish processing plant, so we walked. I held Fred's hand the whole time, afraid he'd fall if I let go.

Sea lions lay on docks floating below the pier, climbing over each other, barking, sleeping, and snorting. We watched one swim round and round looking for a spot to climb on. He got halfway up, looked around and slipped back into the water.

"I'm tired," Fred said.

The only bench we found faced directly into the sun.

I took him back to Su Casa.

Elena was waiting at the door. "Where did you go? It's not good to take him too far. You have to watch him all the time, every minute, all day long."

"I know. I'm his wife." Fred, right there listening, said nothing.

I hustled him to his room, where we could escape Max's demolition derby on TV and Elena's constant talking about Fred, who was their first and only resident so far.

Apparently, she had been talking *to* him, too.

He cleared his throat. "I want to go home. I shouldn't say that."

"You can say anything." Perhaps he believed he was staying there to save me. Or maybe Elena's brainwashing was starting to sink in.

"There's no way out of this," he said.

There wasn't. There really wasn't.

A day later, I was knocking my feelings down with a double shot of whiskey mixed with flat diet Coke. It tasted like Dad's old highballs. I knew it was not the smartest way, but I just could not deal with things anymore.

I had taken Fred to lunch at the Adobe, a white-tablecloth restaurant in Yachats, about a half hour down the coast. Our seats overlooked the ocean. While waiting for our food, Fred's eyes welled up with tears. "I want to go home."

"I'm sorry, honey."

How I wished I could say, "Okay. I'll take you home. We'll tell Max and Elena to go jump."

Our food arrived, and we ate in silence, staring at the breaking waves.

When we got back, Elena met us at the door asking if Fred had had a bowel movement. I had no idea.

She talked on and on about Fred's sadness—in front of him. She suggested I not visit so often because it upset him. Maybe she was right, but I was his wife. What was I supposed to do?

As I turned onto my street coming home from Su Casa, my neighbor Carol called on the cell phone to tell me the dogs were out. I had left one of the back gates ajar, and sure enough, they were gone.

I walked all around the neighborhood with their leashes, calling them and despairing that I would ever see them again. If I had to lose my dogs and Fred in one month, I could not go on.

I walked the neighborhood streets. "Annie! Chico!" I called till my throat hurt. Nothing. I limped home with empty leashes.

But they had beaten me back. They came running out of the bushes and hurried into the house, tongues hanging out. Annie was so dirty she was black from the shoulders down. Soon there was mud on the floors and on the big chair by the window and no one but me to clean it up.

I drank whiskey and told the dogs I would trade lives with anybody, even someone with cancer. I just couldn't take it anymore. All I wanted to do was cry and drink, then go to bed. Forever.

16 Running Away

Once they had a taste of freedom, the dogs escaped whenever they could. In the month after Fred left us, Chico started jumping the chain link fence. Every time I turned around, he was on the other side while Annie, who was shorter, was still confined. If he could jump out, he could jump back in, right? Apparently not. He rustled through the thick growth around the house and ran by, his tongue hanging out, his eyes glowing with excitement. I had spent months taking both dogs to training classes. They could heel, sit, stay and down just fine, but when I hollered, "Come!" Chico would not come.

I needed to "spend down" our savings before we could qualify for government assistance for the nursing home costs, so I hired a local contractor to build a fenced enclosure so tall the pups could not escape. They were coming in about a week.

Meanwhile, I took Chico with me to visit Fred at Su Casa. When the dogs were younger, they rode in their crate, but Chico and Annie had chewed the plastic fronts off, so I couldn't attach a door anymore. He sat in the passenger seat watching the road, looking a little queasy on the turns, but holding it together.

At Su Casa, resident dog Boomer was not thrilled, especially when Chico greeted Elena with full-frontal enthusiasm. Boomer growled while Chico pulled hard on the leash, barking and gnashing his teeth. Elena clutched her dog against her. "I did not know you had that kind of dog," she said, running off with paw prints on her white sweater.

Fred, coming up behind Elena, hugged Chico and laughed as the dog licked his face. We three walked through the pasture, happy to be together again. It was cold, having snowed that morning, so we soon turned back toward Su Casa, where Boomer stood guard at the window. Chico was clearly not welcome in the house. I put him in the car, where he sat up behind the steering wheel like an old man waiting for his wife at the grocery store.

"That's a big dog," Elena said when we went back in. "I wasn't ready for that."

"I'm sorry," I said. "He's still a puppy. He gets excited."

I followed Fred into his room, where he showed me his toothbrush and toothpaste. "What do I do with this?"

I sighed. "Brush your teeth. Put some of this paste on the brush and go like this." I demonstrated.

He stood frozen, confused.

"It's okay. You don't need to do it now. Do you want to listen to music or something?"

He continued staring at the toothbrush. Chico was probably eating the upholstery in the car by now. "Honey, I have to go."

He followed me out, still holding his toothbrush, barely paying attention as I kissed him and hurried to the car, shoving my dog out of the driver's seat so I could get in. The cloth upholstery was fine, except for a layer of fur and drool.

On the way home, Chico lay his head against the back of the seat with a look that said, *I'm so tired.*

But not tired enough. Within a half hour after arriving home, he had jumped over the fence again. I had barely gotten him back in the house when my friend Terry arrived to practice her solo for the next Sunday's Mass. Chico dashed out the front door.

The sun sets before five on the Oregon coast in the winter, and it's dark in the woods. You can't see a black dog. Fortunately, I heard my across-the-street neighbor talking to someone and guessed where Chico had gone.

"Do you have an extra dog over there?" I called.

Sure enough. Paula was barbecuing steaks, and Chico had decided to help. I dragged him home.

In the morning, he jumped over the fence again. I was getting tired of this game.

At Su Casa, Fred looked different. Elena said his eyes used to look happy; now they looked depressed, with dark circles underneath. He shuffled when he walked.

When I suggested we go for a ride, he didn't hesitate to escape.

It wasn't until we were looking at paintings at an art gallery in Nye Beach that I realized Fred, whom I had never seen without full facial hair, except in old pictures, didn't have a mustache. Apparently he had accidentally shaved it off. He still had his beard, giving him an Amish look.

Was it being at Su Casa or his illness taking him down? Elena said he just wanted to sit in his room. I had asked Dr. L. to prescribe an antidepressant, and Fred had been taking it, but it didn't seem to be helping.

We stopped at Starbucks. As we waited in line, Matt, one of my writer friends, passed by us. He touched my shoulder as if to say, "I see where it's at and I care."

Back at Su Casa, Elena told me again that I should space out my visits. If Fred was going to be in long-term care, I needed to let go.

How?

As we sat in Fred's room looking at each other, I asked him questions, trying to get a conversation going. Favorite food? Steak. Color? He didn't know. Elena had told me he had forgotten my name. I tested him.

"What's my name?"

"Ummmmm." He shook his head. "I'm sorry."

"I'm Sue."

He called me Sue a couple times, as if trying to remember it, but it didn't sound the way it used to.

He was withdrawing from me and I from him. We spent two hours a day together and twenty-two apart.

The next morning, I could not see a single reason to launch myself out of bed. I couldn't keep my leaping dog from jumping the fence. My husband didn't live here anymore and didn't know my name. My birthday was next week, and I'd be alone with the dogs. Except for needing to feed those dogs, I might have stayed in bed all day. After Annie ran into the bedroom and nudged my arm, I poured kibble into the shiny metal bowls, showered, ate breakfast and dressed in yesterday's clothes.

The sun was out. I joined Annie and Chico on the deck. In my jeans, T-shirt and two layers of sweatshirts, I was almost warm. I decided to be like the dogs, with no agenda, just living in the moment.

We lived a half mile south of the Newport airport. Small planes and helicopters buzzed over the house. As I gazed at the scattered clouds, I noticed a plane rising straight up, leaving a contrail that started back behind the eastern trees and stretched all the way across the sky like a white rainbow. Over time, the contrail moved with the earth and slid southward, its edges going in and out of the thunder-clouds that had trapped the sun so well it looked more like the moon. Nearby, I saw a patch of colors, not a rainbow but a rain patch of pink, blue, and yellow.

As the rain patch faded away, Annie lay with her head in my lap, and Chico, after a sloppy face kiss, jumped off the deck to play.

Now the contrail looked like vertebrae on a spine being pushed into the gray-black cloud from both directions. In a minute, the left side was gone, the right looking like a frayed piece of wool. The light had dimmed. A cool breeze rattled the wind chimes. Rain was coming. It was time to go be a dog in the house.

17 Broken Record

Nancy, caregiver turned friend, was chatting over coffee with Fred when I arrived at Su Casa.

Elena came running out to the car. "Did Fred really tell Nancy that he wants to go home? She said he did. Maybe she's making it up."

"No, I'm sure he said it. He tells me the same thing all the time. Of course he wants to go home." I could see Fred and Nancy through the window and wanted to join them, but Elena kept talking.

"He's too depressed," she said. "I'm afraid he wants to die."

"Maybe he does."

"Don't say that. You have to talk to him."

"Okay," I said, but I didn't plan to mention it.

Earlier in his illness, Fred had talked about Oregon's 1997 Death with Dignity Act, which allows for physician-assisted suicide. He had voted for it, and I had voted against it. As a Catholic, it would be a mortal sin for me to help him die. But it was moot in this case. Alzheimer's patients don't fit the qualifications. Not only do they need a terminal diagnosis with less than six months to live, but they must be lucid and able to administer the fatal prescription to themselves. That close to the end, they're barely conscious.

I was grateful I didn't have to make that choice.

Fred hadn't talked about suicide lately, but who could blame him for wanting to escape a future living a ghost life in a nursing home?

Nancy was leaving as I came in.

"Thank you for coming," I said.

"My pleasure. I love this guy."

After Nancy left, Fred hugged me. "Help," he whispered in my ear.

I didn't know what to say, except to wrap him in my arms. I was visiting, I was defending him like a mother tiger and trying to make sure he had everything he needed. But I couldn't do the one thing he wanted most; I couldn't take him home.

Sitting in the waiting room before our next appointment with Dr. L, Fred said, "He'll let me go home, won't he?"

"No, you have to stay where you are."

"Why?" He was crying when Dr. L. came in and shook our hands.

Fred moved his mouth but couldn't make words. He finally managed, "I don't want to be here."

The doctor nodded. He confirmed Newport Rehab's low mini-mental score, did reflex tests that didn't seem to get any reaction, and wrote a new prescription to continue the same AD meds.

"Fred is living in an adult care facility called Su Casa now," I said. "I'm wondering if it's too soon. Should he be in a place like that at this point?

He looked straight at me. "Yes, it's time." He turned to Fred. "They can give you the care you need, and it's a lot easier on your wife."

Fred nodded but kept crying.

On the way back to Su Casa, Fred asked, "How are we going to divide things up?"

What things? Did he think I was divorcing him like his first wife did? Was he reliving that time, not able to tell the difference between the two of us?

When I left Fred at Su Casa, he was still sobbing. Elena hugged him as I drove down the hill to church for choir practice. It was my birthday, my first one alone, but I was trying not to think about that.

In the middle of practice, Father Brian came into the chapel to give me a birthday card. Other people started wishing me happy birthday.

"Stop it or I'll cry," I said. But I couldn't hold back the tears. I sobbed on my friend Terry's soft shoulder. I could feel everyone watching. Finally, I grabbed a bongo drum and banged on it. "Let's sing."

I knew people with AD repeated things, but at times I wished we could change the channel and obsess about something besides Fred's desire to come home.

I didn't visit every day anymore. New residents moved in, an old guy who stayed in his room, another man who laughed a lot but had trouble talking, and an elderly couple who spoke only to each other. I had hoped Fred would make some friends at Su Casa, but it wasn't happening.

He kept asking, "How long do I have to stay here?"

I kept saying, "I don't know."

I didn't have to give up french fries or chocolate for Lent that year. This was penance enough.

When I visited a few days before Easter, we had barely sat down when the broken record started again. "What if we just got in the car and drove away? I've been good. What do I have to do to get out of here?"

I led him on a walk around the grounds. It was a beautiful place, lots of green grass sloping down to the river. Boomer chased rabbits and squirrels as Fred lurched along, unsteady on his feet now.

"Let's sit here in the sun," I said, picking a grassy spot on the trail above the river. Boomer hung close for a while before running off.

Fred started in again. "How can I get out of here?"

"I don't know."

We sat in silence for a while. I held Fred's hand, tracing the veins, matching my palm to his. Fred looked like he was about to cry.

"Oh, babe. Come on. It's hot. Let's go get something cold to drink." As we walked back to the house, Fred was teary, his eyes puffy. "Let's go watch TV with the other guys," I said. They were all there, lined up in their wheelchairs. We watched a bit of news. At five thirty, Elena came out with dinner, tuna chunks on peas and a roll.

If only I could tell Fred, "Get in the car. We're going home."

18 Breaking Out

Had I lost my mind or found it? It was April 14, two days after Easter. On Easter Sunday, something had clicked for me. Fred and I went to brunch with friends from church. Although he had trouble with his food, when dressed up and out in the world, he didn't seem demented. He looked good, had fun, even made a joke. I decided he had been institutionalized too soon. I should take him home. We'd need more help, but not all the time, so it might be cheaper than Su Casa. Even if it wasn't, I couldn't watch my husband weep anymore.

That night, I brought Fred to our house for dinner and lied to Elena about where he had gone. He wanted it so badly, and what could it hurt? Yes, he seemed depressed. Yes, he wandered and forgot a lot, but it was all part of Alzheimer's.

The neighbors were talking together across the street when we arrived. We joined the conversation, like old times. Later, Fred enjoyed his homemade pizza and Jell-O salad, and he had fun with the dogs. He kept saying it was so good to be home. But he didn't fight me when it was time to go back to Su Casa.

"Where did you go?" Elena asked.

"Abby's Pizza."

"Oh, we had pizza last night."

She bought the lie. Fred and I were lying together as a team, and it felt good. Why shouldn't I take him home? It was my husband and our house.

This time when I left Su Casa, he was not crying. He was "escorting my lady" to the car. I told him I'd try to bring him home. I knew it would complicate my life. But visits were torture. Maybe in six months, he'd be so far along he'd have to go to an institution. But not now.

In January, when the people at the hospital had asked if I could take care of him, he hadn't been able to walk. Now he was back on his feet. He was not adjusting to life at Su Casa. Maybe he was just not ready. We had been pushed around and told what to do for almost three months. It was time to make our own decisions.

Before we could make any changes, my Aunt Edna died. She was a hundred years old. I flew to San Jose for the funeral.

I said goodbye to my aunt in the casket, watched it be lowered into the ground, and threw a pink rose on top. At the reception afterward, I ate and half-listened to my father tell stories. He was the kind of guy who dominated every conversation. By now, everyone knew about Fred and was sympathetic. I was married but no longer had a husband at my side. If I carried out my plan, he would be home soon. But—

In San Jose, I started having second thoughts. Telling Fred I was considering bringing him home had turned his mood around and given him hope. But maybe it was crazy after all. Alzheimer's is a one-way trip. It only gets worse. We'd have to go through the whole thing again in a few months.

I called Su Casa to check on him. The guy who answered the phone, somebody named Gary, refused to tell me anything about Fred. He cited privacy laws.

"But I'm his wife," I protested.

"Sorry."

"Can I talk to Elena or Max? I don't even know who you are."

"They're not here."

"This is ridiculous. I'll call back later."

"Fine." He hung up.

Pain zinged across my stomach. If Max and Elena were gone, who was taking care of Fred?

When I visited Su Casa the Wednesday after the funeral, I found Fred helping Max build a new greenhouse. When he saw me, he stood smiling with his arms open wide. It was like the old days.

Elena insisted that I stay for dinner. Over pizza and salad, we talked, maybe even bonded a bit. I told her about the funeral. She told me about her family in Mexico. She wasn't a bad person, just not as skilled at AD care as advertised.

Fred didn't say anything about my earlier promise to bring him home. He had forgotten. Every time he got a little teary, I tried to change the subject.

He kept saying, "I lost, I had, I used to." That summed it up pretty well.

Max told me that Gary, the new employee who wouldn't give me information when I called from San Jose, had already been fired. He mixed up the medications, had no respect for the residents, and served a slice of pizza that he had dropped on the floor. He reportedly said that because the residents had dementia, they wouldn't remember ten minutes later. Probably true, but still . . . bye-bye, Gary.

In Fred's room, I played Glen Miller music on his stereo. We sang and pretended to play trumpets, pianos, and drums. We snuggled, kissed, and felt happy. Fred didn't know our own phone number, but he still knew the phone number on the song "Pennsylvania 6-5000." He knew all the words, all the beats to all the songs. Yet when he tried to ask about the truck we used to have, he came out with "book," "milk," and other words that made no sense.

After almost three months at Su Casa, he had no idea how long he had been there and wasn't sure where I lived.

When it was time for me to leave, we hugged one more time.

"You are the love of my life," he said.

"You are mine, too." My throat tightened with tears. I forced a smile. "See you later, alligator."

On my next visit, I asked, "What do you want to do? We could go to the aquarium or the beach. We could get coffee or ice cream."

His eyes lit up. "Ice cream. Yeah."

I drove to Seal Rock, where we bought ice cream cones and sat at a picnic table in the sun. Fred had a hard time getting into the seat. It's one of those things you don't think about, how you have to swing a leg over, balance and swing the other one in.

"This is so good," he said, taking a bite of mocha almond fudge as it dripped into his beard and melted down his fingers. I licked at my marionberry cone and mopped his face and hands with paper napkins.

After we finished our ice cream, we went to Ona Beach. Fred looked around. "I need to—"

"Restroom?"

After he came out of the men's room, I thought we'd walk on the sand, maybe stop at home, maybe visit a friend. But Fred suddenly said, "I think I should go back."

"Really?"

"Yeah, I need to go back."

He was uncomfortable not being at Su Casa. He had forgotten his other home. Our home. Or maybe he didn't know who I was, thought I was another paid caregiver killing time driving him around.

"It was nice of you to come," he said.

Back at Su Casa, nothing had changed. Craig, a new resident, sat playing on his computer in front of the TV. Elena and Max were gone. I had hoped to talk to them, but by five thirty, they still hadn't returned. Their daughter served pizza for dinner. Again. What happened to the nutritious meals they had advertised?

Fred led me into his room, grabbed a stack of paperback books and handed them to me. "I can't read," he said.

I stuffed them into my purse.

"Are they keeping you busy with activities here?" I asked.

"Activities?"

"Like exercises or games or something."

"I don't think so."

"Well, that's not good." I checked my watch. "I'm sorry. I have to go."

"What if I just walked home?" he asked.

He hadn't forgotten his other home. "It's been done," I said, thinking of a local guy with AD who walked ten miles from the Oceanview assisted living facility at the north end of Newport to South Beach to see his girlfriend. By then, his family was in a tizzy, and the police were looking for him.

"I don't know," I said.

But I was pretty sure Fred would not be coming home. When I pictured him urinating on the carpet in the middle of the night a few days before he fell, I knew I couldn't manage it anymore. Sure, I could hire caregivers, but for every Nancy, I got three Bonis who didn't know what they were doing.

I gave Fred another kiss and got in the car. Soon I was heading down the hill again, merging into the afternoon commute traffic.

19 Back in the Classroom

That spring, I guest-taught a friend's writing class at Oregon Coast Community College. The session went so well I got excited about teaching again. I had started teaching weekly creative writing classes at OCCC in 2002 as part of my MFA program and continued after I graduated. I quit when Fred reached the stage where I couldn't leave him alone anymore. With him at Su Casa, maybe I could resurrect my teaching dream.

Chemeketa Community College in Salem was holding a faculty job fair that afternoon. I hadn't planned to go, but I was all dressed up and the weather was great, so I raced home to get my resume and transcripts then drove to Salem, the state capital, about a hundred miles from home.

By the time I got to the college, the job fair was almost over, but I managed to talk to the staff about distance education, community education, and regular English classes. The English department chairman stressed that they prioritized candidates by experience, but they had openings. He was excited about my MFA in creative writing. I did not mention my husband with AD.

I could teach community education classes like I'd done on the coast. Chemeketa paid more. They did publicity and let the instructors attend their teacher training classes for free. All I had to do was send the director a proposal for a class and hope he approved it for the fall quarter.

It was encouraging and exciting. I had used a whole tank of gas and driven two hours each way, but I filled out the application forms and turned them in.

Was this a logical decision? No. It was a desperate deluded attempt to reboot my life despite what was happening with Fred.

I woke up later that week feeling depressed, with a migraine headache making it worse. I spent the morning sitting in the sun with the dogs, sometimes crying, sometimes doing nothing. Everything seemed hopeless, and I felt so alone.

When I decided to drag myself to the post office to pick up the mail, I accidentally left the inside garage door open and the dogs came roaring out. I spent the next hour getting them back.

I hadn't done the dishes in three days. Every room in the house was coated with dust, grunge, and dog hair. Annie had peed through her blanket onto the big easy chair, and I didn't know how to clean it. The empty freezer in the laundry room was mildewed inside and leaking something onto the floor, probably something toxic.

I needed a maid and a caretaker, one of those loving couples from the old movies. "Don't worry about it, ma'am, we'll take care of it."

As for becoming a college instructor in Salem, yeah, right.

May 18th was our twenty-fourth wedding anniversary.

The day before, at Mass, Father Brian had asked for prayers for Fred Lick, who was suffering from Alzheimer's disease, that he find peace and find God in his own way.

In the sacristy after Mass, he told me again that I needed to let go of him.

"I know, Father. But he's still alive. He's still my husband."

He nodded. "He's being taken care of. You need to trust God and take care of yourself."

Joe, the eighty-year-old usher, came rushing in. "Father, I got a problem."

Yeah, me too, I thought as I slipped away.

Over the years, Fred and I had had great anniversaries. We celebrated with champagne on the *Delta Queen* riverboat cruising down the Mississippi, over lobster at a portside restaurant in Gloucester, Massachusetts, and drinking piña coladas in Waikiki. The year before we moved to Oregon, Fred whisked me out of my office at the *Saratoga News* to a posh hotel where he had filled our room with roses and photographs from our wedding. We soaked in a private spa, toasted each other with champagne, and renewed our vows of love.

Today I would visit Fred at an adult foster care home. I would bring a card, our wedding album, and diapers.

He was waiting for me. After we sat on his bed looking at the photos, he said he wanted to go out to dinner. We ended up in Depoe Bay at Tidal Raves, which overlooks the ocean. The steak and crab cakes were spectacular, the staff cheery.

When we got back to Su Casa, Fred was so happy he started tap-dancing in the living room.

A lot of hand-holding, hugging, kissing, and "I love yous" followed. I asked if he was up for another year of marriage.

"Darn right," he said. "You want to stay here tonight?"

Could I? Did I want to? "No, I'm sorry. I can't."

In a minute, he had forgotten his request and calmly said goodbye.

20 Su Casa Is Not Mi Casa

You think you've got all your ducks in a row . . .

As I got out of the car at Su Casa, Elena charged out, raving at me about how Fred had tried to help Jimmy, a very old man with a walker, who had just moved in. "Fred's not stable and he could knock Jimmy down. You talk to him and tell him," she said.

"He won't remember what I say."

"He gets mad when I scold him." She gazed up the road and back at me. "I think he wants to go home. Maybe you should take him home."

Oh my God. Of course he wanted to go home, but she had always said I couldn't care for him by myself. Everyone had said that. Dr. L. had said Fred needed full-time care. I had come to believe it, too.

I thought Max would be more reasonable. He was watching TV with Fred. As I joined them, Max said, "What do you think about just bringing Fred for daycare or something? It would save you money."

"What do I do at night?"

He shrugged.

After these three and a half nightmare months, they had done a complete 180. Did they suddenly think their "sweet" Fred was too much trouble? Was it because he was eventually going onto Medicaid and they wouldn't make as much money off him?

I had just started getting my life together. I was playing more at the church because our music director was fighting a losing battle with cancer. I had applied for that new teaching job in Salem, and I had started writing a book about childlessness. I was counting on

Fred being cared for full-time at Su Casa, but now Max said he was tired of Fred's nighttime exploits.

"He pees wherever he's at, like a damned dog," he protested.

"I understand. He did that at home, too."

All this time, we'd been trying to help him adapt. Now we were talking in front of him about taking him home.

"I need to go to Rite Aid. Fred, let's go for a ride."

He never turned down a chance to get away, and I needed to end this conversation before Fred realized what they were saying.

In the car, he didn't say a word as I drove down the hill into Newport. What could he have been thinking?

He followed me into the drugstore. As I waited in line for my thyroid pills, Fred wandered up and down the aisles.

"Can I help you?" I heard a male employee ask from somewhere near the greeting cards.

"I-uh, I don't know."

Shoot. I jumped out of line to rescue my husband. "We're fine," I said, taking Fred by the arm.

Three more people had joined the long line at the pharmacy counter. I decided to come back another day.

It was dinnertime when we returned to Su Casa. Three old people sat in their wheelchairs waiting for supper while *Star Wars* played unwatched on the TV. Jimmy was up with his walker heading toward the bathroom, but he seemed confused.

"Do you need to use the restroom?" I asked.

"I can't make any sense of what I'm seeing," he said.

"Wait a second."

I found Max in the kitchen making grilled cheese sandwiches. Elena was gone, visiting a friend. Max said he couldn't leave the food because it would burn. I heard Jimmy saying, "I need somebody."

I helped Jimmy into the restroom, hoping he'd know what to do once he got there, and said goodnight to Fred.

Back home, after documenting numerous instances of insufficient care, including no activities, substandard food, and a shortage of staff, I called the state long-term care ombudsman's office and left a message. The next morning "Jennifer" returned my call. She was going to have the licensing people look into Su Casa. It certainly wouldn't help my relationship with Max and Elena, but I had to do something.

Elena still sang the same song when I talked to her on the phone the next day.

"Fred is endangering my other residents. He tries to help, but he doesn't know what he's doing. He gets angry now, especially after you visit."

Angry? Fred? That didn't sound like him.

"He wanders around all night, sometimes with no clothes on. He told me he feels like a prisoner. I don't want to hold him here if he's unhappy. I told him maybe you could take him home."

"Don't say that to him!" I protested. I told her I was looking for work.

"But you're already so busy."

"I can't pay for Fred to live here and have enough to live on."

"That's why Fred could come just for daycare," she said.

She went on and on about how he was bored, except for when he went down to the garden. I tried to explain that there was nothing going on but TV and not even shows he liked.

"Oh, but we have activities," she said. "A half hour of exercise every day."

She took his moods personally, not understanding that all of this comes with Alzheimer's. She said Max had been on duty last night when Fred was up three times. During the day, still watching the residents, Max was probably half asleep. If there was another person working there, I had yet to see him or her.

I wasn't sorry I'd called the ombudsman. But now I had to find an alternative to Su Casa.

* * *

The following evening, Max called me. Fred wanted to talk to me.

"Can I come home?" he asked.

"I'm sorry, no."

He was crying.

"Honey—"

He hung up the phone.

I looked up at the ceiling. "God, I don't know what to do. This is too hard! What am I supposed to do?"

In desperation, I called the Alzheimer's Association hotline. The man who answered sounded sweet. I explained the situation. Fred was having trouble walking and talking, was confused, and until recently the Su Casa folks had said that I couldn't take care of him. Suddenly they had started suggesting he go home, at least during the nights. Now he was begging me to take him home.

I believe the volunteer on the hotline gave me God's answer. He said I had to be very clear. I had to accept that Fred was in the best place for his needs, that "the matter is not open to debate," that taking him home was "not an option." As for Fred's requests, I could tell him I was working on it, we'll see, maybe next week, I have to talk to the doctor, etc. I could use his lack of memory to my advantage to make him feel better.

I thanked him for that clear answer. *It is not an option. You can't do it. That's the way it is.*

After I hung up, I wailed and whimpered for a while.

Then I remembered that Dr. L. had suggested they give Fred an extra tranquilizer before I left for the night. I called Max to tell him about the extra pill. I also made it clear that I could not take him home.

The next day, Max called to complain that Fred had been uncooperative all day. Around four that afternoon, he had run away from Su Casa and headed alone down the gravel road. Elena had gone after him in the car. He didn't get far.

I told Max that Fred needed to be in a locked facility. Max said he couldn't lock the doors under the terms of their license.

That's it, I thought. *I'm going to find another place.* There was nothing on the coast. It would have to be in Albany or Corvallis.

When I told Fred he would be moving, he wept with happiness. He couldn't wait to get out of Su Casa. "You just don't know," he said.

But I could guess. It's a pretty prison when you can't do anything on your own all day every day and you can't leave without an escort.

"If you move Fred to a locked facility," Elena said, "They will over-medicate him, ignore him, and let him die. I have seen it many times."

"I don't believe every nursing home does that. There are some good ones."

She shook her head. "I don't want this to happen to Fred."

"It won't."

He might hate the new place, but it would be more appropriate than Su Casa for his condition. I would not be able to visit as often, but maybe he'd be too busy to miss me. When I did come, I could stay longer and do a little shopping on the way. If Chemeketa approved my class for the fall quarter, I'd be working closer to him.

Would I really be able to drive a three- or four-hour round trip every few days? I couldn't think that far ahead.

21 | Timberwood

I looked at five nursing homes and arranged to move Fred to Timberwood Court Memory Care Community in Albany, up I-5 from Corvallis. Timberwood is its real name.

Timberwood would start at $4,885 per month, plus furnishings and a $500 initiation fee. Expensive, but slightly cheaper than Su Casa. Fred could continue to stay there after we transitioned to Medicaid government financing.

Fred and I chuckled like children with a silly secret because he was leaving, and his captors didn't know it yet. Elena was busy cooking dinner, and Max was working with a friend on new PR photos for Su Casa. I planned to talk to them later.

We had been running around spending money like drunken sailors. The rooms at Timberwood were unfurnished, with big windows, closets, and semi-private bathrooms. We bought Fred a double bed, dresser and nightstand at Roby's Furniture in Newport; they would deliver them to Albany. At Walmart, we bought sheets, towels, blankets, a bedspread, toothpaste, shampoo, and soap. It felt like I was outfitting my son to live in his first apartment.

Fred kept saying, "I love you so much. Thank you so much. That's a lot of money."

"Don't worry about it," I said. "We got a little tax refund from the government."

Very little.

He wanted to pack right away, but I kept telling him to wait two days for the furniture to be delivered to the new place. "Don't say anything to Max and Elena. I'll talk to them."

"I won't."

I wasn't sure he understood what he was getting into, that he was going into an institution full of Alzheimer's patients, that the doors would be locked, and that he'd be seventy-four miles from me and everyone else he knew.

As I sat at a ragtime concert with church friends the day after I signed the papers at Timberwood, the realization dropped on me like ice cubes. Oh! We can't do *that* anymore. Oh, we can't. . . .

Halfway through the concert, I had an attack of restless leg syndrome, a new tic that made it impossible to sit still. The music was fun, but I would lose my mind if I didn't move my legs. My left leg twitched and kicked. I slipped off my shoes and massaged my feet through my stockings, hoping the friends next to me didn't notice. I counted the songs left in the program. Nine, eight, seven—finally, a standing ovation. Thank God it was over, but I was still twitching.

My friends asked how Fred was doing. I was moving him to a better place, I said. They would probably never see him again, but I didn't mention that.

My legs spasmed in the car. I rubbed them with my fists and prayed to get home before I went completely crazy. At the house, I ignored the dogs, threw off my clothes and sank into a hot bath. Relief. So tired.

My unwashed laundry was piled on Fred's bed. There was no need to move it. Ever.

The phone rang early Sunday morning.

Max said, "Fred has packed all his things. Is he leaving?"

Nuts.

"This is not how I planned to tell you, but yes, he is. Not until

Wednesday. I told Fred not to pack. I was going to talk to you after church."

It turned out Max and Elena planned to be gone all day. Who would take care of their residents? Their teenage daughter? Max said he did not know what was different about specialized AD care. I wanted to say, *And that's the problem.*

I knew this was best for Fred. Su Casa had been a prison with nothing for him to do, no one for him to relate to, and no real understanding of his needs. He had been crying, sobbing, and cursing for months, and now he was up all night with no one but Max and Elena to help him.

I would learn later that someone from the state nursing home ombudsman's office had visited Su Casa, issued some warnings, and filed a report. Max was angry, but I have never been sorry that I called them. Years later, Max and Elena were still in business. They never did understand why I moved Fred out of there.

Timberwood offered daily activities, a nurse on duty, good meals, and staff who really seemed to care.

The director, a Filipina woman named Tina, came to Newport to meet Fred and me. We went to lunch at the Red Door Café, which had become my new hangout since Fred left.

She said they would work on his medication so he would sleep at night. She told Fred he could help with their activities, like he had in the San Jose Recreation Department and at the Oregon Coast Aquarium. His eyes glowed with hope and happiness.

While Fred was going to an exciting new life, I would be home with the dogs. No more zipping up the hill to see him or take him to familiar restaurants, church potlucks, or the beach. It sank in like cold rain as I marked and packed his things and considered sleeping in the master bedroom again.

He had been at Su Casa for months, but it hadn't felt permanent.

Because it was possible I might bring him home, I hadn't wanted to disturb his possessions—even though he didn't recognize most of them as his. Now my life would start anew as a woman whose husband was far away in an institution and never coming home.

On June 2, the day before Fred moved to Timberwood, we sat on a bench at Su Casa looking out at the fields and the creek beyond. Boomer sat panting at Fred's feet. We kissed and hugged and held hands, soaking in the sun and letting the warm breeze ruffle our hair.

I couldn't help thinking this was the last time we'd be able to do this, to just walk out a door and sit outside cuddling and kissing. Fred would be locked in at Timberwood. Over time, he would be absorbed into the community there. His memory of me and our house in South Beach would fade away.

Fred was too anxious to sit for long, so we walked, and he asked questions.

"How will I get there?" "Where will you live?" "Where will the dogs be?" "How much longer till I go?"

Inside, Elena was doing exercises with the other residents, simple leg and arm lifts. I joined them, urging Fred to try it. He wasn't interested.

In his room, I played classical music on the radio, hoping it would calm him. He didn't seem to notice. He suddenly got up, swished his toothbrush in the water that was always at the bottom of his plastic cup and brushed his teeth furiously. There was no point in asking why.

I loaded the dining room chair that I had brought from home into the car. "Is that ours?" he asked. Not only was it ours, but we had reupholstered those chairs together.

Finally, it was time for me to go. I put Fred's suitcase and two boxes of stuff into the car—clothes, pictures, CDs, shoes, a melting chocolate Easter bunny. The toiletries would go with us tomorrow.

The staff at Timberwood had told me they wanted me to stay away for a week or more, as long as it took for Fred to adapt to his new home. I needed that week off, too. He wouldn't be the only one adapting to a new life.

God, I prayed, please be with us tomorrow. We had been apart before, but we had always known we'd come back together. It would never be the same again.

On moving day, as I drove to Su Casa, Pat O'Leary, my friend the DJ at "Boss Radio," played "Let It Be." He had heard me sing it before and had received my email message about Fred. I soaked it in.

Fred was waiting. I collected his pills, and off we went. The music on the radio kept Fred mellow the whole trip. He noticed that we were driving a long distance. He worried when we passed the hospital in Corvallis where he went to see Dr. L. and kept going past miles of sheep pastures and grass farms. Open land gave way to shopping centers, restaurants, and nursing homes. I wondered if he'd panic when he saw the MEMORY CARE COMMUNITY sign in front of the long beige building with neatly trimmed hedges. But he didn't react at all as I entered the circular driveway and found a parking space.

Inside, administrators and aides welcomed him. He was soon involved in conversation with the activities director while I hung his clothes in the closet. Lunch at noon was delicious—meat loaf sandwich, macaroni salad, watermelon and orange slices, peaches and cream for dessert.

Roby's delivered the furniture around noon. Fred and I made the bed together. Then he boarded the Timberwood bus for a field trip to an old flour mill turned museum. While he was gone, Tina helped me take the empty suitcases out, and I left. Back on the freeway, I slapped the '50s radio station off, replacing it with soothing yoga music. *It will be all right*, I told myself. *It will be all right.*

22 Our New Normal

When Tina called the next day, I held my breath. Fred had just spent his first night at Timberwood. What if? But the report was miraculous. He had been happy and active. He had accepted my departure with no tears. He had stayed up until eleven thirty visiting with residents and staff and slept straight through to six thirty. No wandering, no crying, no naked walking, no peeing on the floors—and no tranquilizer because they didn't have a doctor's order for it yet. He appeared to be in exactly the right place. Of course, there would be a backlash, but right now, he had everything he needed, so I could get back to work.

I was making progress. The book about childlessness was coming along. I had gotten a poem accepted. The publisher of the *Newport News-Times* had emailed to ask if I was interested in writing for a travel magazine they were starting. Yes. Perfect timing. I felt like a real writer again.

It was great to have a whole day to myself, to not need to run to Su Casa or the pharmacy or anywhere else.

That night, I let the dogs out of the six-foot enclosure into the bigger fenced yard, thinking they'd stick around because it was dark and drizzling. I settled in to read for a while. Annie barked. Chico had jumped the fence. I chased him all over the neighborhood, getting soaked. I called, but he wouldn't come. When a car came up the street, I held my breath. The driver just missed him. When she stopped to scold him, he ran up to her door, and I grabbed him, dragging him home.

As the reality of our new situation sank in, I sat under the eaves with my back against the garage door, crying.

Yes, I could work in peace, but I had no one to help me with everything else. My back ached from Annie jumping on me. People might chuckle over puppies playing hard, but they hadn't watched Chico and Annie thrashing each other, eyes narrowed, teeth clacking. No matter what I did, they wouldn't stop. I had read that pit bulls only fight if you train them to do it. But no one had taught them this.

They had ruined the carpet in the den, destroyed the back screen door, and wrecked the hot tub cover. They had chewed up their crates and the walls of the laundry room. They had destroyed everything they got hold of.

If not for those dogs, Fred might still be at home.

Other single women owned large dogs that jumped into the car and went everywhere with them. But mine wouldn't sit still. They jumped on me when I was driving and practically knocked me over when I opened the door. If I took them to the beach, they fought when I tried to walk them both at once on their leashes. If I let them go, they wouldn't come back.

All this in spite of graduating from obedience classes. I had spent months forcing both dogs into the car, taking one out for the early class and the other for the late one. Fred had only attended the first session and graduation. Unlike the pups, I could not get him to sit, stay, or come when I asked him to, so I did it all myself, envious of those couples who trained their dogs together.

Chico was a model student at doggy school, but when he wasn't running away, he stood at the door looking to escape. Like Fred at the foster care home, he wanted out.

Who would have known when we gathered those tiny dogs into our arms and brought them home, when our church friends showered us with toys and blankets and we put them in a playpen full of pee pads, that fourteen months later, life would have turned upside down while they became one more huge burden?

When I arrived at Timberwood Court after my week of exile, I signed in, wrote a check to pay the June rent with money from our dwindling savings, and punched the code to get into the resident area.

I found Fred sitting at a table in the dining room. He looked confused when he first saw me, but realized who I was as I pulled up a chair and kissed him hello.

I joined him for lunch that day: chicken, mashed potatoes and gravy, carrots, strawberries, and apple crisp. Best three-dollar meal in Linn County.

Afterward I drove him to the mall to buy a new belt. Somehow the buckle on the old one had broken.

"What is this place?" he asked as I parked outside Target.

"Just a store."

Inside, he followed me around like a blind man as I sorted through the belts, trying to find one in his size like the brown leather belt he had broken. I found it way in the back and handed it to Fred.

"What's this?"

"A belt." I wrapped it around his waist as he stood like a child, then led him to the checkout counter to pay for it.

Back at Timberwood, Fred asked, "What is this place?"

"This is where you live."

"It is? No."

"It is. Come on."

My nose was running. Hay fever. Linn County calls itself the "grass seed capital of the world."

I signed us in and led the way back to his room. The staff had brought his mom's matching mauve easy chairs in from my car. Fred sat in one of them and smiled, rocking and spinning. "Where did these come from?"

"Your mother's house. They were in the storage locker."

"My mother?"

"Yes." We settled into the chairs, holding hands, '50s music playing on the radio.

"When can I get out of here?"

My heart sank. "Not right now. You have this illness."

"Oh, yeah."

Outside Fred's room just off the dining area, people paraded by: young aides, mostly women, hair in ponytails, wearing khaki scrubs; food servers in white jackets; administrators in business attire; medical aides in scrubs or jeans; white-haired residents in wheelchairs or bent over walkers, vacant look in their eyes.

Candace, the nurse, with flaming red hair, a deep tan, and colorful skirts, had reported that Fred was confused and depressed. Growing up, Fred had been an insecure, undersized boy with Coke-bottle glasses. Now he was an anxious seventy-one-year-old man.

Before AD, Fred hid his anxiety well. He was friendly and loving and had lots of friends, but he was shy. Now he had no control over anything. It must be horrible to not know or understand from one moment to the next what's going on. Even worse when you're surrounded by other people who are just as confused.

The residents often wandered into each other's rooms. When we were in the hallway, I saw a woman heading into Fred's room.

"Ma'am, that's not your room," I said.

"The guy in there is mean," Fred added.

The woman stared at us and walked away.

Fred's room and Sam's next door were right off the dining area, fair game for anybody. There was a stranger sleeping in Sam's easy chair now.

I liked Sam. He reminded me of my dad, talking all the time about World War II. He was handsome, friendly, and comforting. Fred said he was crazy.

I didn't know about that, but over the next few months, I learned that some of the residents certainly were a little off.

Take Lorraine, running around in her pink housecoat. She kept telling everyone, "I have to go home, I have to go home. My sister's coming to get me." Maybe the sister really was coming, but no one had seen her yet.

Or Aggie, always cackling to herself.

That day, the woman across from her asked, "Are you tired?"

Aggie replied, "What do you think? I'm ninety-one years old. Of course I'm tired."

Sam and I cracked up. "Those ladies always give us a show," he said.

Fred had a different attitude. "They shouldn't be here."

"Why?"

He didn't answer.

Peggy, with flawless skin and curly hair, walked around like a demented doll, smiling but always lost.

Another woman the aides called Grandma had such short hair Fred thought she was a man. No, she's a woman, I insisted. I had seen her without her pants at the dinner table.

You could tell the ones with their faces in their plates had dementia, but with others, like Fred, it wasn't so clear. I assumed the woman who helped me figure out how to play the electric organ was a visitor, but no. She was a resident named Jean.

Every one of these people had a story, a previous life in which they could have been smart, funny, kind, and accomplished. They may have been doctors, teachers, ministers, musicians, artists, or chefs. They were someone's son or daughter, spouse, parent, grandparent, or friend. You would never guess any of that seeing them dressed in oversized baby clothes, their hair chopped off for convenience, lost as they wandered the halls or lay in bed screaming.

One would notice that nearly all were white while many of the workers were black or brown. Was it a matter of money or culture? My guilt deepened as I considered families who would never put their loved ones in a "home," who would take them into their own houses and care for them until the end. But I didn't have a family to call on.

The nursing home residents didn't even get the dignity of being addressed as adults. Staff called them by their first names or "honey," "sweetie," or "doll" as they washed them, dressed them and helped them go to the bathroom, as they held food to their lips and begged them to eat, as they tried to soothe them and assure them everything was all right, when everyone, even the person with the disease, knew it was definitely not all right. How aware were they of what was going on? No one knew for sure. I prayed it was a blur, that they didn't see what I saw.

Sometimes Fred surprised me. One day, we were sitting side by side in his mother's chairs. I had told him all the things I was doing and how hectic my schedule was.

"Do you ever have fun?" he asked.

"Of course," I said. "I'm having fun with you right now."

And I was. My trips to Albany forced me to get off the writing/ choir-directing/ house managing/dog-wrangling merry-go-round, to stop and sit with Fred with nothing to do but be in love.

On the Fourth of July, I came lugging my guitar and music stand. Fred sat in the Timberwood backyard with the other residents. He looked pale in the bright sun. He wore baggy jeans and a stained under-shirt. As we kissed, his just-trimmed mustache stabbed my lips, and the smell of sweat pushed me back. Tears rolling down his face, he thanked me for coming, as if he had thought I would never return.

The staff, wearing red, white, and blue, were setting out water-melon, potato salad, hamburgers, and potato chips.

"It's too hot," Fred complained. He asked for his hat, so I went in.

A tiny woman named Mary sat in the hall in her wheelchair. "Can you help me?" she called. "I want to go to my room."

I looked around for help. The aides were all outside at the party. "Okay. Show me where it is."

I pushed her down the hall as she held up her white-socked feet. In her room—which turned out not to be her room—she wanted to get into a leather recliner.

"Help me, help me," she pleaded.

"Sure." I thought I'd just lift her up, but she was heavier than she looked, and she fought me. I eased her back into the wheelchair and went out into the hall. I saw an aide walking toward the dining room.

"I need some help in here."

The aide followed me in. "Mary, what are you doing?"

"Help me, help me, help me."

"She does this all day long," the aide said.

I was new. I'd learn not to trust what the residents told me.

Back outside, the others sat in folding chairs, their heads drooping. When I handed Fred his fisherman's cap, he said, "This isn't my hat."

"Yes, it is." I had been with him when he bought it.

I rushed through my lunch. Everyone was waiting for me to sing. Sweating, my guitar not quite in tune in the hot sun, I sang country and folk songs and "God Bless America." People moved their lips and beat time with their hands on the tables. Fred sang along. Tina, the director, watched him, hand over her mouth, tears in her eyes.

I would cry later. Here I was, singing "Glory, Glory Hallelujah" to my husband in a nursing home, just like I had for my grandfather. Fred used to come with me sometimes, talking with all the residents and keeping Grandpa company while I sang. I never imagined he'd be the one I would come to visit.

As the party ended, people curled up for naps, but Fred was awake, fussing with his pants, worrying about the grape Popsicle stain on his undershirt. In his room, he started to take off his undershirt, pulled it back on, pulled it up again. I yanked it off and took a red polo shirt out of the closet. Fred stood with his arms at right angles. The sweat smell gagged me as I enclosed it in the clean shirt.

He kept scratching his ankle. I took off his shoes and socks. His feet were puffy, his ankles mottled with blue veins, his heels so dry the skin was flaking off.

I called the nurse to look at his feet. She said she'd keep an eye on them. "Just wear your slippers," she told Fred.

Soon it was time to say goodbye. Struggling to see the white line as I drove into the setting sun, I felt sick. My eyes felt as if I had big chunks of salt in them. Fred was happy when I was there. But it was getting harder every time.

It was like becoming a widow every few days.

23 Separate Worlds

Five weeks after Fred moved to Timberwood, I sat on a bench over-looking Yaquina Bay. I needed to take all the tangled strands of my life, untangle them, and see what I had.

Timberwood was a good place, run by caring people. Fred had been happy at first, but now he was back to constant crying. The staff changed his medications, and he started having panic attacks. They said he tried to strangle Aggie, the ninety-one-year-old who cackled all the time. Sweet, gentle Fred?

Fred wasn't the only one crying. After visits and calls, I wept. I had trouble getting out of bed in the morning. Even taking a shower seemed like too much work. I was barely meeting my article dead-lines. I had submitted a manuscript for a book on freelance writing based on my community college classes and was already on to my next book, but the editor said the freelance writing manuscript wasn't good enough. In my years as a professional writer, no one had ever said that to me before. Now I had a month to rewrite the whole thing, with no guarantee it would be any better.

Fred's nurse suspected that his tranquilizer, Klonopin, was bring-ing him down. I was taking the same thing. Was it making me more depressed? Or was my life just one big suck-fest?

I was lonely. During the day, the handful of other people who lived on my street were all at work. I could dance naked or fall over dead in the front yard; no one would see me. When I wept, nobody heard me except my dogs, who came to lick my face, then ran off to wrestle some more.

I was always busy, but I seemed to be getting nothing done, and then I was back on the road to Timberwood.

Medicaid loomed. Keeping Fred at Timberwood cost almost $5,000 a month. We would soon run out of savings and be eligible for government assistance to pay for Fred's care, but we would be poor. No, *I* would be poor. Fred's expenses would take all the money we got from Medicaid, plus most of his pension.

If you're an unmarried elderly person with no dependents and not much money, Medicaid is not a bad deal. The government will pay your bills, and when you die, they take your house, which you won't need anyway. But what if you are married? What if your wife is fifteen years younger and still building her career? What happens to her while you're spending your life savings and letting Medicaid take care of you?

Everyone kept telling me to get Fred's name off our property. How do you do that to a person who has worked two jobs all his adult life to get to this level of comfort? First he loses his ability to work, then we take away his driver's license, and now we want to take away his money and remove his name from the deed to the house which he paid for. We want to turn him into a non-person, a homeless, helpless indigent with dementia. That is not a respectful way to treat our elders—or their spouses.

When my grandfather lived in a nursing home, I was not the one making decisions. That fell on my father and my uncle. They gathered the family to clean out his house near Santa Cruz and sold it without his knowledge. Grandpa still thought he had a home to go to if he could escape the nursing home, but everything he owned had been thrown away, given to charity, sold, or taken home by family members. I had his bookshelf in my kitchen and his hat rack in my laundry room. At the time, I hated that my parents did that. But now I understood. He was never going home, and they needed the money to pay his bills. If the money from the house had run out before he died, I suppose Grandpa would have gone on Medicaid, too.

But Grandpa was in his nineties. How could this be happening to us? We were too young. We were healthy, yet Fred was in a nursing home, and I was scrambling to pay the bills. I didn't earn nearly enough from book royalties, freelance articles, and the few hours I worked at the church. My class at Chemeketa had been approved and would start soon, but my wages would barely cover my expenses commuting between South Beach and Salem.

If I couldn't make ends meet and needed a full-time job, who was going to hire me at fifty-something when I hadn't had a regular job for years?

People try to get around the system by offloading money or assets to family members and charities, but if you do that within five years of qualifying for benefits, Medicaid says, oh ho, you're trying to trick us, so now you have to wait another five years. You have to be truly poor to qualify. So, despite all that saving and planning you did back in the day, you're screwed.

Until Fred's fall in January, I didn't think I'd have to worry about money for a long time. I could write what I wanted to write and abandon work that caused me stress. Suddenly at fifty-seven years old, I was single again—or so it felt—looking for jobs I didn't want in the worst economic recession since World War II.

I couldn't win, so why bother?

I couldn't even complain to the AD support group anymore. Although I was much younger than the other people there and had different problems—no one else was trying to work or complaining about not having sex—the meetings helped. Now that I wasn't caring for my husband at home anymore, my issues were different, and the leader told me it was time to move on.

Timberwood had a family support group, but I didn't want to

drive seventy-four miles to Albany for night meetings. So I saved my sorrows for my appointments with Dr. Smith.

Meanwhile my editors and parishioners still expected me to perform. It was all robot work as I made phone calls and wrote my articles, as I played the piano every weekend at church, as I walked and fed the dogs, as I wished for someone to come take over my life and make all the decisions for me.

24 Catherine's Hands

Almost two months into Fred's stay at Timberwood, I hadn't heard about any more panic attacks or murder attempts. Fred seemed calm and content.

I watched the Timberwood activities director engage him in easy word games. She asked him and another man to set the tables for dinner. She had to direct them every step of the way, but they could do these things, as opposed to being out in the real world where it was constantly "I can't."

It was a quiet visit. I put lotion on Fred's rough feet. I didn't want to touch them. I tried to remember Jesus and the feet he washed. He didn't say, "Oh, you have nasty, dirty feet." He washed his apostles' feet with love. But did they smell bad and have toenail fungus?

We sat in the courtyard. Blue sky, wispy clouds, temperature just right. So much more peaceful than the outside world. Sometimes I wished I could move in and let the aides take care of me, too.

I told Fred he looked good and asked if he felt good. He said, "Yeah, I feel good. This is a good place. You did well."

He had what he needed at Timberwood: twenty-four-hour care. They were not just keeping him alive, but paying attention. I couldn't give him that. The workers in their khaki scrubs had nothing to do but take care of the residents. If one activity didn't work, they tried another. If somebody wanted something to eat and it wasn't meal time, they got him a sandwich. If somebody needed a hug, they were there, even if it was two in the morning.

It felt like family. Not like Su Casa, where it felt as if Fred had been kidnapped and told, "We're your family now. Forget about those other people." The workers at Timberwood understood that the residents had real families, but they would take care of them when their families couldn't be there.

We goofed around a lot during our visits. I told stories about the dogs and events at home, wanting to make Fred laugh. I made silly noises, and he copied me. We howled like wolves. We sang, and sometimes we danced. As suppertime approached, we sang with a Broadway CD as Fred set the tables. Later, I would remember this as the summer we had fun together at Timberwood.

When I visited, Fred told everyone, "This is my wife," as if they hadn't seen me before. But I couldn't take him anywhere and say, *Hey, this is my husband.* I did have a husband, but he lived in a bubble.

One day at the Farmers' Market, the woman I was helping run the authors' booth asked me, "Are you married, single, or what?" I wore a wedding ring, but there was no husband in sight, and I talked as if I were single. I could understand her confusion.

Freaking Alzheimer's.

While Fred thrived, I struggled. I was grieving even though Fred was still alive. I was juggling too many balls and didn't dare drop any of them. I needed another set of hands, but all I had was my own.

Chico had a new hobby: touring the across-the-street neighbors' house to see what he could find to eat. They left their doors open on warm days. Paula was taking a nap one afternoon when she became aware of someone staring at her. She awoke to find Chico's brown eyes fixed on her. Surprise!

The next day, Chico escaped twice. The first time, I found him near the mailboxes eating a slice of wheat bread Paula had put out for the birds. The second time, I crossed the street and knocked on the siding by the open door. Who greeted me? Right, Chico. He had just cleaned out the cat's food and was slurping up its water. I don't know where Joe and Paula were or if they ever discovered they had had a visitor.

Meanwhile, back at home, Annie was digging holes. She could get her whole head and shoulders in them now, but she was having so much fun I didn't have the heart to stop her. So what if she dug up the yard? I lay on the deck watching the fog move in from the west, about to overwhelm the sun. Did anything matter anymore?

Catherine, our music director at church, was dying of pancreatic cancer. I had already started playing the piano and leading the choir for most of her Masses.

Tall and thin, she had a radiant smile and walked around singing. She dressed like a 1950s spinster librarian, but she loved her husband, Jim, who had died of a stroke a few years earlier. She cared for a houseful of special-needs kids and welcomed everyone to her woodsy home. She went contra dancing with friends. One night at a bluegrass concert, deep into her cancer treatment, she stood in the back and danced.

"Gotta do it while you have the chance," she told me as I stood on the sidelines listening.

Catherine played the organ at her husband's funeral a few years before Fred went to the nursing home. The person she had asked to play was late, so she jumped up and said, "I'll do it" to a great round of applause. If she missed a note, nobody heard it.

I thought she was crazy to put herself under so much stress.

I teared up when I played the piano at the funerals of people I had never met. How could I play if I had actually known and loved the deceased? At my mother's funeral, I sat mute beside my father, watching a stranger play. Would I do the same when Fred died?

The day after Catherine's husband's funeral, during a TV commercial with the sound muted, I mentioned this to Fred. He put on a shocked face. "You're not going to sing and play at my funeral?"

"What? Do you want me to?"

"Well, of course."

"How can I sing when I'm wailing over your loss? Wouldn't you rather I throw myself on the floor, moaning that I can't live without you? Screaming, 'Come back, Fred, I can't go on'?"

Soon we were both laughing as I resurrected every bad movie funeral scene I could think of. The widow either weeps or stands in stony silence. It's the stranger who suddenly bursts into "Amazing Grace" as the mourners place roses atop the casket.

"Besides," I added. "It would be hard reading the sheet music through that black veil."

Fred guffawed, slapping his leg. "This is terrible. We probably shouldn't be talking like this."

"Yes, we should, considering that death is all around us these days. If we don't laugh, we'll go crazy."

"So you're not going to sing at my funeral?"

I swallowed. "I don't know. Besides, you're not allowed to die."

With that I punched the remote control button to bring back the sound as our TV show returned.

I played at Catherine's funeral, leading an expanded choir of past and present singers. That evening, I approached my first Saturday vigil Mass in Catherine's place, exhausted and anxious, my throat sore. The roses and hydrangeas from her funeral perfumed the air around the piano. As I played the opening song, I felt Catherine standing behind me, encouraging me, her long fingers guiding my small ones. When our communion hymns ran short, I improvised as the notes flowed through me.

After Mass, a woman said she loved my piano playing. One of the choir members hugged me and said she wanted me to know how much they appreciated me. I appreciated them, too.

With Catherine gone, I expected to be offered the music director's job. But our pastor had other plans. I was not going to be *the* music director. My friend Mary Lee, who had been leading the contemporary choir at the ten thirty Mass, and I would both be music ministers, sharing the work. We would alternate Masses, and I would lead the children's music for the religious education program.

My pay went up a little, but not much. Father Brian pulled out a chart from the archdiocese and showed me that if I had a degree in music, I would earn more. Unfortunately, my bachelor's and master's degrees were in writing. Mary Lee had a PhD in music.

Still, it was amazing after all these years to get paid for playing the piano. I knew my skills didn't match up to other church pianists'. While they had taken lessons as children and gone on to earn university music degrees, I had taught myself, stealing moments at the piano whenever I could. My fingering was awful, my pedaling all wrong, and I had to practice every day to hit most of the right notes on Sunday.

Now that I was getting paid for it, I ought to be perfect, right? I kept having nightmares in which I couldn't find my music, couldn't get to the church on time, or showed up and found someone else playing my songs.

But I loved to play the piano, and I hoped I could make up with my singing for whatever I lacked on the keyboard.

Adding my new church responsibilities to my writing, dog wrangling, and household chores, plus overseeing Fred's care, blasted my anxiety to a new level. Thank God I had my pills.

25 Hypnotized

My psychiatrist, Dr. Smith, moved to San Diego the summer Fred moved to Timberwood. In late July, I met my new therapist, Reatha Ryan, a psychiatric nurse practitioner who supplemented medication with hypnosis, behavioral conditioning, and other techniques.

Reatha, a brown-haired woman about my age, exuded peace. Like Dr. Smith, she had a therapy dog, Harry Happy Hound, a seven-year-old golden retriever. We met in Dr. Smith's old office with the same peanut-butter-colored leather couch and brown walls, but she had added a big green recliner. As I relaxed into the soft cushions, I knew this experience was going to be different.

We started with EMDR—eye movement desensitization and reprocessing—which is a method of helping patients process traumatic experiences from the past. Essentially, the memories are transferred from the fight-or-flight area of the brain to a place where they can be processed into healing. Sometimes patients follow a light moving side to side with their eyes. In this case, I held a pulsing knob in each hand. My palms tickled as the pulses alternated.

As Reatha led me through a guided meditation, I relaxed. Thoughts and memories poured out. In my mind, I went to a comfortable place by a river and described what I saw, heard and smelled.

I slipped into the river. I talked about how I loved to float. . . .

Afterward, we talked about learning to let things go, to ride the tide of uncertainties without trying to control everything.

The hour passed quickly. I came away feeling happier and more relaxed. No one changes overnight, but Reatha had accomplished more in one session than Dr. Smith had in years.

At my next appointment, Reatha tried hypnosis.

After asking what I wanted help with, she had me sit back in the recliner. She told me to stare at a point on the wall. I chose the corner where the white ceiling and the brown walls came together. Take deep breaths, she said. Relax. As my eyes grew heavy, she encouraged me to close them and picture myself going down stairs, a ladder, or an elevator. I chose a ladder.

She asked me to picture a safe place. I pictured the spot where I used to sit in the backyard reading or writing before the puppies started jumping all over me. It was sunny and warm. She had me describe the smells, colors, and sounds. Green grass, blue sky, waves, wind.

Tears leaked out of my left eye. She asked me to picture God there with me, protecting me, offering unconditional love. Bigger tears escaped both eyes. She told me to touch my thumb and forefinger together. Any time after this, I could do that and go back to the safe place.

She had me rest one hand inside the other and picture the wise woman within me. My wise woman looked like Tess from the TV show *Touched by an Angel*. We were in a car. Tess was driving. She told me, "You don't have to do everything."

Reatha asked me to remember the last time I had felt severe pain and grief. That was Thursday leaving the nursing home. I let out big sobs.

What would I like to say to Fred if I could? What else? What else? What else? What had I never told him? Sobbing, I told all. I even talked about my abusive relationship with the guy I dated before Fred. I told Reatha how I had been afraid Fred would leave me if I insisted on having children, and now I didn't believe he would have because he loved me so much.

She gave me a pillow and told me to hug it as if it were Fred. Tears poured down my cheeks and down my neck. She handed me a Kleenex. Hypnosis was nothing like I'd seen in movies and TV shows or stage shows where hypnotists supposedly got people to tap dance or quack like ducks. I knew exactly what was happening. I could end it at any time, but I wanted to do the work, to finish what we had started. I wanted to feel better without drugs.

After much crying and talking, she took me back to my wise woman, my safe place, and God. She said to picture myself surrounded by a color. I chose blue. She talked me back up the ladder from one to five, by which time I would open my eyes and feel clear-headed and refreshed.

Wow. I couldn't believe I had let all that out. Reatha said I had done really well. And yes, people often cried. I had a lot of pain to release. She gave me water and urged me to be careful for a while until I was fully awake.

For the moment, I felt freer. *Don't let Reatha move away,* I thought.

Before I left, she wrote me a new prescription. Although I was still taking Klonopin during the day, she switched me to trazodone at night.

"It's not as addictive, so you can use it as needed."

"Okay." It was another drug with more possible side effects, but I already felt so much better. Reatha had become my wise woman.

I didn't get my writing work done that day; hypnosis was like having surgery. I didn't just jump back into work. I needed to untangle a lot of knots, most of which no one else even knew were there.

26 Medi-screwed

Eight months after Fred started full-time care, I met with a Medicaid worker at the Senior and Disability Services office in Toledo. I had "spent down" our savings to the required maximum. I had made lists of income and expenses. I expected this heavyset gray-haired woman to look at my efficient paperwork and say, "Good job." But no, she scolded me. She told me that the "spend down" was only supposed to be on Fred's care, not dog fences. Great. Now the money was gone. I had already put $40,000 into Fred's care, and our savings would only cover one more month.

Medicaid was going to allow me $300 for my utilities, not including cable or Internet, plus money for the mortgage. When Fred couldn't drive anymore, we had traded his pickup and my Honda Accord for a single car, a Honda Element for which I was making $300 monthly payments.

"How will I handle my car payments?" I asked.

"I don't know," she responded.

"Would I be allowed money for food?"

"It's up to them."

Who was "them?" What kind of system was this?

She asked me how much Social Security I got. I stared at her. "I'm fifty-seven. I'm not old enough for Social Security."

She rubbed her eyes with the palm of her hand. "I'm so tired."

"Me too." But I had questions. I needed someone who cared, who wanted to help me make sense of all this, not someone who just wanted to get my signature on the papers and go home.

I hadn't been a housewife, but I hadn't been a high earner either, and in the last couple years, Fred's care had taken a lot of my time. I couldn't afford many hours of paid help at $20 an hour. Even with him in a nursing home, I spent hours on financial and insurance matters, and I lost a whole day of work and a tank of gas every time I visited him. Who was going to pay for that gas now?

"Will the money I earn be subtracted from the money I get from Fred's pension?"

"I don't know."

"Could I have a hearing to go over my expenses and how I will survive?"

"I don't know."

I was willing to be as frugal as possible if allowed to live a reasonable life for a woman my age who was still trying to work, but I probably looked like a spoiled trophy wife in her weary eyes. I had a new car, a master's degree, a big house with a hot tub, and more income from various sources than she ever dreamed of having.

The woman was old enough to retire but probably couldn't. When I whined about my expenses, she said she had no TV or computer herself. She was shocked at my $30-per-hour pay from the church, even though it was only a few hours a week. She was working so hard, probably for much less.

What if I gave up on Medicaid and tried to pay everything myself? Fred's city pension and Social Security would cover the nursing home, but that would leave nothing for me unless I traded my writing and music for a full-time job. Living-wage jobs were scarce on the Oregon coast. I could divorce Fred so that I wouldn't be responsible for his expenses. But then I wouldn't have his health insurance.

When my father died, I would inherit enough money to keep me going, but I hoped he would stay alive for a long time. I couldn't bear to lose both him and Fred.

I needed to earn more money in a hurry at exactly the time I was so deep into grieving and depression I could barely function.

Impossible choices.

I drove home down the Bay Road and walked into the house sobbing.

There were phone messages: A friend at the historical museum wanted me to do a free performance for the holidays. No. No more freebies. A satellite TV company wanted Fred to call them back. He didn't live here anymore.

I called the Medicaid woman, fighting my tears, to ask again whether my earnings would be subtracted from what I could keep out of Fred's pension. She replied, "I can't tell you that. My computer's down."

"I just want a theoretical answer."

"Well, I can't determine that. It may not be dollar for dollar."

That was not an answer. I wanted to know what was going to happen, and nobody would tell me.

When I telephoned our friend David, who was also our lawyer, to complain about my latest Medicaid encounter, he asked how I had spent down the money. Did I buy something I wanted for the house? No. Did I do something fun with it? No. I just built a dog fence and paid bills.

"Well, at least you got the bills paid," he said.

He explained how he would set up an income cap trust from which I would pay Fred's bills. Because of his pension, Medicaid probably would not give us enough money to cover everything, but whatever they gave us would help.

"I'll write a letter to Senior Services on your behalf."

"Thank you."

I did the math and surrendered to reality. Uncle Sam's deal was the best option. I would do the paperwork and try to stop hating the tired worker at the Senior Services office.

Fred had given me a taste of the good life. We had traveled and bought the things we wanted. We bought our cars new, never used. Fred collected wine. I collected antique glass. We had a hot tub, TV, and Internet, and did not worry about spending $30 for lunch.

I sat on the loveseat with my arm around Annie and looked around my living room: green walls, mauve carpet, piano and guitars, TV and DVD player, mahogany dining room table and chairs, china cabinet full of vintage glassware.

Growing up in a family that pinched every penny, where our parents laughed when we asked for anything extravagant, I was forever surprised by Fred's generosity. While I never had cash to spare, he always had a wad of twenty-dollar bills in his wallet. Sometimes I had to stop him, to say, "No, I like it, but I really don't need it." But if I wanted something, Fred bought it for me. Like the piano he had given me as a wedding gift, the antique ukulele for my birthday, the $300 mandolin I had been drooling over one day at the music store in Corvallis.

Fred and I loved to roam the antique stores. He'd look for my ruby glass and the clip-on or screw-on earrings I wore in those days. I would hunt for shot glasses to add to his collection, which filled a floor-to-ceiling display case in the den. We both collected musty-smelling classic books.

We loved wandering through the past, whether it was the cast-offs gathering dust at secondhand stores or century-old buildings we toured on vacations in the Northwest, Southwest, New England, and the Deep South. We marveled at castles in Portugal and old cemeteries in Costa Rica.

We walked hand in hand on the beach at Waikiki and hiked through the snow in British Columbia.

But that was over now. My only travels were between South Beach and Albany, and I needed to cut expenses, to go back to the frugality of the days before I met Fred, when sometimes I had to choose between milk and crackers because I couldn't afford both.

In my writing classes, I used to joke that I could afford to be a writer because I had Fred, my "sugar daddy." Don't quit your day jobs or expect to get rich off writing anytime soon, I told them. I knew all too well that most writers couldn't live off their writing income.

Even together, we were never wealthy, especially back in San Jose, but in Oregon we had been able to live comfortably and splurge a little bit. Alzheimer's took that away.

A few days after my miserable Medicaid meeting, I took Fred to see Dr. L. It was a short visit. Dr. L. asked Fred what activities he did; Fred couldn't name any. The doctor looked at his eyes, thumped his knees, and said he still needed to take his pills or he'd forget who I was more quickly. Come back in six months.

It had been a day for taking care of business. Fred's beard was growing back after an aide had shaved it down to a goatee. He kept rubbing the stubble. He smelled awful. When was the last time he had a shower? He didn't know. I talked the Timberwood director into getting Fred more showers. I filled out the paperwork to start paying his monthly fee through Medicaid.

Fred looked thin. His glasses were bent. He took them off and said he could see. "Yes," I said, "And I can see your pretty eyes." Now that he didn't read, he didn't need glasses anyway. He'd completely forgotten about his cataract surgeries.

We held hands. He said, "I love you so much." I hugged him, despite the stink and the bristly beard. Then it was time to leave again.

Back on I-5, I suddenly felt unreasonably happy, giddy even. I laughed at bumper stickers and baby sheep, hummed a song from church. I had forgotten my tranquilizers, so I'd missed my midday dose. Trazodone gave me headaches, so I was back on Klonopin several times a day, but my pills were at home on the kitchen counter.

Now, on the freeway, I was laughing for no logical reason. Was Klonopin causing my depression, I wondered. Or was I just happy to get away from Timberwood?

Just when I expected Medicaid to start paying Fred's bills, the woman from Senior Services said I still had too much money. Therefore, I did not qualify for benefits. When I said her numbers were all wrong, she wouldn't listen to me.

She kept pointing to the numbers on her forms. "See, it's right here in black and white."

"No, no, I don't have that much money. It isn't there." I burst into tears.

She patted my knee. "I don't mean to make you cry. I'm sorry. I have five- hundred-plus cases and three income cap trusts, and I only work six hours three days a week. Plus I'm covering for employees who are out sick."

"That's a lot," I said.

"The idea is not to impoverish the spouse."

"But that's what's going to happen."

"What about your Social Security and Medicare?"

"I'm not old enough." I was tired, but surely I didn't look sixty-five.

We had $6,000 left in savings. Timberwood cost almost $5,000 a month. After that, it would take all of Fred's pension to pay for his care, with only his minimal Social Security and my piddly income to cover the rest of our expenses. Not enough.

Thank God for David. His letter convinced my Senior Services worker that we did indeed qualify for Medicaid. About $2,000 a month would go into the trust account. As trustor, I would use it to pay part of his nursing home bills while paying the rest out of his pension and using my own account to take care of my expenses. It was a financial divorce, and I was getting the short end. I would make it work, but it wouldn't be easy.

I stopped at the Social Security office in Albany on my way to Timberwood. A uniformed guard greeted me at the door. In the office, a clerk asked me to swear under penalty of perjury that I had no felony convictions, that I had my own means of support, and that no one else had expressed a desire to handle Fred's finances. They would mail a letter to Fred, giving him ten days to protest my taking care of his income. As if he could read and understand such a letter.

When I visited that day, I did not tell Fred I had gone to Social Security or that I had separated our bank accounts. He asked, "Are we still solvent?"

"Well, just keep paddling," I said.

When I paid Fred's bill, Kim at the front desk also handed me bills for the dentist and Fred's phone. I wanted to scream, "Stop!" I already had a pile of bills to pay, and I needed gas for the car.

It was a beautiful day, sun shining through the clouds, trees starting to turn yellow and red. But I couldn't stifle the tears.

27 Outnumbered

We never thought our dogs would get so big. Because they were part terrier, we figured they'd be medium-sized. We were wrong. When they were up to twenty-four and twenty-seven pounds at three and a half months, I told the vet they weren't going to get much larger. He laughed and showed me their massive paws. Their legs were so long they looked like those jacked-up trucks with the giant tires, and they could already reach almost everything in the house. A year later, they were big dogs, both over sixty pounds and still filling out.

I had planned to take Chico to church for the blessing of the animals, then drive him back home, grab my guitar and go to choir practice. I had my guitar tuned, my music ready. But Annie refused to stay home, and I couldn't manage both dogs. Bribes, bitch-voice commands, and brute force failed.

I was just outside the back door, trying to negotiate with the dogs, when Chico charged me from behind. I went flying into the wall of the house with a horror-movie scream. I hit the new concrete with my right wrist, glasses and knee. My knee was okay, but my glasses were bent, and my wrist immediately went numb and started to swell. Choir practice or hospital? Hospital.

The ER doctor said I had a sprained wrist. I was supposed to wear a splint for at least a week. No typing or piano playing. No yoga. No lots of things.

Not fun. But I could practice doing things with one hand, good research for a character in the novel I had started.

That Sunday, I laughed when I discovered after church that I'd been wearing my dress backward. Standing on the altar singing the psalm, I felt gorgeous, in spite of the big white splint on my wrist. But the front was in back, the back in front. No wonder my dress felt so tight around my neck.

The sprained wrist made everything harder, including the drive to Albany. I had to turn myself into a human Slinky to turn the key and shift gears, but as long as I was driving in a straight line, it was not too bad. On the turns, I discovered the usefulness of elbows and knees.

Later that week, I was struggling to bag soggy dog poop in the rain one-handed when a squirrel chirped and Chico ran toward the fence. "No!" I shouted as he struggled to get past the ladder I had set up to block him. "No!" as he went over. "Shit!" as I realized I would have to chase him. Goodbye to my tightly scheduled day.

It was raining hard, a real gully-washer. And cold. I threw on my coat and my old slouch hat, grabbed the short you're-in-so-much-trouble leash, and set off to fetch my dog. I saw him in the tall weeds beyond our fence, but he took off, plunging through the brush.

I splashed through people's yards, calling for Chico. I looked down into the creek behind my neighbor's house and hoped he wasn't there. I listened for rustling in the bushes and heard nothing but rain and the ocean slamming the shore.

"Chico!" I called, my purple sweat pants stuck to my legs, my feet sloshing in my wet shoes, the splint on my wrist damp.

No response.

I walked around the block and back three times, getting wetter each time. I would catch a glimpse of my flying black dog, holler his name, and he would zip out of sight. Meanwhile, Annie whined from the pen. Each time I returned to the house, she looked at me, hope in her eyes. It turned to fear when she saw Chico was not with me.

The chase seemed futile. I opened the garage and the back of the car, hoping to lure him in. I saw him. He saw me. I rattled a bag of dog food. He zoomed off in another direction.

Dear God, I would never catch him. I was wet, cold, and discouraged. If I lost Chico, my heart would break. I loved both dogs, but Chico—oh, Chico was special, so loving, so handsome, and so obedient when he wasn't running away.

I didn't know what to do. I went into the house, used the bathroom, and traded my soggy clothes for dry ones. I borrowed one of Fred's hats and put on my dirty green slicker. As I took another walk around the block, the rain stopped, and a faint sun came out. A crabber who lived nearby asked if I was looking for a dog.

"Yes, I am."

As he talked about how my neighbors' dogs were always getting loose, Chico appeared out of nowhere. He ran up to the husky, white-haired man, growling, his soaked fur standing up straight.

"Chico!" I yelled. "No." He had never shown aggression toward any human before.

The man just stood there jawing. Chico ran past him into his workshop. I followed and finally caught him as he stood sniffing a pallet, fascinated by the fishy smell. "Don't hurt my wrist, don't hurt my wrist," I chanted as I hooked him onto the short leash.

Chico walked calmly next to me. He seemed perfectly content that his great adventure was over.

I led him through the house and let him into the pen. Annie dashed past me into the house. With a voice from the devil deep inside me, I roared, "Get out!" And she did.

I needed a break.

I left both dogs outside while I drove away to get the mail from my post office box and deposit checks in two different banks, one to make my business solvent, the other to keep the mortgage payment from bouncing.

At dinnertime, when I let the dogs back in, Chico rested his muzzle on my knee. I hugged him. His fur was dry now, although his collar was still damp. I gave the dogs their food, said grace, and thanked God for bringing the three of us back together.

With the early winter darkness upon us, the dogs fell asleep in the living room, Chico by the stove, Annie on the chair. I retired to my desk, wondering how many more times I could do this.

Chico's tags were gone. Instead of jingling, he walked in silence. After searching the yard, I gave up and wrote his name and phone number on his cloth collar. He had jumped the fence a day earlier, so I figured the tags were lost in the forest.

A couple days later, while cleaning up the yard, I discovered something shiny sticking out of the dog droppings. Oh my gosh, Chico's rabies tag. In another pile, his license. In yet another, his microchip tag. Annie had eaten them! What a stomach that dog had. She had not only eaten them but digested and excreted them. Wearing plastic gloves, I washed off the poo and analyzed what was left. The license had lost all its color, and the microchip tag was illegible, but the rabies tag looked clean as new. All we were missing was Chico's name tag.

When he wasn't running away, Chico chewed on things, too. While I was working in my office that morning, he had quietly shredded pieces of yellow foam rubber from the cushion of the big chair in the living room.

People kept telling me the dogs would mature. If they lived another week, they'd be eighteen months old. Meanwhile, it was like having twin toddlers in the terrible twos.

28 Giving Thanks

"What's your favorite color?" I asked Fred, trying to spark a conversation.

"Eight."

"Do you remember your first wife, Annette?"

"No." He was quiet for a minute. "What happened with her?"

"You got divorced; she didn't want to stay married anymore."

"Oh."

I reset his radio station to the oldies station Fred liked. Fifties crooners Steve Lawrence and Eydie Gorme filled the silence.

"Do you like my new bracelet?" I asked, pointing to my splint.

"What happened?"

"I wrestled with the dogs, and they won."

He chuckled. "What kind of dogs do you have?"

I started to remind him that they were his dogs, too, but what was the point? Chico and Annie were lost in the tangles in his brain. "Big dogs," I said. "Come on. Let's go for a walk."

The section of the building where Fred lived was built in a square around a courtyard garden. We walked a lap, holding hands. Merritt, one of the sharper residents, saw us and said, "Oh, the sweethearts."

I smiled and squeezed his hand. Fred's hands were soft, mottled with liver spots and red blotches, lined with veins and knuckle wrinkles. When we matched our palms together, our fingers were exactly the same length. Our gold wedding bands clinked against each other.

But verbally, we couldn't always connect, and this was one of those afternoons when I kept looking at my watch.

A little after four, I said I had to go, and Fred walked me to the door. We kissed. I said, "Good night, honey."

The door closed gently between us and I walked through the lobby into the sun. It was like visiting someone in prison. They couldn't come out, but I could go in. I had my date with Fred, then emerged into a completely different world.

I was eating dinner at home when the phone rang. Timberwood Court. Chelsea, one of the night aides, said Fred wanted to talk to me.

He was crying and struggling to use the phone. I asked him what was wrong. "I don't know," he said. He just kept crying.

I told him about the rain and about Chico running off again.

"Who's Chico?"

"Big black dog I can't see in the dark except for his eyes."

My attempt to make him laugh didn't work. He continued weeping.

"Oh, honey, you'll feel better in a little while," I said.

"How?"

"Well, I always feel better after a good cry." I didn't know what to say. What could I do from so far away? By the time I got to Albany, he might be fine. "Maybe a cup of tea or hot chocolate would make you feel better."

"Maybe."

Chelsea came back on and said she could make him some hot chocolate.

"Thank you." I told Fred, "I'll see you in a few days. I love you."

And they were gone.

"Shit," I said to the furniture. I took my plate to the microwave to reheat. "God, please watch over Fred," I prayed. Then I forced myself to focus on my pasta and on the Sunday travel section I had been reading. I felt like the evil wife who had dumped her husband in a nursing home. My dinner tasted like glue.

* * *

On my next visit, Fred was calm and more clear-headed than usual. We walked around the building, pausing to sit in two wing chairs near the exit.

"How long have I been here?" he asked.

"Five months."

"Boy, that other place. How long was I there?"

"Five months."

"This is a good place. Thank you for sticking with me through all this. . . ." He broke down in tears. Today he understood that he had Alzheimer's, that he was living in a nursing home, and that I was still with him. Not knowing might hurt less.

He had gone with the other residents to a pumpkin patch, and he looked forward to the Timberwood Halloween party. "Can you come?" he asked.

"No. I have to work."

"I guess I won't get a turkey dinner this Thanksgiving."

"You will. They'll have it here. I'll come."

"That's good."

In the quiet, I felt tired. These visits wore me out. I had to keep Fred entertained and avoid telling him anything that would worry or confuse him. I sorted my thoughts like cue cards. Nope, can't talk about that. Nothing about money, nothing about home repairs. Nothing negative about his kids. Ted and Michael had visited once since he moved to Timberwood. Both in the restaurant business, they had taken us out to dinner and critiqued the food and service all evening while Fred sat silent and lost.

Some of our church friends from Newport had come to see Fred. I was beyond grateful. I knew how hard it was to sit there trying to think of something to say.

I told Fred about playing music for a funeral and having this intimidating piano teacher sitting right next to me. I'd been a nervous wreck. Turned out the guy was even more nervous because he had to play after me. Fred laughed. Thank God he could still laugh.

In November, things were looking up. Although I still paid the bulk of Fred's nursing home bill, almost $3,000, Medicaid picked up the other $2,000, which was something, and I did get to keep the money I earned with my writing and music.

My wrist still ached, but I could play the piano again.

Despite what I had told Fred, I hadn't planned to attend Timberwood's midweek Thanksgiving dinner. I was supposed to be at a liturgy meeting, but when the church secretary told Father Brian what was happening in Albany, he told me to go be with Fred, forget about the meeting.

Thank God I did go. Everybody's family came. The place was jammed, the parking lot full. I found Fred standing up against the wall, looking forlorn because he thought I wasn't coming.

We ate turkey, mashed potatoes and gravy, carrots, sweet potatoes, rolls, cranberry sauce, and giant slices of pumpkin pie off paper plates with plastic utensils. We held hands and joked with our tablemates.

Many of the guests left right after lunch, and about half of the residents went to sleep or settled in to watch *Anne of Green Gables* on the big-screen TV.

Among those who remained behind were the middle-aged daughter and son-in-law of a sweet old woman who walked bent over like the letter R. I'll call her Violet. They sat together on the couch for a long time, but then Violet's loved ones signaled the aide waiting nearby.

The aide asked Violet to come with her for a minute to help with something.

"No, we're leaving," said Violet.

"It'll only take a minute, and I really need your help," said the aide.

"Well, all right."

She led Violet to another room while the daughter and son-in-law hurried to the exit.

When Violet returned, they were gone. She searched everywhere for them, saying, "They wouldn't leave without me." For over an hour, she walked around the building, bent at a right angle, whimpering her daughter's name. The aide said it broke her heart. Mine, too.

After a while, Violet said, "I'll have to walk. It's fourteen miles, but I have to go home. I've got my purse and my Bible. I'm all ready. I just don't know how they could leave me like this."

Would it really have been worse to tell her the truth? By the time I left, Violet was playing Scrabble with the activities director, but she kept looking around, still wondering how her daughter could desert her.

Meanwhile, Aggie was having a tantrum, a new resident named Loy kept yelling and trying to hit people, and Lydia pushed a wheelchair over "Grandma's" red, swollen toes. Grandma screamed and burst into tears.

Mary, who sat closest to me as we watched *Anne of Green Gables*, kept saying, "Hi, hon," complaining that her back hurt, and asking if she could go home with me.

"In a few minutes. After the movie," I lied.

An aide came by, and she started up with her. "Hi, hon."

When she told her about her back hurting, the aide said, "Oh, I'll go get you something." She never returned.

I learned later that Mary had had back surgery, and she really was in pain. How many times did the staff tell them lies? And didn't they know that sitting in a hard chair was the worst position for an injured back?

An aide brought Lydia over to sit beside Fred.

"No. There isn't room," Fred declared.

"You don't want me here," she said.

"No!"

She wandered off.

To distract him, I took Fred with me to the office to pay his monthly bill.

"How much?" he asked.

I told him.

"How long. . . ?" He couldn't spell out what.

"Your illness?"

He nodded.

"Nobody knows. Let's go back and watch the movie."

29 Over the Fence

I had pulled every muscle hauling giant boards from the lawn to the fence, blocking Chico's most recent favorite jumping place. When that didn't stop him, I added an eight-foot stretch of lattice from the garden shed. Surely he was secure now.

It was a blindingly sunny early December day. I cleaned up dog droppings and relaxed on one of the old creosoted railroad ties by the back fence. Chico approached his jumping spot. Annie grabbed his collar and hauled him back. The dogs erupted in a flurry of teeth and growls. When the fight got too intense, I got up and called them in. "Annie, come. Chico, come. Cookie time."

Annie flew across the deck and into the pen, but Chico had other ideas. I watched in horror as he squeezed himself into a five-inch gap between the boards and the fence and hoisted himself over, disappearing into the thick growth.

Enough of this. I was not going to walk all the way around the block again. While Annie wailed and whined, I grabbed the loppers and Fred's leather gloves and started chopping a path between my yard and the adjoining property where Chico usually went. Most of the berry vines and alders were mine anyway. They were leafless now, so dry I could snap the thinnest branches with my hands. The rest I cut, thin ones, fat ones, straining my wrists, feeling the thorns grab my pants and my mother's oversized green sweater, raking my face.

As I chopped, the dog sometimes passed nearby. I forced myself to stay calm. "Hey there. Look, a path," I said. He went on. Fine. He knew where I was.

With each step I took farther away, Annie, back in the pen, grew more desperate, her cries echoing through the forest.

I chopped my way back and forth, back and forth, always finding another branch to remove as the thorny cuttings grabbed at me. I yelped and swatted at them as if they were a swarm of bees.

My wrists ached, my mother's sweater was dotted with bits of wood and thorns, and my feet were wet where the moisture had leaked through the worn areas of my secondhand boots, but the path was done.

I lay on the deck resting my back and waited.

After a while, I heard the hard breathing and jingling tags of the escaped dog. He had come in through the gate and casually crossed the yard.

I got up, jogged to the open gate, wedged it shut, and quietly grabbed a leash. Chico's tongue hung long as I pulled him into the pen where his sister waited to sniff him all over.

Now Annie wanted to go on an adventure. She followed me into the house and stood under the coat rack, pushing my jacket with her nose.

"In a little while," I said, going to the back room to finish my Christmas cards. My hands shook so badly my letters came out scraggly. I had written half a dozen cards before my writing evened out. By then the dogs were asleep. We had all had enough exercise for the day.

The following day, I was back at Timberwood where John, one of several entertainers who came every week or so, was playing music again. He had a voice like melted butter and flat-picked his guitar so well I studied his technique, hoping I could learn a little bit. The twenty-one residents in the audience sang along. A couple of the men in wheelchairs patted their hands to the rhythm.

Back when I used to perform at nursing homes in California and Oregon, I heard residents say, "What's she doing?" or "When's she gonna go home?" or "I'm hungry." Sometimes they screamed, covered their ears, or got into fights with other residents. I just kept singing.

John handled it well. When Pauline came walking toward him with no sign of going around, he calmly made room until an aide or another resident led her away. When Mary said, "Hi, hon" and "Hey, that was pretty good" after every song, he thanked her every time.

Fred sat in the front row, singing loudly, his jaw and neck tight. I sang with him, adding harmony wherever I could, letting myself forget everything but what was happening right then and there.

Afterward, we ate ice cream.

Back at Fred's room, we found a new guy named Ted wearing Fred's jacket. He had Fred's Christmas cards in his hand. He was certain he was in the right room.

"That's not yours," I said.

He slowly took off Fred's jacket and sank onto the bed. "Nothing makes any sense. I feel as if I have lost everything. My woman, my home, my things. Nobody wants me around."

I put my arm around him and said I liked him.

He turned to Fred. "Will you be my friend?"

"Okay." But then Fred grabbed for his cards. Ted would not let go.

Before they came to blows, I called an aide to take Ted away.

At Timberwood, I was not responsible for anything except being Fred's wife. When problems arose, I just had to find the staff member in charge. Lying on Fred's bed with the sun shining in, I felt like a kid.

I was going to hit darkness on the way home, but I had arrived late, and I wanted to spend enough time to make the trip worthwhile.

I wore a nametag this time because Fred didn't know my name.

The room down the hall was empty. The woman who'd lived there had died. There was nothing left but a portable heater and a cat bed with a stuffed toy cat. By next week, someone else would be moving in. Fred had no idea.

When I went out to the car, it was like I'd been catapulted out of a dark theater in the middle of a movie. For a few minutes, I didn't know what to do.

It was Sunday afternoon. Chico was gone again. Before I left for church, I had put a nylon harness on him, which seemed to hobble him enough to keep him home.

When I returned a little over two hours later, I found a silver ring sitting on the laundry room floor. All of the nylon parts were gone. Annie trailing behind me, I went over the frozen mud outside, but I couldn't find anything but metal rings and clasps.

The fences might not even be there for all the good they did.

Joe across the street saw me walking around with the leash.

"He's out again?"

"Yes."

"You know, I caught him trying to kill my cat. And I saw him going after another dog over on Cedar."

"Oh, my God. I had no idea." I watched as his small gray-and-white cat walked up behind him and rubbed against his leg.

"One of these days, somebody's going to shoot that dog," Joe said. "Especially if he goes after their animals."

"I'm trying, but he keeps getting loose. He jumps right over a six-foot fence."

"He's part pit bull, ain't he?"

"Half." Chico looked more like a black Lab, but his wide-spaced golden eyes gave away his bully heritage.

"Well, I don't know what to tell you, but if you can't keep him in, somebody's gonna get hurt."

It was the last straw. I loved that dog so much, but I knew Joe was right. No matter what obstacles I put in the way, Chico got out. When

I was gone all day visiting Fred, I had no control over what he was doing. I couldn't keep chasing him.

I heard a neighbor dog barking down the street. I hurried in that direction and found my dog sniffing at a candy wrapper. "Let's go for a ride," I said, dragging him home and loading him into the car.

As I drove him to the Alsea River kennel up Highway 34, I listened to his panting and fought not to cry. I knew I couldn't keep him. I needed to find him a home where he had all the room he needed to run. But that day I just needed to stop worrying about him for a while.

He sat on the passenger seat with his head against the cushion, looking like he might be sick. He knew this wasn't good. I was crying, and we were riding down narrow roads he had never seen before. This was not a trip to the beach.

At the kennel, Chico's head hung down and his tail wedged between his legs as a worker dragged him to his cage while dogs of all sizes barked. I said I would pick him up in a week.

I had tried my best, but with Fred gone to a nursing home, I was outnumbered and overpowered.

Back home, I missed Chico, but I couldn't believe how much easier it was with just one dog. Annie slept inside on the big chair that first night. She looked for Chico, but seemed to be glad to be the only dog, to not have to compete for attention or food. When we went for a walk, I didn't have to struggle to separate them. But this respite was temporary. I needed to find a permanent solution.

In freezing weather, I took Annie to the house up 98th Street where she and Chico had been born. I knocked on the door. The young man who had sold us the dogs opened the door.

"Hi. I'm Sue Lick. My husband and I adopted two puppies from you almost two years ago. This one and a black one."

"Yeah, I remember." He bent down to pet Annie. "She got big."

"They both did. Anyway, my husband's in a nursing home now.

The black dog, Chico, keeps running away, and I just can't keep him anymore. Is there any chance you would take him back?"

He sighed. "No. I'm sorry, but I've got little kids and too many dogs."

Annie's dog-mom came out onto the porch. Mottled brown and black, she was exactly the same size and shape as Annie. I had hoped for a sweet reunion, but Annie went after her mother, growling, teeth bared. I apologized and dragged her away.

I imagined Chico whining all night at the kennel. He didn't even have his own blankets. In my rush to get him out, I hadn't stopped for anything. I had wanted this to be a quick, clean break. But he couldn't stay at the kennel forever.

On Annie's third night in, she wanted to go out at four in the morning. I took her out back, admiring the stars and the half-moon, shivering in the twenty-degree weather. She disappeared into the darkness, then came racing in.

The next morning, I found piles of vomit on the lawn. She had thrown up big chunks of Chico's harness. It had taken four days, and I was sure there was more to come.

30 Weepy Christmas

Fred and I were in his room holding hands and listening to the radio when Pachelbel's Canon came on. It was the song we walked down the aisle to at our wedding. We both started humming along.

As I felt his arms around me, I couldn't stop the tears. "I'm sorry," I said.

"It's okay." He held me tighter, his own tears coming.

I tried not to cry at Timberwood, but sometimes I couldn't help it. It was Dec. 17, the twenty-sixth anniversary of our first date. We used to celebrate and reminisce about that night, but now the date didn't mean anything to Fred.

He had been crying and shaking when I arrived. He was more confused than usual. He kept asking me how I got there.

I led him out to the Christmas party taking place in the dining room. Aides served cookies, cream puffs, M&Ms, punch, and coffee. Santa and Mrs. Claus handed out gifts, mostly pajamas, blankets, and stuffed animals which family members had brought in earlier.

Santa was all hearty ho, ho, hos, but the residents didn't understand what was going on. They needed help opening their gifts, then just left them sitting on the tables. Eugene, at the table with us, spent half the time with his head on his arms, dozing. Once, he looked up and said, "Right about now, I'd like to find myself a nice shady tree and catch me some Z's."

Me too.

I had brought Fred the green sweater I'd knitted for him when we were first married. He kept asking me who made it. I kept telling him I did. I feared it would get lost or destroyed in the Timberwood laundry, but I had to let it go.

As he opened his Christmas cards, Fred got stuck on simple words, like a child just learning to read.

At home, I cried every time I opened a card, most of them addressed to both of us.

On our rainy afternoon walk, Annie darted in and out of the weeds, sniffing and pawing at anything that smelled interesting: dog droppings, clumps of leaves, a plastic coffee cup, a candy bar wrapper, a tuft of rabbit fur. I scanned the wet concrete for newts like the ones that dotted my yard these days. They look like slick-skinned lizards with orange bellies.

We walked until my dusty green raincoat was washed clean, my lungs filled with cold, fresh air.

I had been giving Annie so many privileges. The loose leash. Paws on the sofa. My plates to lick. I hated to rein her in and make her "heel" and "sit," but I knew I had to keep up the training. For practice, I let her run to the end of her leash and called, "Annie, come." She trotted back to me, tail wagging. I pet her wet head. "Good girl."

When we got home, I rubbed her dry and laughed as she dragged her blanket over to the couch. Soon she was sound asleep.

In the mornings, I was glad to see her, and she was glad to see me. It was not like facing Annie and Chico together, both vying for attention, pawing the door, jumping on me, banging into me on their way to the kitchen. Annie trotted out onto the grass, did her business, ran to the fence and back, barked a time or two, then scooted back into the house.

Without Chico, I could work unimpeded. I could eat unmolested. Annie came over and put her head on my lap, looking for a treat, but I just told her no, and she went back to her blankets. Things were more peaceful for Annie, too. She could eat her food in leisurely bites. With Chico around, it was a contest. As soon as he emptied his bowl, he would turn to hers. I knew she missed him. Coming back from our walks, she poked her nose into the bushes around our fence, looking for him. I missed him, too, but I didn't miss the daily hand-to-paw combat.

I was losing my dog, but losing my husband was much worse. I'd try to work, play music, or read and suddenly burst into tears. I missed Fred. I missed our life together. I missed having a family.

On this first Christmas alone, I went through the motions of decorating and sending out cards like a robot, wishing the holidays were over.

My father, in his late eighties, didn't travel on his own, and my brother was hosting Christmas at his own house for his family, Dad, and the in-laws. I wouldn't want them on the road in December anyway, with 1-5 snowed in just north of the California border and the coast route drenched in rain and hurricane-force wind.

Friends invited me to spend Christmas with their families, but I had church music to play, and I needed to visit Fred. Even if he didn't know it was Christmas, he was still my husband.

Gone were the days when Fred and I sat together in our bathrobes on Christmas morning handing each other gifts, thanking each other with hugs and kisses.

With Fred and my mother gone, I didn't have many gifts to unwrap. On Christmas Eve, I opened Aunt Suzanne's package first. Portuguese sausage. Five twenty-dollar bills. A black scarf with music notes on it and a bag of rocky road candy.

My friend Georgia gave me two bootlegged CDs.

Dad sent a check for $300, which I would use for a new vacuum cleaner.

That was it. I tossed the wrapping paper into the recycle bin and moved on.

My eyes puffy and sore from crying, I soaked in the bathtub and shaved my legs. I met choir friends for dinner at Lee's Wok, then played at the ten o'clock Mass. The notes for the familiar Christmas carols fell under my fingers easily. After Mass, I stayed up and played a little more piano at home. As long as I focused on the notes, I could forget everything else.

After church on Christmas morning, I hit Highway 20. The sky was blue, the ocean a darker blue. I had a sack lunch, a thermos of iced tea, more gifts for Fred, and Georgia's Ray Charles and Patsy Cline CDs to listen to on the way.

It was beautiful out, but I wanted to cry. I wanted to go back to the old days in San Jose and have Mom make dinner. Turkey, gravy, stuffing, mashed potatoes. Rolls with real butter. Salami. Pickles. Olives. Stuffed celery. Green Jell-O salad. Pumpkin pie. Fudge. Both sets of grandparents and my aunts and uncles sitting around the table. Instead, I ate a ham sandwich at a deserted park on the way to the nursing home, where it was just another day.

I was so tired that afternoon, I fell asleep on Fred's shoulder. Aggie shouted, "Boo!" and woke me up.

"Let's go to your room," I said, yawning.

In his room, his hands shaking, Fred handed me a stack of unopened Christmas cards. "What should I do with them?" I read the cards to him, trying to explain who the senders were—his children, my aunt, friends from the aquarium. He was worried. Did he have to respond? No. Should he just toss them? No.

We opened my gifts for him, a book and a shirt.

"I have nothing for you," Fred said.

"That's okay," I lied.

It was just another afternoon at Timberwood, short-staffed because of the holiday. We hugged, held hands, and sat around as usual.

Violet walked around with her Bible and her purse, ready to go home.

"How are your dogs?" Fred asked.

"Fine."

Fred needed a shave. His hair looked flat and greasy. He asked me about his kids, and I had no answers. When I had called Michael in Portland to ask about Christmas, he had told me, "I have plans."

Ted had sent fruit from California, but Fred wasn't sure who he was anymore. Gretchen sent a card to her dad. None of the kids had responded to the cards and cash I had sent them.

Fred's nails were jagged. I got the scissors out of my purse and trimmed them. We listened to Christmas songs on the radio. The staff led a Christmas carol sing-along. We dozed in front of the TV until it was time for me to leave. The road looked icy, and it was getting dark.

I passed cars full of wrapped gifts and a house where I could see what looked like Grandma opening packages in the rocker by the window. I hurried home to Annie and leftover Chinese food.

31 | Oh, Chico

"I hope you're relaxing or doing something fun," said my friend on the phone message two days after Christmas.

"Ha!" I responded. At that moment, I was covered in mud. Shortly after I brought Chico home from the kennel, both dogs had escaped. I had managed to lure Annie into the car near the property behind mine. She was soaked and covered in black goo. Chico was still out there somewhere.

I took Annie home and rubbed off the top layer of mud, then went out to look for Chico. When I looked back, I saw I had forgotten to close the gate. Annie zoomed toward freedom. I had never run so fast in my life. I won the race by a dog's nose. Slammed the gate shut, pushed the clamp down, and collapsed on the wet grass and pine needles. I was already so dirty it didn't matter.

Meanwhile, I had a load of laundry in the washer and another in the dryer. I had cleaned my way up to the kitchen, vacuumed out the pellet stove, and refreshed the chemicals in the spa. With Fred gone, I had to do it all. At three thirty, I would start cooking the turkey I had bought for my post-Christmas dinner. Relaxing? I don't think so. Fun? A little.

I had put an ad in the newspaper and hung up flyers seeking someone to adopt Chico. I worried that a potential owner would see my ad and decide to meet my black dog at this point. *Um, well, he's not here, but this is his sister. . .*

As dusk approached, I was just muttering, "Chico, where the heck are you?" when he trotted onto the porch. I opened the door a crack, grabbed his collar and hauled him in. "You're driving me crazy," I growled as I toweled off the muck.

He wagged his tail.

So now both dogs were clean and warming by the pellet stove. The turkey was in the oven. One load of laundry was done, the next was in the dryer, the third in the washer, and I had changed the sheets on my bed.

When my friend called again, I settled on the floor between my dogs with the phone, glad to hear another human voice.

The next morning, I was opening my mail when the phone rang. Shirley at Dr. H.'s office had seen my Chico flyer at the post office and was interested. They had a fenced yard and a four-year-old black Lab-pit bull mix who needed a companion. Perfect. Her husband Larry would be over that afternoon.

Larry came early. I had been standing by the pellet stove with the two dogs, taking pictures and crying over the potential loss of my buddy Chico. When I opened the front door, zoom! Both dogs escaped. Larry laughed. Not funny. While I searched for them, getting drenched in the rain, Larry climbed up on the back of his truck, cleaned out part of my overflowing gutter, and fixed the part that was bent. I envied Shirley for having such a husband, the kind I used to have.

When I returned with empty leashes, he said, "I'll come back later."

"Sure. I'll have him ready." I hoped.

Larry drove away, and I searched for my dogs in my car. I found them running across the yard behind mine. Both dogs were soaked and muddy. I opened the door and Chico jumped in, but Annie didn't join us until I started to drive away.

"Come on!" I called.

She scrambled in. Now my car was a mess, too.

At home, I separated the dogs, Annie in the yard, Chico in the house and watched for Larry's truck in the driveway.

When he returned, Chico jumped all over him in joy. So far so good. Then Larry brought in his dog, Thomas.

Chico went ballistic. Trying to hold him back, I fell and lost my grip on his collar. Chico bolted after Thomas, grabbing him around the throat. This wasn't play. He was going to kill him. His jaws were locked as the other dog whimpered. I tried to pry them apart.

Somehow in the scuffle, Chico bit my right leg, but finally I got him to let go of the other dog. Larry rushed his dog out of there, said he was sorry, and fled. I threw Chico out back and hurried to the bathroom to doctor my bloody calf.

My dog was a menace. Yes, he was sweet around me and Annie, but I couldn't keep him in, and he would have killed Thomas if I hadn't stopped him. What if he went after another animal or human while he was running around the neighborhood? I'd be responsible, and he'd be euthanized. I should take him to the animal shelter right now. My baby. My puppy. Annie's best friend. He was a killer.

The only question was whether I should wait until the newspaper ad ran out or get it over with.

As I pondered, my stupid Christmas clock started playing "We Wish You a Merry Christmas." Shut up!

Chico's bite left a half circle of four tooth marks, one deep and black, the others red, surrounded by a darkening bruise. I was not crippled, but it hurt, and the wound would leave a scar.

The next morning, I called Shirley to apologize. She said her dog was missing some fur and had some abrasions. He had trembled for hours. When I asked her if I needed a tetanus shot, she said yes, *today*. So I went. It made it all very real. I had been bitten by a dog. My dog. When I got there, Shirley hugged me, no hard feelings.

From the doctor's office, I went to the local animal shelter, my absolute last resort. The woman at the desk said they were at capacity. She put us on a waiting list. Another dog leaped against a chain link fence. I said my dog did that. Everything I said was another notch in the forget-about-it meter.

She gave me a list of other shelters to call. The one in Corvallis only took dogs from Corvallis. The ones in Eugene and Salem were closed that day. The one in Portland required a behavior test, which Chico would probably fail.

When I got home, my neighbor Joe beckoned.

"Did that guy take Chico?"

"He tried to kill his dog, so no."

"Well, that's too bad."

Chico was looking out the gate. Hearing us, he jumped and escaped again. Joe drove away in his pickup while I sat in the weak sun, feeling helpless. Every time Chico approached me, if I showed any interest, he ran away again.

I told myself I didn't really care at that point if anything happened to him, but I was afraid he'd do more harm. He had hurt me and the other dog in a few seconds.

Eventually he came back and I grabbed him. I tied him to a long cable. I couldn't deal with it anymore. I called the kennel and loaded Chico into the mud-coated car. He sat with his head against the seat, moaning.

The staff welcomed him, and Chico sniffed noses with the other dogs. I heard him whining as I left. I had failed. But I couldn't think, couldn't work. I worried all the time.

After my leftover turkey dinner, I put away some of the Christmas decorations. The rest I put in a box to give away. I didn't need them anymore.

I curled up in a blanket to watch an old episode of *Thirtysomething*. Annie sat in my lap. Now it was just us. No more Fred, no more Chico.

* * *

Two weeks later, I found a shelter in Salem that would take Chico.

When I picked him up at the kennel, he jumped into the car and gave me a big lick on the face. As we approached home, he put his paw on my knee and his nose near my cheek. It killed me to think that I was taking him to a shelter the next day and I would never see him again.

Annie kept trying to get her brother to play, but he wasn't interested. Chico followed me around, leaned on me. As I talked to my father on the phone, I lay on the couch. Chico put his paw and his head on me. He was really beautiful. He easily sat, lay down, and let me hook up his leash. He heeled well. He was so good. Except that he needed to jump the fences and in a flash he could hurt another dog or a human.

I knew it would be hard to see Chico again and then give him up. If I could have had someone else do the handoff, I would have.

There were so many parallels with Fred. When my husband asked, "How can I get out of this?" I had no answer. Chico, if he could have thought like a human, would surely have wondered what he'd done to be exiled. I had to leave both my strong males in the valley, locked up, after trying so hard to keep them.

I watched Chico and Annie lying back to back and head to head, licking each other. Damn. Maybe someone in Salem could give him the home I could not provide.

I got a stomachache thinking about it.

The next day, as soon as I got to the desk at the shelter, a young woman in scrubs took my puppy away. I said, "Goodbye, honey," but I'm sure he didn't hear me. That was it. He was gone, and I was doing paperwork, turning over his blankets and leash, and stuffing his pronged collar into my purse because they wouldn't take it.

I lied when the receptionist asked me whether Chico had ever bitten anyone, just as I had lied at the kennel when I said his shots were up to date. Almost but not quite.

I asked the woman how long they would keep him before they euthanized him. She said they'd keep him as long as they had room. They had adopted out six hundred animals the year before. Sometimes the volunteers liked the animals so much they took them home. They all liked Chico right away as he placed his big paws on the counter.

The form I signed said I was not supposed to call them to ask what happened.

I started sobbing before I reached the car. I parked in a deserted construction lot a block away from the shelter. I couldn't drive until I stopped crying.

I knew Chico was just a dog. Giving up a dog was nothing compared to the pain suffered by people who lost their homes in earthquakes, hurricanes, or fires, people who were hungry or dying in wars, but Chico was my baby.

I cried for a half hour in that parking lot among the dump trucks and bulldozers, then slowly drove back to I-5, hoping the fences at the shelter were tall enough to hold my boy.

32 Back to School

From the first night teaching my community education creative writing class at Chemeketa Community College, I loved everything about the place. I loved the red brick buildings, the parking permit I stuck on the bumper of my car, and the code that let me use the copier in the hall. Everyone was friendly, smiling at me. I was all dressed up. Like a teacher.

I was living the life I had envisioned before Fred got sick.

It took a little over two hours to drive there from my home on the coast. Working in Salem was not practical. My expenses would exceed what I earned. But I wanted to be part of this place.

The first night, I had only four students, two men and two women, but more showed up at subsequent sessions. All good writers, they included a teacher, a contractor, a housewife writing a children's book, and a man who liked to write poetry. They were surprised that I had driven all the way from the coast.

"Catch it while you can," I said. I explained about Fred. They sympathized.

Driving that far at night in the winter was dangerous, especially the last hour on Highway 20, the tree-lined, two-lane road that paralleled the Yaquina River all the way to the ocean. Even if it wasn't raining or snowing, I feared a deer or an elk would jump out of the trees. People died on this road. Every year, several vehicles crashed head on or ran off the pavement into the river.

I had traveled Highway 20 so often to visit Fred that I knew the landmarks: Burnt Woods Café, Ellmaker State Wayside, Eddyville, Chitwood Bridge, Toledo . . . but everything looked different in the dark. On that first January night, I felt thankful to those families who had left their Christmas lights up. I passed little settlements of houses and imagined how glad people traveling over this road on horseback would have been to see houses and lights.

When a car approached in the other lane, I could see its head-lights way around the bend. It was raining just enough to have to use the wipers. I couldn't tell puddles from pavement from black ice. Could I really do this every week?

At Timberwood the following week before my class, Fred and I sat in his room in his mother's easy chairs. We had walked across the street to the grocery store for odds and ends. Now, conversation all used up, we were quiet, holding hands. The radio was off. Fred seemed thoughtful.

"What are you thinking about?"

"Oh, lots of things," he said. His left hand began to shake, and a tear spilled down his cheek.

I breathed deeply, seeking the stillness I had found earlier in yoga class, as he struggled to find words.

"I want, I want, I can't. I don't know how to do anything. I want to ask things . . . I want to ask people. . . ."

"Do you want to talk to Tina or somebody else in the office?"

"I don't know her name."

"Filipina, dark hair, real friendly."

"Yes," he said, his eyes full of tears.

He wore a T-shirt under a blue V-neck sweater and the black jeans that had appeared mysteriously in his room a few weeks ago. I didn't know whether they belonged to someone who had died or someone alive who was missing his pants. His goatee and his hair looked good. He was still a handsome man.

I took him by the hand and led him beyond the locked door to find Tina.

"She's gone for the day," said Kim at the front desk.

I led him back to his room.

He had been in good spirits when I arrived. Now he was crying. I could feel him trembling. Perhaps when we had gone out shopping, he compared himself to other people and realized he was different. He didn't understand what was wrong with him, but he knew he had lost everything.

As we sat in his mother's chairs, I touched his knee, forgetting he was ticklish there. Instantly he stopped shaking. He didn't like me to do that, but if it worked . . .

"What do you want to do?" I asked.

"I-uh, I don't know. I can't—"

I held my breath, wishing his words out. He could still say, "I love you." He said that often. But he couldn't tell me what was bothering him.

It was getting dark. It was time for me to go. I led him to a table for dinner. We hugged. He started to cry again. If only I could think of a joke, something to make him feel better. I told him to be good, and I let go.

Before I went out, I looked back. He was just standing by the table. He was inertia.

I had to teach my class. I couldn't be crying. Should I stay overnight in Salem? The weather was nice enough, no rain or ice. But it was a long, hard drive.

Forty-five minutes later, I was at Chemeketa, organizing my papers, distributing the handouts, and writing on the whiteboard. A new student walked in. "Are you the teacher?"

I sniffed back my tears. "Yes, I am."

It was like that week after week after week.

* * *

Another week passed. At almost ten o'clock, I still hadn't gotten myself up. Annie started barking as Paula across the street left for work. Moaning, I slid out of bed and prepared to drag myself to Timberwood.

To keep myself awake, I counted cars like my Honda Element along the way. I saw four.

Fred must have had one of his nighttime rampages. The framed beach photo on his wall was upside down. The fronts were torn off his Christmas cards. I found the one from me on the floor between his dresser and the wall, along with his shaving brush and a pair of soiled underpants.

He was wearing the black jeans that weren't his, a paint-stained, blue T-shirt, and his heavy black coat. He kept taking off his pants and his underpants, trying to show me some problem he couldn't explain.

The three-thirty activity was "spa day." Westy, the new activities director, gave us lotion to massage into each other's hands. But Fred didn't get the concept. His hands went right to his belt.

"No," I said. "Don't take off your pants. Give me your hands."

He started taking off his slippers.

"No. Give me your hands."

Finally I managed to get some lotion on his fingers. He kept trying to rest his hands on my slacks. I told him I needed to keep them clean for my class, but he stained them with lotion anyway.

"Is that my shirt?" he asked, fingering the blue dress shirt I had on. He had given it to me years earlier because it was too small for him.

"Yes, it is. Do you want it?"

He didn't respond.

I turned on the radio. When the news came on, he went to turn it down, but I wanted to hear. We seemed to be having some kind of stock market crash, sparked by problems in Europe. Stocks down. Petroleum sales down. Unemployment up. Toyota had recalled eight models of cars with sticking accelerators; now another model had brake problems. Also, there had been an earthquake in Humboldt County, California.

That was my world, not Fred's. Not anymore.

All of his pockets were empty. His back pocket, where he had always kept his wallet, was flat. He had no possessions now. Nothing. He was wearing someone else's pants. It didn't matter.

As I was leaving, Fred zipped up his coat. "Is it cold outside?" he asked.

"Yes, but you're not going anywhere."

"Can't we go out?"

"No, it's almost time for your dinner."

"Can't you stay for dinner?"

"I didn't make a reservation."

My dinner would be an apple on the way to the college and a slice of pizza in the cafeteria.

33 The Jitters

I had started spending the night after class at Motel 6 in Salem. It was too wet and dark to drive back to South Beach. The motel was in a dodgy part of town. One night, someone tried to bash in the door of the room below mine. Another night, I heard a commotion and then the police were at my door, asking what I had seen and heard. "Just slamming doors and people yelling," I said.

In the mornings, beer bottles and cigarette butts covered the landing.

The motel was off I-5 just past a bridge where homeless folks camped with their sleeping bags and shopping carts. Men in stocking caps walked the street during the day. I saw curses spray-painted in Spanish. I missed my house. I missed Annie, who was being fed by the neighbor. I considered driving straight home in the morning without stopping to see Fred. He wouldn't know the difference. But I would.

When I woke up on Feb. 4 at Motel 6, my heart was beating too fast. Sitting on the toilet, I felt dizzy. I was trying to do too much. In addition to writing, playing music, teaching, and taking care of Fred, I was trying to kick my tranquilizer, Klonopin. Reatha, my therapist, refused to renew the prescription I had gotten from Dr. Smith. It was too addictive, she said. Taking it was like being drunk all the time.

Forced to choose between quitting Klonopin and finding a new shrink, I chose to quit, but it was more difficult than I had expected. My psyche was permanently stuck in crisis mode.

Deciding I needed to relax before going to Timberwood, I drove to nearby Mt. Angel, a retreat center and seminary where most of Oregon's priests trained. It was close, admission was free, and I needed a break.

I drove past Chemeketa Community College and a string of shopping centers and turned onto a road that led into the foothills. I passed a Christmas tree farm and green pastures with the snow-tipped Cascade Mountains in the distance. Clouds jetted across the blue sky like angels in a hurry.

I followed the signs to Mt. Angel, a small town known for its annual Bavarian Oktoberfest, and continued on past St. Mary's church. When I saw brown-robed monks stopping to pray at little enclosures with statues that represented the Stations of the Cross, I knew I was almost there. I parked, entered through the bookstore, and walked into the open area near the church.

"Wow," I whispered as I opened the heavy wooden door. The Abbey Church was filled with beautiful wooden alcoves and altars and the biggest organ pipes I had ever seen. "Holy shit," I blurted, then looked around, hoping the monk praying in the far pew hadn't heard me. I knelt and prayed a while, feeling the peace of the place seep into me.

Emerging from the church, I heard singing and went that way. The singer was a giant Chicano seminarian taking out the garbage and singing in a high falsetto.

Suddenly I wanted to join the Benedictine nuns who lived down the road or at least move to somewhere in the Salem–Silverton–Mt. Angel area. Work on a newspaper. Play music. Grow flowers. Mt. Angel was only forty miles from Portland, and there was so much in Portland for writers.

But what about Fred? What about Annie? What about my job at Sacred Heart?

As I drove south on I-5 toward Albany, I had all kinds of writing ideas. So many possibilities. Laughter bubbled up for no reason. Was it cutting my Klonopin dose in half or just getting away?

I started singing, "Blue skies smiling at me. . . ."

But I was far from done with Klonopin. Over the next two weeks, I had wild dreams. I felt jittery. Hot flashes had me tearing off my clothes down to my underwear at home. I planned to go to a quarter of a pill, barely a crumb, soon. I wanted to finish this withdrawal business, but I clung to the peace that came with those little pills.

Full of nervous tics, I chewed on my lips, pushed at my teeth, and felt my mouth fill with saliva. My stomach hurt. Even though I was eating too much, I lost weight. I was tired and wired. I didn't play as well at church, and I was anxious teaching my class. A student would say something, and I couldn't remember what she just said.

One morning after class, I stayed in my Motel 6 bed a long time, feeling weary and nauseated. Church songs played over and over in my head until I wanted to rip that part of my brain out.

At checkout time, I drove to the Oregon Garden in Silverton, up the same road as Mt. Angel. The gardens were not blooming in February, but it was still quite a sight, eighty acres of themed gardens and an amphitheater used for weddings and other events.

In the midst of all this beauty, I felt sorry for myself. Even when the roses looked dead, the gardeners took loving care of them. I needed someone to take loving care of me.

The oak grove and the eucalyptus trees reminded me of home in California with their smell, their twisted trunks, and the branches reaching into the sky.

A blue jay passed in front of me. A hawk soared over my head and settled in the branches of an oak. When it spread its wings, I glimpsed a flash of red.

I inhaled the sharp, clean air and walked until I had seen every plant. I wanted to stay there forever, but I needed to visit Fred and go home.

At the entrance to Timberwood, a woman who was visiting her dad asked me if I was Fred's daughter.

"No, I'm his wife."

"Oh, I'm sorry. You look so young," she said, punching the buttons to let us in.

Inside, John was singing and playing. Fred, fixated on the music, sang along. Taking a seat next to him, I joined in. He looked at me with an expression that seemed to say, "Who are you?" When I touched his arm, he pulled it away.

During a break, I asked him, "Do you know who I am?"

"Of course."

"Well, who am I?"

"Uh, uh."

"Do you know I'm your wife?"

"Yeah, I know that."

I didn't believe him.

An hour later, when I got up to leave, he just said, "Okay, bye," and joined the men at his usual table in the dining area.

By Feb. 25, I had been taking a quarter of a Klonopin pill for a week. When I ran out in another week, I'd have to manage my anxiety on my own. I only felt the effects sporadically now. My heart would beat too fast. I'd start to sweat and feel anxious. I'd close my eyes and breathe until I felt reasonably okay.

Reatha had given me some breathing and tapping exercises to use when I got panicky. That week I used them all. On Wednesday night, I sang for the kids, then hurried to the chapel to set things up for choir practice. I started to go over the songs before the choir got there, but my heart was thumping so hard I had to go outside and breathe.

Walking around the ministry house, I tried the butterfly hug. You cross your arms across your chest and start patting yourself, one side then the other. It's like EMDR, moving troubling thoughts to a calmer section of the brain. You can also pat your knees so it's less conspicuous. Reatha said she had a lawyer friend who always did it before she went into court.

The other technique was blowing out birthday candles. You take in a big breath and forcefully blow out every bit of air.

I also tried alternate nostril breathing from yoga. Back in the chapel, I started doing yoga postures. My heart kept thrumming. As the singers arrived, complaining about the cold, I was sweating. They made hot flash jokes. I couldn't wait to get out of there.

In the morning, I relaxed at home. The weather was balmy. I sat outside with Annie, enjoying the songs of robins, goldfinches, and jays. I spread out my mat and did yoga on the deck. I was supposed to go to a church ladies' lunch that day, but I canceled. I didn't go to yoga class either. I just wanted to stay home for a while.

I hadn't cried much lately. A few tears came out, but not that long, sobbing, end-of-the-world crying I had been doing before. Had all the tears I'd gushed in hypnosis cleaned me out? Was I calmer because I was quitting Klonopin? Or was I just learning to accept my losses?

I was still taking a quarter pill but would finish in a couple more days. Now every time I took that sliver of orange pill, I wondered if I needed it. It didn't seem to do anything good.

That week at church, withdrawal might have added to my distraction and my almost forgetting to play the memorial acclamation. There I was on my knees, my mind busy thinking about something else, when I realized Father Brian was saying the words that cued our song. I jumped up and played, boggling the introduction.

My teeth didn't seem to fit in my mouth. I was constantly aware of my upper front teeth poking into my lower lip and my jaw jutting too far forward. My tongue kept pushing at my teeth, wetting my chapped lips and swimming around in what seemed to be too much saliva. Was this still the withdrawal from Klonopin?

I forgot to take the Sunday pill until late in the evening and decided it was a good time to skip it, since I hadn't noticed any difference.

There was a difference.

The next day in yoga class, I knew the teacher could see that my jaw and tongue never stopped moving.

Afterward, at Walmart, a panic attack hit me. My heart beat too fast, my hands went numb, and I was sure I was going to faint. Leaning against the vacuum cleaner shelf, I forced myself to take slow deep breaths until I felt a little better, then walked around the hardware department blowing out invisible birthday candles.

The morning after my last winter quarter class at Chemeketa, I could see no reason to get out of my bed at Motel 6, at least not until the maid kicked me out. I was done teaching, and no one expected me anywhere. I hadn't gotten much sleep. All night, my legs were jumpy. I'd taken a bath at one in the morning because I couldn't lie still.

Eventually I scrabbled through my bag for the granola bars I had brought for breakfast. Then I dressed, packed, and left. Just outside my door, I found a big Coke cup full of water with a cigarette butt floating in it. I heard a rumbling noise and saw a maid coming toward me with her cart.

"It's all yours," I said, heading for the stairs to the parking lot.

Goodbye, Room 223, cheesy motel with the broken chair and the cigarette stain on the bedspread, with the neighbors going in and out all night. The term was over, and I wasn't going back to Chemeketa. It was just too hard.

34 Let's Jump the Fence

I had always considered Friday the twelfth a lucky day, but so far, this March Friday wasn't looking good. I woke early, thinking I could get some work done, but I closed my eyes and an hour passed. When I woke again, I couldn't move.

Wind had banged against the windows all night, tossing my deck chairs onto the lawn, tearing branches off my trees, and shredding my daffodils. I had gotten up at one o'clock because my legs were so twitchy I couldn't lie still. Now they felt like sacks of cement.

I kept calculating the time. If I get up now, I can still write a little before I shower, drive to Albany, grab a quick lunch and visit Fred. If I get up now, I can write a little, skip lunch, and get to Fred fifteen minutes later than usual. If I get up now, I can dictate something into my recorder on the road . . .

When I finally dragged myself out of bed, I opened the shade in the living room, cranked up the pellet stove, and settled in my office to write. Annie followed; I had forgotten to feed her. Back to the kitchen.

God forgive me, I did not want to visit Fred. I did not want to make that long drive again—or face what waited at the end of it.

Now the dog was barking, seeking attention.

Two hours later, at Timberwood, Fred jumped up from the couch, saying, "My wife's here." He was watching a cartoon on TV. I settled on the couch next to him. We kissed and held hands. He kept saying, "I love you so much." I started feeling sleepy and relaxed.

An aide tapped me on the back. "He needs more shampoo."

"Next time," I said.

"What do you think about shaving off his mustache and goatee?"

"No."

In the lull after the movie, I tossed a plush basketball to Fred. Soon I was passing it around to the others, but the old ladies quickly tired of the game. We retreated to Fred's room.

"Let's jump the fence and run away," he said.

There was no fence. It was raining hard outside, icicles sliding down the window.

"No, let's stay here." I lay on his bed. He gave me an awkward back rub, his hands barely touching me. He couldn't see the tears in my eyes as I thanked him and sat up. "Let's listen to music."

Although Fred knew I was his wife, I wasn't sure he knew which wife I was. When I told him I had celebrated my birthday, he asked, "Did the kids come?"

"What kids?" I muttered, then backtracked and said, "No."

A hawk soared overhead as I lay on the deck while Annie lolled on top of the hot tub cover. In the pine-scented spring breeze, my yard felt like the campgrounds where my family stayed when I was a kid, set free in nature. That little girl in pedal pushers and curly hair had so few worries. She could spend her days swimming, fishing, reading, writing, drawing, and singing. She made little sculptures out of bark and pinecones. What happened to that child?

In spite of the sunny weather and beautiful surroundings, everything seemed pointless. My work had been a total loss the past year and continued on the same path this year. Yes, my book on freelance writing for newspapers had been published, but the editor had left it full of typos, and I was not free to travel around promoting it. Between the recession and the growth of the Internet, newspapers were dying anyway. The travel magazine I had been writing for had stopped giving me assignments. I still had a few freelance gigs and my church job. I was writing a little poetry. But I felt like I was treading water while the tide pulled me farther and farther away from shore.

I visited Fred for two or three hours a week. When he knew me, we held hands and said we loved each other, but I left him teary-eyed in a nursing home and returned to this big house where I was alone day after day. I couldn't stand it.

I thought about ending it, ending my life. I had enough pills. I had knives. It just seemed so much easier to disappear. Let someone else figure everything out. I needed to go away, to fade into the blackness forever.

But I would break my father's heart. He had already lost his grandfather and brother to suicide. He would never get over my mother's death. I knew if I could hang on, things would be better later. I dragged myself up and into my office. I couldn't write, but maybe I could get my taxes done.

Taxes saved me. It was slow, frustrating work, made more frustrating not just by having to hunt for the numbers but because at every step, I had to wait for my slow computer to proceed. Gradually, the refund number at the top of my screen grew. When I put in how much we had spent on nursing homes in 2009 (could it really be $52,000?), the number zoomed up to a $7,800 refund from the federal government and more than $3,000 from the state of Oregon. Oh, my God! I could buy those new glasses I needed and a new computer, too.

Maybe. My audit risk was high because of my business loss and the huge medical expenses I was claiming. But I had the numbers to prove I deserved that refund.

Then I remembered the unsympathetic Medicaid worker. If I got a big tax refund, did I have to give up my share of Fred's pension until the refund was spent? Rats.

It would turn out that I did have to sacrifice some of my refund, but on that desperate day this one bit of good news saved my life. That and Turbo Tax, with its reassuring comments, like, "Good job! You just increased your refund."

I got off the ledge, but each time I fell into a funk, I eased a little closer to the void. I could feel the dirt crumbling beneath my feet.

My phone rang. It was Johanna, one of my most dependable singers at Sacred Heart. Her forty-four-year-old son had just died of influenza. I could hear the shake of tears in her voice. It hadn't been long since she had lost her other son; I didn't know what he died of, but he had been far too young.

I needed to stop feeling sorry for myself. Some people had real troubles.

35 Playing in the Sand

"Hey, you're here!" Fred said. "Come sit down."

"I can't. Traffic was awful, and we have a doctor's appointment. Are you ready? Do you need to go to the bathroom or anything?"

"Yes."

I watched the clock as he closed himself in the restroom. We were definitely going to be late.

"You okay in there?" I called.

Nothing. I was about to barge in when he came out.

"Let's go."

I pointed to his crotch. "Zip up."

Leading him into the lobby, I grabbed forms from Kim at the front desk, strapped him into the car, and drove as fast as I dared. We were late, but it didn't matter. We waited in Dr. L's office for a half hour. Fred became agitated. He wanted to come home. He said he wanted to see the ocean again.

I sat holding his hands, comparing the tan skin of my hands to the pale skin on Fred's hands and arms. His muscles, always strong, looked withered now.

We sat in those same two chairs, Fred next to the desk, me at his side. The same fire engine pictures, the Cote d'Azur painting, and other artifacts lined the walls next to the red container for used needles. It looked the same, but I had seen the progression of Fred's AD over the last five years. When we first met Dr. L., Fred spoke easily, describing his work at the aquarium, asking intelligent questions about Alzheimer's. Now I could feel him trembling. He couldn't stop shaking and couldn't form a sentence.

Dr. L. arrived. As always, he shook our hands before settling in his chair.

"Good morning, Fred. How are you doing?"

"I-I don't know."

"Well, let's just try a couple things. Okay. Touch your nose and then my finger."

Fred waved his hand around, confused.

Dr. L. made a note, then asked Fred about his activities.

"I don't know."

The neurologist turned to me.

"Life must be easier for you now that he's in—Timberwood?"

"Yes, Timberwood. In some ways, I guess. In others, not so much. He wants to go home. I always feel guilty."

"I understand. But he's getting the care he needs."

"I know." I cleared my throat. "How do you think he's doing?"

"It's progressing as expected. There's not much else we can do."

Fred stared at the bookshelf across the room. I didn't know how much he understood of our conversation. "Well, thank you," I said.

"Hang in there." He patted me on the shoulder and showed us to the exit.

On the way back to the nursing home, it was sunny but not hot. As soon as Fred got into the car, he started fiddling with the temperature controls, trying to get cold air. I locked the master door lock for fear he'd pull the passenger door handle in his search. As I drove, I tried to coach him. "Pull that thing there. No, no, that thing. Pull it this way. No, that's the glove compartment." My maps fell onto the floor. I watched, helpless, as Fred stepped on them with his food-stained slippers. He never wore shoes anymore.

We stopped at the Sweet Waters diner for dessert. At another table, men in baseball caps sat and jawed. Lots of teasing. They talked about sports. I watched Fred slop ice cream over the side of his dish. He lifted big goopy chunks into his mouth, splashing the excess back onto the bowl and table. He panicked and started to choke when he got a cherry stem in his mouth. I silently cursed the cook who placed the cherry in his way. I had to wipe ice cream off his arms in front of those manly men. Then I waited outside the bathroom while he washed his hands before we went back to Timberwood.

It seemed like I had had to watch out for Fred ever since I met him, feeding him names when he forgot, keeping track of his schedule, making sure his pancake syrup was heated the way he liked it, and that he didn't eat nuts because he was allergic to them. How long had I been doing that? Where was the line between being a loving spouse and being a caregiver?

Perhaps it's when your spouse stops watching over you, too. When he forgets you can't digest dairy products and don't like lemon meringue pie. When it's all one-sided.

Returning to Timberwood after lunch, I nestled against him on the sofa. He told me he loved me. I told him I wished I could do more for him. Tearful, he shook his head. "No, you're doing enough."

No, I wasn't.

He was wearing someone else's undershirt—round collar instead of his usual V-necks—and those black jeans that weren't his. Grated carrots clung to his suede slippers.

Every time I visited Fred, I was checking things. What did he have on, did he stink, did he need a haircut, were his nails too long, did he need more diapers, was everything he had last week still in his room? Were there new symptoms the doctor needed to check? Was the staff offering the activities listed on the schedule?

Someone had to make sure everything was as it should be. I tried not to think about who would do this for me if I ended up in a nursing home someday after Fred was gone.

* * *

At my April 1 appointment with Reatha, I spoke slowly, reluctantly, in a low, weary voice. She asked me to rate my mood on a scale of one to ten, one being don't want to live anymore. Two?

I felt too blue to cry, too worn out to talk about it. Reatha went over her notes from my last hypnosis session; it sounded like something from another person, all this business about breathing out my anxiety like a gray fog, breathing in light and peace.

What had happened between that hypnosis session and now? Another visit to Fred—after he pushed an old lady down. Another night broken by church choir nightmares and frequent awakenings. Computer troubles. Being alone so much I couldn't stand it.

"Would you like to try the sand tray?" Reatha asked.

"Maybe." I had always wanted a sand tray. When I went to the beach alone, I often wrote my problems in the sand.

She led me to the kitchen, where she kept a rubber container full of clean white sand.

On each side of the tray, she showed me drawers full of toys: dolls, little houses, fake plants, animals, jewels, and a blue scarf to imitate water.

She invited me to play like a child. Then she settled back in a chair to watch. On the beach, I wrote my words in private then erased them so no one else could see them. This was different. But if therapy is to work, you have to try it. I had done pills, hypnosis, EMDR, butterfly hugs, and biofeedback where I worked on breathing and relaxing until the meter showed my heartbeat settling at a calm pace. I had cried oceans of tears, completely letting go. I had to try the sand tray.

I pulled a little house out of a drawer and plopped it on the left side of the tray. I found a yellow dog. Annie. I drew a winding road in the sand with my hand. Thiel Creek Road. I was re-creating my home. I walked toy Annie along the road to where she was born.

Now what? I pulled out a turtle. I buried it in sand up to its neck. I remembered playing on the beach with my mother and brother while Dad fished at the shoreline. I remembered warm sand above, cool sand below, that tight feeling when you're buried, knowing you could move but not wanting to break the smooth sand covering you. I released the turtle, had Annie lead it home. The dog and the turtle both looked down the chimney. I brushed the sand off the turtle and put it away.

I pulled out another dog, a German shepherd, but it had a dark back. Chico? Annie led it down the road to where they were born then turned and led it back home. I rustled in the box, looking at all the people until I found a dark-haired girl. Me. I put her in front of the house. Then I found a red-haired boy with glasses. Fred. His hair was brown, but this doll was close enough. I put him there, too. I planted flowers and trees. I placed other houses down the road. Then I announced I was done.

Reatha had watched it all. In therapy, a house is not just a house; a turtle is not just a turtle. In fact, she said the turtle signified the wise woman.

"I just thought it was cute," I said.

She asked me to describe what I had there. I started to cry. I had recreated my home the way I wanted it to be, with Chico and Fred still there.

The sand tray had opened the door to my feelings.

Clearly I was grieving, Reatha said in her comforting voice as she held me and patted my back. "It's all right."

I was grieving about more than Fred. More than Chico. I was grieving a way of life that had disappeared. Where was the woman who made wall hangings and other crafts with her hands, delighting in touches of cloth and yarn and jewels? Where was the woman who felt free to play?

Reatha said she would take a picture of the sand tray for my files.

We would do it again another time. I wondered if I would just keep creating the same picture.

Our time was up. I went out into the world feeling better, as if my wounds were still there but bandaged and ready to start healing. I had a lot to think about.

The sun broke through the clouds. I stopped in Seal Rock and bought myself a root beer float, then drove to Lost Creek State Park, a mile down the coast from home. Storm-driven waves came all the way up to the cliffs, so I stayed in my car. The ice cream tasted tangy and felt crunchy from the root beer. The root beer turned creamy from the melting ice cream. It went to all the wounded places and soothed them. Later, I would suffer terribly from gas, but now I savored my treat and let my mind wander.

When I said I couldn't write, Reatha had asked, "Do you have to?" I was still pondering that as I sipped my root beer float. What if I just quit? But then I started making deals with myself. What if I just wrote a poem every day for the April poem-a-day challenge? And well, what if I just finished my next book? And maybe I could keep doing my blog. . . . Eventually I was back to doing everything I'd been doing, but because I wanted to, not because I had to.

Sun glowed golden on the waves. The water churned and crashed and spread across the beach like a blue-and-white quilt. I pulled out my notebook and started to write.

36 "Was I There?"

It was May 18, our twenty-fifth wedding anniversary. A year earlier, when Fred had been at Su Casa, we had had a good time looking at our wedding pictures and remembering the day when we said our vows beside a pond and partied in our backyard with all our friends. "Remember when Debbie played the wrong song for the procession?" I asked. "Remember how Scotty played the piano and my grandparents danced in the patio? Remember the Portuguese feast Pat Silva cooked for us? Remember how happy we were?" He remembered it all. I even took him out to dinner that night, and it was almost like old times.

But now at Timberwood, Fred didn't know who I was. I tried to give him an anniversary card, but he didn't understand it was from me or what it was for. He didn't know that I was married to him. When I sat down next to him, he moved away.

An accordion player and her guitar-playing friend were entertaining. Fred sat up front and sang along. I couldn't get him to look at me.

When the music ended, I hugged him and asked, "Do you know who I am?"

He stared at me. "I'm sorry. No."

It was the first time he really didn't know me, not just my name, but that I had any connection to him at all.

I had brought our wedding album. I showed it to him, hoping it would jog his memory. He appeared to be interested in the pictures.

He recognized his parents. After a while, he seemed to recognize me in the wedding dress. Maybe.

I had thought about having a party like most people do for their twenty-fifth. Thank God I didn't.

We threw big surprise parties for my parents' twenty-fifth and fiftieth anniversaries, huge expensive fiestas with tons of food and gifts and all the friends and family there. We danced and took photographs to treasure. But that could never happen with Fred. As I sat beside him in his mother's easy chair, flipping the plastic-wrapped pages of our wedding album, my throat ached with tears.

I had had this vision of listening to our wedding music and everyone looking at our pictures together, but Fred didn't share our memories anymore. He looked at those pictures and asked, "Was I there?"

He didn't recognize his own children.

When we ran out of photos, Fred wanted me to take him for a ride, but it was late, and I was barely holding back the tears.

Unaware of our anniversary, Tina, Timberwood's manager, brought me a new Portable Orders for Life-Sustaining Treatment (POLST) form to fill out. This is the pink form that tells paramedics and doctors what we want them to do in a medical emergency. If Fred's heart stopped, did we want CPR? Did we want tube feeding, a ventilator?

Of all days to ask if I wanted to pull the plug if my husband stopped breathing.

After I filled out the form, checking "no" to the life-sustaining options because Fred had told me that's what he wanted, I said a quick goodbye and hurried to the car, already sobbing. Before I could start the engine, Tina was at my window, waving the form. I had forgotten to fill in one of the blanks. I rolled down the window, fighting to gain control.

"I'm sorry, sweetie," she said.

"Me too." I scribbled something, handed back the form and got myself out of there.

On the way home, I cried so hard I felt like I would break into a million pieces and die. It hurt so bad, surely I couldn't survive it.

Before my next visit to Timberwood, I took a skidding turn off Highway 20 at the sign to the Harris covered bridge. I passed the Tum Tum Christmas tree farm. Fred and I used to cut down our Christmas trees the first week of December. He'd wear his corduroy coat and carry the big saw. We'd get mud so thick on our shoes they were hard to lift. We'd drink hot chocolate and sing Christmas carols as we drove home and set up the tree together.

It was June now, the Christmas trees small, the grapevines beside the road loaded with grapes, the alders in full leafy regalia. A good day for exploring.

Someone was hammering on a play apparatus by the big white house just past the bridge. I snapped pictures of the house and walked the covered bridge over the river. The water looked cold, clean and green. The sun warmed my back.

Eventually I had to go to Timberwood, where I would play my guitar and sing, but Fred wouldn't know I wasn't one of the paid entertainers.

In mid-June, I drove to California for a journalism conference at Stanford.

Fourteen years earlier, we had caravanned up I-5 with a Ryder truck and a Honda Accord, suffering one breakdown after another, but we were in it together and our trip became a fond memory we used to share.

Now I was driving back to San Jose alone.

I didn't pack my grief for this trip, but it snuck in anyway. I could feel it pushing my shoulders, my head, and my neck. It hid in the cracks of everything, more pervasive than the dog fur clinging to my clothes and the car seats. My husband didn't even know I was going on a trip. I couldn't call when I arrived and hear him say, "Hel-*loh*" in that special way.

Amid the greenery of Oregon spring, I had expected to relax, but there was a memory in every pocket, every suitcase, and every crevice of my car.

We had been to all these places together. He had bought me this coat one cold Christmas. Memories crowded in, trips we took by car, plane, and train, hand in hand, knee to knee, singing to the music.

Now there was just one voice, one pair of hands gripping the steering wheel. The white skin beneath my wedding ring hurt.

At the conference, I learned something important. It wasn't about marketing, how to write a query letter, or how to incorporate "new media" into my stories. It was that I had lost interest in being a journalist. I had published a book about it, but I didn't want to do it anymore.

I spent the rest of the week with my father. When he asked how the conference had gone, I just said, "Fine" and changed the subject.

It was nice hanging out with Dad, not being alone. At lunch on the wharf in Santa Cruz, I said, "I've lost my traveling buddy." My father reminded me that he had lost his companion, my mother, too. Like me, he lived alone. At least for now we had each other.

As long as I was busy with my father and the conference, I didn't have time to think about Fred's situation, but driving home up I-5, I could hardly think of anything else. In Canyonville, Oregon, I visited an antique store, remembering how much fun it had been to wander through old books, dishes, and vintage clothing looking for treasures.

Our whole house was furnished with antiques we had bought together at the antiques warehouse in San Jose, secondhand stores, and garage sales, or inherited from friends and relatives. Every night, I ate alone at the mahogany table and sat on the matching chairs Fred and I had dressed up with maroon leather seat covers. The furniture reminded me of our grandparents' homes, but they were gone, and so was Fred.

I walked through a city park where children played baseball while their parents cheered. I stood on the stage and looked out at the empty amphitheater. I watched a couple walking together in the distance.

Damn.

I stopped at Timberwood on the way home. Fred wanted out. He was wearing his scarlet Hawaiian shirt tucked into those black pants that didn't fit. His socks had red gooey stuff on them, and his slippers were coated with eggs and maple syrup. He smelled like sweat and urine, and he had a bloody spot on his cheek, with no idea where it had come from.

I had just driven seven hundred miles, but I led Fred to the car. Big band music playing, we drove east along a two-lane road called Grand Prairie Drive. It took us toward the farm towns of Sweet Home and Spicer. Wide open spaces. Grass and grazing cows. Eventually the road connected with Highway 20 and brought us back to Albany.

I had to say goodbye. Annie was still at the kennel, and they closed at five.

Fred and I made a clean break. We made palms-together namaste signs, hugged, kissed, and said goodbye. I thought it was all right, but when I looked back, he was crying.

I'm never going to forget that image of Fred with his head bowed down, weeping.

On the way out, I ran into Loy's wife. "This is really hard," she said.

"It's awful. How are you doing?"

She just shook her head.

37 All It Takes Is a Dog

On July 13, I sat on Reatha's leather couch and said I was feeling about eight out of ten, ten being ecstatic and zero killing yourself. Sure, I had gotten down to a one a few days earlier when life felt too hard and nothing meant anything anymore. But I was past that.

"Did you consider suicide?" she asked.

"Well, maybe a little, but now I'm good."

She looked worried; she made notes on her paper. We debated drugs. My Cymbalta should be helping, but maybe I needed something different to even out my moods. She wrote a prescription for citalopram, brand name Celexa.

"Is there anything in particular you want to work on today?" she asked.

"No. I'm fine. I just want to get back to work."

"Tell me about when you were feeling down."

I sighed. "It was just the usual garbage. I'd been to visit Fred and . . ."

I babbled about Timberwood and church and the dogs, and the hour passed. Thank God my insurance was paying for these sessions.

Five hours later, I sat on a picnic table in the park above Ona Beach crying. Below me in the grass, Annie chewed on a steak bone she had found in a barbecue pit.

I stared at the river silvering in the dusk, wind-rippled in the cool summer breeze. Annie and I were the only ones left in the park—unless someone was sleeping in that eighteen-wheeler in the parking lot.

My feet were bare. I had peeled off my wet shoes and socks after Annie dragged me into the water.

Loneliness pulled me down like a weight on a drowning woman. Earlier, I'd eaten a tasteless dinner of cardboard pork chop and bland tuna casserole when what I really wanted was to go out to dinner. I wanted to get dressed up and eat somewhere with white tablecloths, where the air smelled of pasta, garlic, tomato sauce, and red wine. I wanted to listen to music and feel special. I wanted to kiss and feel a man's hands on my body.

My back ached from my morning visit to the chiropractor. I had been feeling dizzy, so he had worked on my neck, cracking it left and right, then pushing at my spine, forcing my lower back to line up. Later, I had gone to yoga, where the world spun every time I lowered my head.

I had chosen Ona Beach just down the road from home because I couldn't stand one more walk on our usual route.

It was getting dark. Annie had finished her bone. "Let's go," I said, leading her to the car.

At home, I changed into dry clothes, watched a talk show on TV, ate mint chocolate chip ice cream, and washed my dishes. That took me up to a three or four.

On my next visit to Timberwood, I drove Fred around for a while. Fred tried on shoes at the Heritage Mall, but nothing fit, and he didn't understand that he couldn't wear shoes with laces anymore because he couldn't tie them. Back at his room, he kept asking about his kids, so I called his daughter Gretchen on my cell phone and let her talk to him. At one point, Fred said, "Sue was here. She's my—" He looked at me. "What relation are you to me?"

"I'm your wife."

After the call, I took out my guitar and played a couple songs in the dining room. But Sam was having a meltdown. Another resident kept yelling, "Help me, help me!"

Pauline came up close. She touched my guitar and then my arm. I could see Fred getting ready to grab her. I hurriedly finished my song and held her cold, thin hand.

Lydia approached with her walker. "Make the screaming stop."

I didn't know whether she meant me or the help-me lady.

Mary came up behind Fred. He spun around and hit her. The aides jumped in. She wasn't injured, but my sweet, gentle husband's face had suddenly turned mean.

Time to stop the show. We went back to Fred's room. I got my stuff, and he escorted me to the door.

"What if I just walked out?" he asked.

"Oh honey, I'd hate to read about you in the paper as a tragedy," I said, messing up the door code twice before I got it right. Holding the door with my foot, I let him grab me for one last kiss, one last "I love you." Then I shut the door on his tear-streaked face.

Two weeks later, Fred asked me what kind of work I did.

"I'm a writer."

"Oh."

If Fred didn't know who I was, should I try to become a friendly visitor, someone with whom he had no history? Could I do that? Was that too much to ask of myself, of anybody? Could I pretend I was no more attached to him than I was to Sam or Jean or Mary? But he was my husband. Wasn't it my job as his wife to do whatever I could, whether he knew me or not?

How could I visit appropriately without breaking my own heart or upsetting him? I supposed I was on the right track telling funny stories about my dogs and talking about the weather. It had to be better than pushing him, saying, "You know, remember when we went to Costa Rica?" No, he didn't know. I could say, "Once upon a time, I went to Costa Rica. Have you ever gone there?" and see what he said, if any wisp of our time at Punta Arenas was still in his memory.

To the staff, I was still the wife, but to the husband with dementia, I was a stranger.

With my grandfather, I was the lady in black because I wore a black coat that last rainy winter when I came to visit and play music. My status as granddaughter was completely erased from his mind. Who was I to Fred now?

The following week, I was heading for Timberwood again. Annie watched me getting ready, head on her paws, already looking lonely. "Come on," I said, grabbing her leash.

Overjoyed, jumping and wagging, she beat me to the car and took her place on the passenger seat.

When I brought the dog in, Fred was thrilled. He couldn't stop petting her. We walked around outside. We sat with Annie in the lobby and in the dining room. The whole visit was about the dog. When people asked if this was his dog, Fred claimed her. He didn't remember her name, but it didn't matter.

Everyone wanted to pet her. Merrit hugged her, Jean reached out for her. But the miracle was Pauline. Before she saw Annie, she had been shuffling along, headed toward Fred, saying to no one, "It's so chilly." It was not chilly; it was ninety degrees out. She was in another world, and then boom, she saw Annie, smiled, and started making sense.

"Oh, you're a pretty dog. Such a sweetheart." She petted her. She was normal.

It made me want to turn Annie into a therapy dog. Music was good, but this seemed better. Annie was such a comfort to residents, staff, and visitors.

Fred must have petted her for an hour and a half out of two hours. When real therapy dogs visited, he got only a brief hello before they had to move on to the next resident, but Annie was there for him.

Fred seemed to know who I was. We kissed and hugged as well as we could with one of us holding the dog. He laughed as Annie poked her head up between us. Just like the old days.

When I left Fred, he was calm. He grabbed me back for an extra kiss. The effect of the dog was amazing. Fred and Annie hadn't seen each other in a year and a half. I didn't know if they remembered each other, but it didn't matter. They were both living in the moment.

Fred wanted Annie to keep coming back, but the poor dog was exhausted. On the way home, she lay with her nose between the seats, her paw on my thigh. I rubbed her head. "I know how you feel, girl."

I was the youngest person attending the Saturday brunch for families of Timberwood residents. With Fred's early onset and our difference in ages, I was younger than most of the children of the residents.

We gathered in the lobby, where our family members inside could not see or hear us. Tina talked through a long agenda that included changing the door codes, welcoming a new activities director, looking for a new in-house nurse, and new forms we had to fill out to order diapers. It went on and on until I had a blazing caffeine headache. When it finally ended, I slipped out for chocolate peanut butter fudge pie and iced tea at Sweet Waters before going in to see Fred.

I found him sitting in the sun in the courtyard. He was wearing two layers of yellowed undershirts and his pajama bottoms inside out with nothing under them. He was uncombed and unshaven. An aide told me he didn't want to get dressed.

"I want to go home," he told me. "I'm fine. I'm good. I'm okay."

"No, not today," I said.

"Well, when?"

"A little while longer."

The lies people tell their loved ones to get through the moment.

We went in. The new activities director was out sick, so nothing was happening. We sat in Fred's room for a while, holding hands and listening to music.

He stared at me as if trying to figure out who I was. He looked up at the picture over his head of the kids. "There's you," he said.

"No," I replied, pointing to the picture on his dresser. "That's me."

The glasses Fred was wearing weren't his. I held them over my own glasses. They didn't seem to make much difference except for being dirty.

"They work," Fred said.

I handed them back. I didn't know whose they were. Maybe the owner had died. Since his cataract surgery, Fred didn't need glasses, but he'd worn them since he was three years old. He probably felt naked without them.

Timberwood had lost eight residents in the last six months. Six had died, and two had moved to the "Maple" wing, where the most unmanageable residents lived. The staff couldn't name any names because of privacy regulations. One week they were there; the next week I didn't see them. I wanted to know what happened.

Fred looked at my wedding ring and seemed surprised that our rings matched.

"That means we're supposed to be together," I said.

I sometimes fantasized about Fred suddenly getting well and questioning me about everything I had done with his money and his things, about all the choices I had made. I shed happy tears at the thought of having him back, but a part of me was a little afraid. Would he be angry at me? Would I measure up?

38 You Talking to Me?

Tension filled the Embarcadero hotel meeting room as potential volunteers dipped a tentative paw into the world of Oregon Coast Therapy Animals. After Annie's success at Timberwood, I had thought I might train her as a certified therapy dog. Now I was having doubts as the therapy dog veterans described the requirements, including classes, fees, tests, and a busy schedule of visits to schools, hospitals, and nursing homes. Where would I find the time?

To take dogs into places where animals didn't usually go, they had to be certified as healthy, be clean from nose to tail, and behave well at all times. The owners had to undergo criminal background checks, and the pet partner teams had to be insured. All OCTA members were required to join Delta Society, which oversaw a national pet partner program.

And yet, the rewards seemed tremendous. At Timberwood, I had seen residents who never talked to humans talk to Annie. I had watched people who always seemed to be cranky soften as they pet her smooth tan fur. I had felt the peace and light that a dog brings into a room. Everyone brightened when therapy dogs came to visit. It seemed worth the effort to use that power for healing and happiness.

Plus we'd get name tags, a spiffy green shirt for me, and a vest for Annie. We'd go to parties and meet new friends. Annie could have more car rides. Oh, happy dog.

I was pleased to see my friends Lyn and Darrell from yoga class at the orientation. Perhaps people who were drawn to yoga were also drawn to doing good deeds with their dogs.

I came home to a restless, crazy dog that grabbed paper from my recycle box and made me chase her around the house to get it back. I took her for a walk in the rain, stopping often to ask her to sit, stay, lie down, or come. She did well, giving me a look that seemed to say, "That was fun. What next?" Maybe this would actually work.

On a chilly morning, Annie and I reported to the playground at Yaquina View School for our practice test before our evaluation as a pet partner team. Annie greeted our evaluator by jumping up and licking her face. Not good.

"She never does that," I lied.

A half dozen other dog owners watched as I backed up ten feet and called Annie, expecting her to run full-tilt toward me, just as all the other dogs had. But no. She decided to stay where she was and pretend she couldn't hear me.

How many times had we done this trick on our walks? I'd release the leash and walk away. Then I'd call Annie, and she'd zoom back to me. But now, surrounded by obedient golden retrievers and their owners, she did not come until I pulled the rope and reeled her in. We tried it again. No go.

Therapy dogs are not allowed to wear the pronged metal collars that Annie had worn since we went to obedience school. They were considered too harsh, and people might get their fingers caught. I had tried a nylon collar. When she decided to go somewhere, it was like trying to stop a Buick. When she spotted the neighbor's cat, I thought I was a goner. I outweighed Annie by a hundred pounds, but she packed at least a hundred pounds of determination in that burly tan body.

For our test, I borrowed a harness that an experienced therapy partner guaranteed would work. Annie pulled me across the pavement. And now she refused to come.

My pup could sit, stay, and lie down with the best of them. She seemed to have the right temperament for a therapy dog, but she couldn't be pulling people around, and she had to come when I called. Score zero for the pooch.

I got in trouble, too. I needed to temper that mean-Marine voice our dog trainer had taught me to use. I needed to say my commands firmly enough to get results but not so firmly that I scared old people and children.

We had two weeks before the real test. We were doomed.

"I don't think this is going to work" I told the evaluator.

She nodded. "Annie's pretty energetic. Maybe you could try another time."

"Thanks."

We walked across the playground to the parking lot. "Well, you'll just be my therapy dog," I told my pup as I opened the car door and she jumped into my seat.

39 Onesies

After choir practice a couple days later, I got a sudden urge to go to the beach. It was August, and darkness came late. Newport was full of tourists enjoying the sand and surf I rarely visited without the dog.

I parked and walked the sandy steps past the Visual Arts Center onto Nye Beach. Bonfires crackled, lovers kissed in the orange light while others walked hand in hand. I kicked off my shoes. The sand felt cool and soft under my feet. The waves swished in and out like layers of silk slips lit by amber lights from the hotels above us. To the north, the beacon blinked at the Yaquina Head lighthouse.

I got this vacation feeling, remembering romantic evening walks with Fred by the water in California, Cape Cod, and Hawaii. I could almost hear the ukulele music.

As I stood at the edge of the surf, a man approached. I got nervous. I hoped he would pass by, but he didn't. He stood right next to me. Up close, I realized he was a teenager, wearing a black suit jacket over his jeans. He sucked on his cigarette and blew out a cloud of smoke.

"It's beautiful here, isn't it?" he said.

"Yes, it is."

We were silent as he smoked. He reminded me of Michael, my stepson.

"Where do you live?" I asked.

"Salem," he said. "You?"

"I live here."

"Sweet."

He said he had lived in Newport years ago, and he was always drawn back to the coast. "Well, have a good evening," he said and walked on.

This experience, no more than ten minutes, was a revelation. The beach was right here whenever I wanted it. I didn't need a husband or a dog to keep me company.

I walked slowly up the sand, thinking of new possibilities. Perhaps I should go to a bar or restaurant to hear music. It would feel good just to soak in the atmosphere. It would be better with someone, but I could go alone. I could put on the new hat I'd bought at Fred Meyer on the way home from the beauty salon and talk to strangers, like I just did.

New haircut. New hat. New life.

At Timberwood, Martin was wearing blue fleece overalls with a zipper down the back. You could see the outline of his diaper. He walked like a baby, rocking from side to side, making slow progress.

Martin rocked close to Betty, who was wearing a one-piece sweat suit, also with a zipper down the back. She reached up and grabbed the tab on his zipper. He hollered and swatted her skinny arm away. An aide jumped in to separate them. Betty went on her way, talking to herself, while Martin rocked back toward the sofa.

Onesies. Baby clothes, except they had zippers instead of snaps. They made dressing easier for the staff and kept the residents from undressing themselves. Up until this week, I had tried to keep Fred in regular clothing, mostly jeans and polo shirts. But I was beginning to see the need for a change.

It was getting hard to dress Fred. A year earlier, when he first moved to Timberwood, he could easily shed his pants and put on another pair. He knew how to button the button and zip the zipper. He could thread his belt through the loops. Now he just stood there. Or he sat with his feet outstretched and flexed, waiting for me to pull his dirty pants off and slide the clean ones on. It was like trying to dress a two-hundred-pound doll that kept interrupting you with complaints and unexpected twitches.

The staff kept asking me to buy bigger clothes. Toward the end, most dementia patients stop eating and waste away, but Fred was at the stage where he forgot he had already eaten, so he ate again and again. Now he couldn't understand why he couldn't button his jeans over his belly.

He walked around holding the waistband of his pants. I couldn't tell whether they didn't fit or they were wet. Usually the latter. So we had to change pants again.

Sweatpants might help. But even sweats required getting up and sitting down.

Was it time to put him in man-sized baby clothes? They looked comfortable. Alzheimer's patients eventually don't recognize themselves in a mirror, so maybe it wouldn't bother him. Fred had trouble telling his clothes from mine when we were sitting together. Would he sit on that couch all day feeling the fleece, wondering whose it was?

In lieu of other activities on this Saturday afternoon, the aides seated the residents in front of the Oregon State Beavers football game. But even Fred, who used to spend his fall weekends watching one football game after another, had no interest. He couldn't follow the game anymore.

The staff had disappeared. Did the aides leave everyone alone in the living room because there was a visitor who would step up if anything happened? I watched Mary, who kept trying to stand up, and two other women quarreling on the sofa, wondering if I should go find someone who worked there. If Mary fell or the women started hitting each other, what would I do?

Every day at the three o'clock shift change, there seemed to be a gap. The morning crew was leaving, and the people who worked three to eleven were checking in. Both groups gathered in the dining room to do paperwork, compare notes, and socialize. Who was watching over the residents then? I was.

Signs on the door into the locked area asked for donations of pens, paper, and other craft supplies. We paid Timberwood an average of $5,000 a month. *The staff could buy their own darned colored pens*, I thought as I got up to find an aide to watch the residents.

The next afternoon, Annie led me through an opening in the bushes at Ona Beach a few miles south of our home and onto a vast stretch of white sand split by a saltwater creek that flowed from Beaver Creek to the ocean. Hundreds of gulls had gathered on the water. A half dozen pelicans stood among them, tall and long-beaked.

"Annie, look!" I shouted over the cacophony of bird noise.

We moved slowly toward the creek.

The birds let us get within ten yards before they rose up in a whoosh and flew toward the surf, gulls squawking, pelicans flapping their massive wings.

Annie strained at the leash. On impulse, I let her go, the first time I had ever done that at the beach. I didn't see any other dogs or people, and I wanted to see how well she could swim.

She zoomed across that belly-deep water, barely touching the sand below. Her eyes glowed with joy as she rousted the birds again.

As she got farther away, I called her name. She chose not to hear me. Shedding my shoes, I plunged my bare feet into the creek. The cold water felt so good I wanted to splash around like a kid.

Annie flew past me, spraying my glasses and shirt with water. She paused to drink, then started toward the waves.

Yikes. Annie didn't know anything about waves, rip tides, and outgoing currents that might drown her. She scared the birds into flight again, stopped, wheeled around and ran toward three people just coming onto the beach. I was too far away to do anything except shout a useless "Off!"

They petted her and she ran back toward me, crossed the water, and bounded away in the other direction until I could barely see her. Her tan fur matched the sand.

"Annie!" I called, starting toward her. But I had been with dogs long enough to know that if you run toward them, they'll keep going, thinking this is a game. So I turned back, running across the sand, through the creek, and toward the entrance.

Annie sped toward me, but veered off at the last minute toward the deeper part of Beaver Creek. I hurried over to find her on the shore, nose plunged into the beach grass, hunting some enchanting smell. I clicked the leash on and pulled her toward the water. Now we would see if she could really swim.

The sand gave way beneath my toes. As soon as the water grew too deep to walk, Annie started to paddle. It was the most beautiful, most natural thing. Her paws stroked smoothly through the green water, her chin resting on the surface, no effort at all.

I was soaked up to my hips but happier than I'd felt in ages.

"You're swimming!" I shouted, hugging her wet fur. She licked my cheek.

When we came out, we sprawled by a log, both of us wet and covered with sand. Sitting there on a warm fall day under a blue sky etched with white clouds, I felt young, strong, and blessed. Anything seemed possible.

40 Holding On to a Ghost

Fred looked around Dr. L's office as if waking from a dream. "We've been here many, many times," he said.

A nurse checked his vital signs. BP 128/70, pulse 60. Normal.

Dr. L asked Fred to touch his thumb and forefinger together. Confused, he held up his hand and shook it. When the doctor grabbed his fingers and moved them for him, he could do it, but still didn't understand what he was supposed to do.

The doctor watched him walk back and forth, then tapped his arms and knees. He agreed with my assessment: more confused, speech worse, movement less fluid. The disease was progressing, no meds could stop it, come back in six months, next April.

I led Fred across the parking lot to the Honda I'd been driving back and forth between South Beach and Albany.

"Is this your car?" he asked as I unlocked the passenger-side door.

"Yes." We had bought it together in Newport the year before he fell. I had used his money and had put his name on the pink slip with mine, but he had never driven it. The new-car smell was long gone, the seats and floors coated with dog fur, pine needles, and stray stove pellets.

We had missed lunch at Timberwood, so I looked for a restaurant in Corvallis near the medical center. I almost pulled into Izzy's Pizza, then remembered it was all buffet, self-serve. Too confusing for Fred. We wound up at Shari's, where several old folks with walkers and wheelchairs were already seated at the tables.

The menu was a spiral-bound book, confusing to anyone. Fred kept looking at the pictures.

"Pancakes," he said.

"Do you want pancakes?"

"Yes." Then he saw hamburgers. "I want this."

"You want a hamburger?"

The young ponytailed server arrived, pen poised to take our order. "He'll have a mushroom Swiss burger. Salad with ranch dressing."

"Coffee," Fred said.

"Cream?" she asked.

"Cream."

He always drank his coffee black. "You want cream?" I asked him.

"No."

I could see the waitress looking around at other tables where customers were waiting. "I'll just have a club sandwich with fries." I handed her my menu and reached for Fred's. He wouldn't let go. "We don't need this anymore, hon." I pulled until I got it loose. "Sorry," I told the server.

"No worries."

Fred's salad came with big chunks of cucumber and carrots. I cut them up for him, then removed the onions and lettuce from his burger and cut it into quarters.

After a few bites, he set down his burger and said, "I gotta go."

I led him to the bathroom door, then waited. Time dragged on. Should I go in and help?

Going out to lunch used to be our thing. At the least suggestion, we'd head to one of the local diners where we'd josh with the waitresses and chat with folks at nearby tables as I gorged on Monte Cristo sandwiches and french fries while Fred ate a burger or his favorite breakfast, the "two two two": two eggs, two pieces of bacon, and two pancakes with as much black coffee as he could get.

It used to be fun. I was proud of my man. Now it was like taking out a two-year-old, except two-year-olds can learn.

It probably confused people when I said I had lost my husband, but I had. It didn't matter whether he was in a cemetery or a nursing home; he was gone.

Waitresses and customers passed by as I waited for Fred. After ten minutes, he came out, and I led him back to the table, but he wouldn't sit.

"Let's finish our lunch," I said.

"I'm done."

I looked at my cold fries and sandwich and called the waitress over. "Can I get a box and our check?"

"Sure."

But it took too long. Fred was already at the door, and I was afraid he'd go out and get lost. I left a twenty-dollar bill and hurried to catch him.

In October, I went through the papers in Fred's office. I shredded reams of old insurance forms and bank statements. I packed up pictures and memorabilia to send to his children.

As I studied bills and notes in his handwriting, I sighed. He used to write so neatly. Now he couldn't sign his name. I was not sure he knew his whole name anymore.

I visited Fred later that day. I held his hand and kissed his bristly cheek. But I was holding on to a spirit caught between this world and the next. When he said he wanted to go home, I gently guided the conversation to another topic. When he insisted on coming with me, I hugged him and said I was sorry.

I couldn't bring him back to the life he used to know. Even if I put him in the car and drove him to the house where I sat in my bathrobe going through his stuff, he would not know how to live there anymore. He would stand in the living room, lost, waiting for me to tell him what to do. I would get busy. He would wet his pants, fall, or start to shake, and there would be no young people in khaki scrubs to rescue him.

Dear God, I prayed, please watch over all the ghost people like Fred who are neither alive nor dead and help them to move one way or the other. Please help me to not feel so guilty as I pile up his things and give them away.

41 Jingle Bells

On Oct. 20, Timberwood was filled with people in purple Alzheimer's Walk T-shirts, purple flowers, purple balloons and tablecloths, purple ribbons, more purple than you've ever seen. Most of the residents had no idea what was going on. Fred certainly didn't.

Staff loaded residents and loved ones into the bus for the short trip to the Heritage Mall. A wheelchair-bound woman who whined all the time sat behind us, crying out at every bump and turn.

The staff had set up a table in the center of the shopping mall with brochures about Alzheimer's and about Timberwood. One-third residents, one-third family members and one-third staff comprised our team. We walked laps around the mall, sipped free water from a hamburger place, and got our pictures taken.

Cruising through the Ross store, one of the residents grabbed a cart and pushed it to the exit. She couldn't get it out because it had a big pole that hit the door frame. Bang, bang, over and over until I took it away from her. The aides were busy watching Merrit, afraid she might shoplift some of the merchandise. I was surprised. This quiet, dignified woman had always seemed like she didn't have AD at all.

It was interesting being out in public with the residents. AD patients aren't usually so visible. You can't always tell who's who. We were all wearing the same purple T-shirts. When Fred wasn't talking, people might not have suspected he had the disease. But we had Violet all bent over, Pauline in her wheelchair, two women in straw hats, and Rachel babbling. People must have wondered.

We walked slowly past stores that sold clothing, cell phones, video games, and shoes.

"Where are we going?" Fred asked.

"Nowhere. Just around the mall."

"Look at all this." He gestured in wonder at all the shops and read random words off the signs. "Sale!" "Mattress." "Orange."

"Yeah," I said, leading him along, hoping he wouldn't decide he wanted to go into any of the stores.

An hour later, we were loading the bus to go back to Timberwood.

In the dining room, we sat amid the purple mania, eating from heaping purple plastic bowls of vanilla ice cream covered with whipped cream, mini M&Ms, caramel and chocolate sauce.

Was it worth the effort? Hard to tell. The staff raised some money selling raffle tickets. We had each paid twenty dollars to participate in the walk. Maybe somebody at the mall noticed and thought about Alzheimer's for a minute.

That Thanksgiving, I took the train to San Jose to spend the holiday with my family. From the time Dad picked me up at the train station until he dropped me off three days later, it felt good not to be alone, to have my father, brother, aunts, and cousins around. They asked about Fred. They asked why I was still in Oregon.

Because Oregon was home now.

I didn't see Fred's kids that Thanksgiving. I depended on my father for transportation, and I had only a few days before I had to get back to Oregon. I felt guilty but didn't have the strength to reach out. I needed them to reach out to me, but they didn't.

When I returned to Albany at twilight three days later, I stopped at Timberwood before heading back to the coast.

After eighteen hours on Amtrak, I could still feel the rocking of the train as I walked through the lobby.

Fred was watching TV, wearing his dingy undershirt and new too-big jeans that were falling off him.

We went into his room, sat in the mauve chairs, and sang along with the radio. We held hands, hugged, and danced.

The residents were gathering for dinner, and we joined them.

Martin greeted everyone, saying, "Hi, hi, hi." Sam complained that he was cold. Mary set out silverware, running it all through her fingers. Rachel was laughing.

Aides went around distributing pills.

One of them approached us. "Sue, did anyone call you?"

"No."

"Fred had seizure activity last night," she said. "His arms and legs were shaking, his eyes rolled back in his head, and he lost consciousness for about fifteen seconds."

I really felt the room rocking and rolling then.

Fred interrupted. "Are you talking about me?"

"Yes, we love you," the girl said. She left us pondering the news.

What did this mean? Who could I ask? Later, on the Internet, I would learn that AD patients are almost ten times more likely to have seizures than non-epileptics without AD. None of Fred's doctors had ever mentioned that.

I hadn't planned to stay for dinner, but they had an extra plate, and the beef stroganoff looked good, so I stayed.

One of the aides said Fred had been talking about me earlier. She had asked who his favorite singer was. "Sue," he had said.

We ate in silence, smiling at each other every now and then. It was nice being there after dark, holding hands, making a connection.

But for how long?

On Dec. 3, I had cataract surgery on my left eye. I was young for it, but the Graves' disease, put into remission with radioactive iodine treatment, had permanently affected my vision, so here I was with the eighty-year-olds. The handsome Dr. Haines from Eugene came to Samaritan Pacific Communities Hospital in Newport once a week to do one cataract surgery after another.

The operation was relatively easy. Minimal soreness afterward, the vision in that eye significantly improved. The biggest problem was figuring out how to function with one eye done and the other still so nearsighted I couldn't see past my hand. But the cataract in my right eye wasn't advanced enough for surgery yet. I ordered a new lens for my regular glasses and removed the left lens on my computer/piano glasses. My eyes struggled to work together, and I avoided driving at night.

A week and a half after my eye surgery, I headed east to Albany. It was not my usual day or time, but the phone had been ringing all the previous day with calls from Timberwood. Fred had been hitting people and refused to take his meds. He shoved an aide up against a counter. An hour later, he was smiling and happy. Then he was crying.

The previous night after supper, they had put Fred on the phone. He was sobbing. We had had heavy rain with thunder and lightning. I didn't dare drive Highway 20 in the dark. I promised to come first thing in the morning, one-eyed or not.

When I met Rebecca, the activities director, in the lobby, she told me she had spent hours sitting with Fred, trying to calm him down. She got him to take a tranquilizer, but he couldn't stop crying. He was shaking. At one point, she saw that he was clutching his jacket and couldn't open his hand.

But now he was fine, all smiles and happy to see me.

We went out to the deserted activity room. When I couldn't make the TV work, I started singing "Jingle Bells." Fred joined me with a bass part he remembered from singing with the barbershop chorus. I moved from that into "Jingle Bell Rock." I sang every lively Christmas song I could think of. I didn't know all the words, but it didn't matter. Fred and I sang together and connected with harmony like we never had before.

I had worried about whether I should bring Annie or my guitar to give us something to do, but God seemed to be saying, "Just take yourself." It was enough.

An aide came to fix the TV, and we settled in to watch an old episode of *Gunsmoke*. But the music lingered in the air.

On the night we had first met at a party at my brother's house, when Fred was still married to Annette, and I was dating a druggie named Gerry, I had sat in the middle of the crowd singing Christmas songs. After we were married, Fred and I performed Christmas music with friends at parties, nursing homes, shopping malls, and anywhere else people would listen. Music remained the shining thread that held us together in spite of Alzheimer's disease. When in doubt, we sang.

That day, Fred seemed clear-headed. He even had a sense of humor. When I said I had to go, he said, "No!" but he was smiling.

I drove onto the freeway behind a truck bearing a sign that said GBF—Glory Bee Foods, glorybee.com.

Amen.

42 Scram, Santa Claus

I was back at Timberwood on Dec. 17 for the Christmas party, Fred's second one there.

All week, it had been one crisis after another. When Timberwood appeared on my phone's caller ID, I steeled myself for disaster. I missed the days when they called about shampoo or haircuts. Now he was falling and fighting with people.

The nurse had called that morning to tell me he had fallen again. Now I could see he had an abrasion on his forehead and another on the top of his head, both bloody and oozing through a smear of yellow ointment. No one, including Fred, knew what had happened. He told one person he fell, another that he hadn't.

Leaving Fred with the others in the dining area, I slipped away to the restroom, hoping as always that no one would come crashing through the unlockable door. If I could have avoided using the restrooms there, I would have, but it was a long drive and my bladder was full. On my way back, I looked around Fred's room for blood to try to figure out where his head hit. I didn't find any.

The Christmas party took less than an hour. Family members came. Santa and Mrs. Claus arrived, ringing bells, shouting "Oh, _____, I've got a present for you!" Santa posed for photos, urging the residents to smile. Most of them had no clue what was going on, and I worried about how Fred was taking all this commotion. I kept thinking, *Get that f-ing Santa Claus out of here*! These people weren't children. Why did the staff think they would get excited about Santa Claus?

The aides passed out cookies and candy. Fifteen minutes later, they were cleaning up, asking, "Did you have a good Christmas?"

The gifts I had brought for Fred confused him. He smiled at the pictures in the book on puffins. I had actually given it to him years ago, but he didn't remember. He also seemed pleased with the new sweatshirt, a gray zip-up hoodie that would keep him warm. "Did you bring these?" he kept asking.

Sam's daughter broke down during the party. Her mom had died a month earlier. Sam looked unshaved and disheveled. He kept yelling at people.

That afternoon, while we watched TV, someone stole Fred's new sweatshirt. I had left it on his bed after the party, but when I went back to his room, it was gone. I suspected staff. When I told Tina, she apologized and said she would replace it. She never did. I let it go.

I talked to Tina about money, too. Medicaid had sent me a letter saying that next year they were only going to pay $102 per month on Fred's nursing home bill. Even if it was a mistake, it would take months to set it right. The little economies I had been making, such as canceling my newspaper subscription and cutting back my cable TV service, wouldn't make much difference if I was a thousand dollars short.

Later, it would turn out to be an error, and I didn't miss a payment, but I felt doomed at that point.

Returning from the office, I found Fred dozing in front of *Bonanza*, twitching and clutching at his black pants. The weather forecaster on the radio had predicted snow. I needed to get home before the highway turned to ice. I kissed his head and said, "See you later."

Two days before Christmas, I got another call from Timberwood. Fred had been violent again, hitting and threatening aides and other residents. Kelli, the new nurse, wanted my permission to give him an antipsychotic drug.

"Go ahead," I said.

When I checked the local news, I learned there had been a head-on collision on Highway 20. The road was going to be closed for at least two hours. I waited until one o'clock to leave for Timberwood. Unable to face another visit alone, I took Annie with me.

The residents sitting around the living room were happy to see my dog, figuring she was there to visit everyone. She went from one to another saying hello, then settled in front of Fred. He laughed as she licked his ear. He didn't know who I was, but he was tickled to see the dog. He kept petting her, saying, "She's so good."

Somebody asked him if she was his dog. "No, it's hers," he said.

Leaving that afternoon, I saw a sympathy card on the front desk. Aggie had died. I wanted to cry. One by one, they all would die. Fred, who had always been so healthy, might last longer, but our turn would come.

From I-5, I could see the snow-covered Three Sisters mountain peaks. I turned onto Highway 20 at twilight, joining people driving home from work, most of them unaware there had been a head-on crash here earlier in the day. Annie slept in the back seat. I reached back and petted her soft fur.

I got sick that Christmas. A cold led to bronchitis, which led to a persistent cough. I coughed my way through the Christmas Eve Masses and let a music teacher friend handle the Christmas morning music while I lay plastered to my sheets until eleven. I considered staying home all day, but I dragged myself and my Jell-O salad to my friends David and Sandy's house in Newport. Since Fred had moved to Timberwood, I had spent most of my holidays with them.

Their tiny living room was a sea of wrapping paper and presents. Besides David, our lawyer, his parents, his wife Sandy, their two kids, and their widowed neighbor Orpha were there. Also Ziggy, their little black dog, three cats, and a hamster. My borrowed family.

I watched Sandy and David prepare dinner together, taking turns basting the roast in the oven and conferring on which bowls to put things in. Fred and I used to be like that, hosting parties as a team. But now I sat with Orpha and David's parents and watched Thomas play a video he'd gotten for Christmas.

When dinner was ready, we gathered around the big table, said grace, and feasted on roast beef, scalloped potatoes, green beans, Jell-O, and hot rolls. We popped poppers and played with the little toys we found inside. We oohed and aahed over the dozen different types of cookies Sandy had made for dessert.

While Sandy and David did the dishes, I played Christmas songs on the piano as everyone sang along. Then we retired to watch the movie *Shrek* on their big-screen TV.

When it was over, I headed home.

I sat in the glow of my Christmas tree lights with Annie and unwrapped food, money, clothes, books, bath soap, candles, ornaments, and a framed photo of me and Fred. If I tried hard enough, I could almost see Fred opening his own presents in the big chair in his red bathrobe. I could almost smell his Dutch baby popovers cooking in the oven. It felt wrong to be opening presents alone.

I was so tired. I had been waking up coughing every night for a week. I went to bed at nine o'clock, glad Christmas was over and I could relax into "ordinary time."

43 Off the Cliff

On New Year's Eve, I was waiting in line at a gas station in Corvallis when my cell phone rang. The marketing director, the only one on duty in the office at Timberwood on the holiday, said they had called an ambulance to take Fred to the hospital. She couldn't tell me what was wrong, only that he was complaining of pain in his belly.

The remaining twenty miles to Samaritan Albany General Hospital seemed to take forever. I ran into the ER, out of breath. Fred lay on the first bed, a doctor leaning over him.

"Hey," he said in a weak voice as I clasped his hand.

I looked at the doctor. "What's going on?"

Imagine having a patient who cannot tell you anything, not where it hurts, when it started, or what happened before. "It's hard to tell," the doctor said. "It could be appendicitis. We'll do a CT and find out."

I settled into the chair beside the bed to wait.

A half hour later, an orderly rolled Fred back in a wheelchair. The doctor followed. "Well, it's not appendicitis. His prostate is enlarged and blocking urination. We need to drain his bladder. Then we'll talk."

While three people held him down and a nurse shoved a catheter tube up his penis, Fred screamed, "No! No! Please, no!" Dark yellow urine gushed from the tube into a plastic bag. The nurses said they had never seen so much urine come out of a person. The normal adult bladder stretches to hold a maximum of about sixteen ounces before it gets expelled involuntarily. But that hadn't happened. The enlarged prostate had blocked the path between bladder and urethra so completely that Fred might not have urinated for days. No wonder he was hitting people.

The staff at Timberwood apparently had no idea. Fred had been relatively independent compared to other patients. He didn't need help going to the bathroom. They didn't know that nothing was coming out.

"We'll keep him catheterized for now and send him back to Timberwood with medication that should shrink his prostate a bit," the doctor said.

"Why is it so big?"

"It's not uncommon in men his age."

"But is it—cancer?"

"Not necessarily. But in light of the bigger picture—"

Fred's hands were trembling. He made gurgling sounds.

"He's having a seizure," the doctor said.

It wasn't the type of violent convulsions I had seen with other people who had epilepsy. I wouldn't have known it was a seizure if the doctor hadn't pointed it out. I was grateful he was there at that moment, resting a comforting hand on Fred's shoulder until the shaking eased.

"Change of plans," he said. "We'll do a head CT and keep him overnight."

"Thank you." Feeling a little shaky myself, I sank back into my chair until the orderlies came to take Fred to a room upstairs.

He remained unconscious in what's called a postictal state. "We can bring in a cot for you if you want to stay," the nurse said. "But you don't have to. He's not in any danger. He'll probably sleep for at least another eight hours."

I gazed at my unconscious husband. It was cold in that room, and I needed to get away for a while to process what was happening. "I'll come back in the morning," I said.

I spent the night at La Quinta Inn, celebrating New Year's Eve with

a box of powdered donuts from the 7-11 store and Dick Clark's *Rockin'
New Year's Eve* on TV. I had no one to kiss when the ball dropped in
Times Square, heralding the beginning of 2011.

It was hard not to compare that New Year's Eve with the turn of
the millennium eleven years earlier. On Dec. 31, 1999, Fred and I had
been in Oregon for three years and had looked forward to many more
years enjoying our life at the beach. We had our house, our dog, our
work, and our music. We had traveled the world together and were
going to Costa Rica in the spring.

New Year's Eve 1999 called for something more than our usual
snacks and champagne in front of the TV, so we bought tickets for the
celebration at the Newport Performing Arts Center. It was an elegant
affair. Fred wore his blue suit. I put on my long black velvet skirt and
my glittery top.

In the candlelit lobby, the guests hovered around tables stacked
high with hors d'oeuvres and glasses of champagne. On the main
stage, a jazz band played standards while a rock band warmed up in
the studio theater.

As midnight approached, we filled our glasses and gathered on
the stage with the band to count down the minutes. "Five, four, three,
two, one, Happy New Year!" We sipped, we kissed, and we hugged.
The band struck up "Auld Lang Syne," and we danced, singing into
each other's ears, happy, in love, a little drunk, and hopeful for this
new time just beginning. Around us, other couples did the same.

We had no idea that eleven years later Fred would lie unconscious
in a hospital bed while I ate donuts alone at La Quinta.

The next morning, Fred spoke mostly gibberish. The doctor on duty,
Dr. Singh, didn't seem to hear me when I insisted he had not been this
way two days earlier.

"Due to his advanced Alzheimer's," she said, "we will treat his
symptoms, but there's no need to do an EEG and other tests. I will

send the physical therapist in to check his mobility. If he can get up and walk, he can go home today."

"He lives in a nursing home."

She looked at her chart. "Yes, I see that."

And I could see that she was on her way out the door. "Wait. He's really different than he was a couple days ago. His memory was shot, but he could speak well. He usually knew what was going on. . . ."

"Yes. I understand. I will send his discharge papers later today."

I wanted to scream, but she was gone, and I didn't want to upset Fred or his roommate, a middle-aged man speaking quietly into his phone. I resumed my seat in the plastic chair beside Fred's bed.

He had fallen off the cognitive cliff. Now he made up words and animal sounds instead of English and looked at me as if I should understand. His hands shook so violently I had to feed him the macaroni and Jell-O an aide brought for lunch.

"Come on, honey, just a few bites," I urged, but he was a moving target. Most of the food fell on his hospital gown and his blankets.

He kept trying to wiggle out of bed, activating the alarm. He tugged the wires to his heart monitor and fussed with his catheter. I reached for his hand and guided it away from the tubes and wires. "Leave it alone, babe."

As soon as I let go, his hands started moving down again.

We waited three hours for the physical therapist.

The young man bustled in. "Hello! Is this Fred?"

"Yes."

"Well, let's get him going."

"Can you stand up?" he asked.

Fred stared at him.

"Come on, babe, try to stand up," I said, tugging at his arm.

He didn't move.

"That's okay. We'll just give him a boost."

Together, the physical therapist and I raised him to a sitting position and eventually to his feet. Holding Fred by a strap around his waist, the therapist walked him from the bed to the door and back.

He smiled at me. "Once he gets the concept, he can walk just fine."

"Right," I said, sick at how much my husband had changed overnight. How would he function at Timberwood now?

Over the next few weeks, Fred could not urinate normally, so he wore a catheter. He tried to pull it out and frequently succeeded. The female aides would gang up on him in his room to reinsert it while he screamed and struggled as if fighting for his life. Suffering infections and frequently backed up with urine, he kept returning to the hospital. The aides started dressing him in a onesie borrowed from another resident so he couldn't get to his penis. I had put off ordering them, but now I purchased two onesies online. Whatever dignity he had before was gone.

More than half of men in their seventies suffer from enlarged prostates, according to the National Institute of Health. Those without dementia notice the problem and see a doctor. They get treated with medication or surgery. Fred's problem had turned into a crisis because no one knew about it. He was still going into the bathroom on his own, but he couldn't find the words to tell anyone nothing was coming out. By the time he went to the hospital, his bladder was permanently damaged.

The nurse at Timberwood arranged an appointment for Fred with a primary care doctor whose office was nearby. I drove him there and led him into the waiting room, where he wouldn't sit still for a minute.

"What is this place? What are we doing here?"

"It's a doctor's office. We have an appointment."

"No. I want to go."

I could feel everyone in the waiting room watching me and my husband wearing a blue onesie. Please call us in, I prayed.

Finally a nurse led us to an examining room, where we met Dr. G., a middle-aged man with a crew cut and black glasses. He shook my hand and tried to shake Fred's, but he turned away. I couldn't get him to sit, so we stood.

Holding onto my husband lest he bolt, I waited for Dr. G. to speak.

He punched buttons on his computer, then turned to me. "Fred has a severely enlarged prostate and can't urinate on his own."

I nodded.

"Usually in such cases, we perform surgery to remove the tissue blocking the urethra. There are also a number of medications we could try to shrink his prostate, but in this case, in view of the big picture, surgery is not advisable. It might just be better to take out the catheter and let nature take its course."

My heart pounded. "Wouldn't he die?"

Dr. G. nodded. "Yes. His bladder would fill and overflow, his kidneys would shut down, and he'd pass away in a few days. We would make sure he didn't feel any pain."

What? Oh my God.

Fred's advanced directive specified he did not want any extraordinary measures. No respirators, no CPR, no feeding tubes. The doctor was trying to obey it. But the form didn't say anything about urinary catheters, and Fred was standing right there, confused and frightened but very much alive.

I knew what it felt like to have a full bladder and be unable to go to the bathroom for a few hours. What if that was multiplied by days or weeks? I couldn't think of a more horrible way to go.

My head was spinning. "Can we check with a specialist before we make a decision?"

"Sure." He typed a note. "I will make a referral."

I led my husband back through the waiting room. He could barely speak. And yet, coming out of the doctor's office, he pointed out a contrail in the sky. One of those little moments of *oh, he's still in there.*

He was otherwise physically healthy. If I let him die of a full bladder instead of making him comfortable with the catheter, wouldn't it be euthanasia? Wasn't I violating the rules of my Catholic faith? I consulted the Alzheimer's Association website. It said that limiting treatments was not euthanasia, that it let the disease take its natural course. That Sunday, I asked my priest. He told me to search my heart.

My heart wanted an easy way out. Most of us in our Alzheimer's support group hoped that a heart attack or stroke would take our loved ones before the Alzheimer's got as bad as it was going to get. But this was just an enlarged prostate.

At Timberwood, the man I loved walked around in his onesies, bent over and clutching at his penis. He battled with the aides and the nurse. Over the next few weeks, they kept sending him back to the hospital by ambulance to reinsert his catheter while I boomeranged between South Beach and Albany.

Every time the phone rang, it was Timberwood.

When I got home from the evening Mass on a Saturday in late January, there was a message on my phone. Fred had gone to the hospital again. No urine output all day, just a little blood. They would call back to let me know what was going on.

I waited. At nine o'clock, I called Timberwood. The night staff knew nothing. I called the hospital. An ER nurse said Fred had two clots blocking his catheter, and he had a urinary tract infection. He was agitated, swinging at people and trying to get out of bed. They had three guards and a nurse holding him down. He had been given Ativan, Vicodin, and Haldol. As soon as the drugs took effect, they'd send him back to Timberwood.

As I hung up, I collapsed into my chair, sobbing.

Every time this happened, I thought he was going to die.

44 Suprapubic

A french fry sat in the space between the seats in my car. My owner's manual was bent up from Fred clutching it. It had been a long day that started with a visit to a urologist.

I liked Dr. O. A no-nonsense woman with gray-streaked hair, she was smart and sympathetic. She never once said, "In view of the big picture . . ."

She showed me an ultrasound image of Fred's urinary tract. I couldn't make out what it showed, but she said Fred's prostate was huge. His bladder had been stretched so far out of shape that it might never function normally again.

"Prostate surgery might not do any good at this point," she said.

"So he'd have to keep wearing the catheter?"

"Yes. With the catheter, there will inevitably be infections, which will soon become resistant to antibiotics."

"Right."

"There is one thing we can do. It's a minor procedure in which we would insert a catheter through the pubic area directly into the bladder instead of the penis. It's called a suprapubic catheter. It would be more comfortable and less likely to get pulled out."

"Do you recommend that?"

"You're the decision-maker," she said.

Oh, my aching head. I needed to think about it.

I felt totally alone in this. I suppose I could have called Fred's children to help me make the decisions. Maybe I felt that if they cared enough they would already be there with me, that they would have been there all along. Maybe I knew they would insist I keep their father alive.

I could have asked my own family, too. My father might have sided with Dr. G. *Let him go.* Maybe not. When my mother was dying of cancer, when her doctors had insisted there was no hope, he still believed she could be saved—right up to the moment she died. He chided me when I talked about Fred as if he were already gone. "Don't talk like that. He's not dead yet."

But the man I had married *was* gone. The shell he'd left behind could not help me decide what to do, and the doctors were pressing for an answer.

Fred, sedated with Valium, lay naked and calm on the table in Dr. O.'s office. He didn't know where we were or why we were there. As Dr. O. replaced his catheter, she kept up a steady chatter, talking about food, dogs, and the weather to distract him.

In the car, when I leaned over to help Fred with his seat belt, he hugged me, not understanding what I was doing. A few minutes later, he looked at me as if he had just noticed me. "Hello!"

Our busy day wasn't over yet. We were going to a follow-up appointment with Dr. G. that afternoon. I bought burgers, fries, and soft drinks at Burger King to eat at Timberwood between appointments. At a table in the dining room, Fred tore his hamburger to pieces. He spilled his fries and drank only a few sips of Dr. Pepper. I wolfed my food down. We were running late.

"Let's go to my room," Fred said.

"No. We can't. We have another appointment."

Wishing I had a minute to empty my own bladder, I led him back to the car and drove to the medical complex.

Dr. G. echoed everything Dr. O. had said. Ruined bladder. Catheter forever. Maybe the suprapubic would work. Maybe I should let Fred go.

Back at Timberwood in the late afternoon, finally done with our appointments, I was so tired I knew I'd cry if anyone said a kind word to me. I took Fred to the activities area, kissed him goodbye, and headed out.

Tina caught me. "What did the doctors say?"

"Oh." I cleared my throat. "His bladder is shot. The urologist wants to insert a catheter directly into his bladder. She thinks that would be easier. Dr. G. thinks we should just remove the catheter and let him go."

Tina covered her mouth with her hand as tears filled her eyes. "I'm so sorry."

"Thanks. Does anybody else here have a catheter?"

She thought for a minute. "Just Frank. But he's gone."

"Gone? Where?"

"I'm not allowed to talk about it."

Privacy regulations. From the look in her eyes, I guessed good old toothless Frank the baker had died.

Dr. O. had made the suprapubic surgery sound like a simple procedure. Suprapubic catheters were often used for men who were paralyzed or who needed permanent catheterization, she said.

Researching online, I read posts by men who loved their suprapubic catheters because they gave them more comfort and freedom. It seemed like an easy solution to Fred's problem. Maybe we should do it.

That weekend, I was sick again. I knew it was going to be dicey playing the Sunday Masses. I had a cough and a runny nose. My chest hurt to the bottom of my ribs. At the first Mass, the choir's singing was off pitch and sloppy. At the second Mass, I started coughing during the homily and couldn't stop. I hurried out. In the vestibule, with its holy water basin and pebbled concrete floor, I coughed so hard I felt like I was turning inside out.

Through the beveled glass window, I watched Father Brian doing his homily. I didn't want to miss my cue, plus I was freezing, so I went back in.

Sermon over, I resumed my seat at the piano. I started coughing again, put my head down in my lap, and thought about going home. I coughed a cough drop onto my red tweed skirt and put it back in my mouth. My fingers were sticky and wet, and I couldn't see through my tears. I had nine pieces of music left. If anyone else could have played for me, I would gladly have surrendered my piano bench.

Afterward, people told me to get better.

How could I when I never got any rest?

Three days later, Dr. G. called me at dinnertime to talk about Fred's catheter problems. He was still pushing euthanasia. The Timberwood staff and I were torturing Fred with the catheter and all these trips to the hospital. The suprapubic catheter might be more comfortable, but Fred would try to pull that out, too. "In view of the big picture . . ." Dr. G. said again. Take out the catheter, let his bladder fill. Give him enough pain medication that he wouldn't feel anything, and he would drift away, dying of urinary retention. But it was up to me.

Why did it have to be up to me?

I walked around my kitchen saying, "Oh, my God" until it was time to sing for the kids at church. I squeaked through two songs on my own and did two songs with CDs. Catholic karaoke. As we sang, I forgot about Fred for a few minutes.

Choir practice followed the children's music. Halfway through, my phone rang. Timberwood. They had transported Fred by ambulance to the hospital with no output again. I prepared to head east, but before I hit Highway 20 and no cell service, I called for an update.

The hospital had already sent him home. I turned around.

When I arrived at Timberwood the next day, the nurse caught me at the door.

"We're sending Fred back to the hospital," she said. "We already called the ER and they're expecting him."

"What? Why?"

Catheter problems again.

"Don't call an ambulance. I'll take him," I said.

Mistake. Fred, who didn't recognize me, refused to get into the car. He clung to the door frame as a couple of aides fought to get him to bend and slide in.

At the hospital, parked at the emergency room entrance, he wouldn't get out. He held on with everything he had, terrified. A security guard helped me get him loose and into a wheelchair.

Who could blame him? Once again, he was stripped and placed on a gurney where nurses shoved a catheter up his sore penis. This man who never cursed hollered the whole time. "No! Fuck you. Leave me alone. Don't. Fuck!"

I don't even have a penis, but I could feel it.

Like the others, this ER doctor wanted to drain him and ship him back.

"No way," I said. "This keeps happening. Something needs to be done."

"Insurance won't cover it," he said.

"I don't care."

Fred stayed at the hospital, alternately sedated and wild while I sat beside him, staring through the bars on his bed. This could not go on.

Dr. O. called. She had an opening for the next day. She needed a decision about the suprapubic catheter. There was a good chance it wouldn't work, she said, but Fred was never going to urinate normally again, so this was our only option.

Was there a choice? I was exhausted. I was still sick. I was alone, and everybody wanted me to make decisions. I wasn't ready to let Fred go.

"Do it," I said.

That afternoon, when I came back from lunch, he recognized me. He said very clearly, "I'm in trouble."

"Yes, you are," I said. I grabbed his hand as it wandered toward his catheter.

"They're going to do this minor surgery," I began, but I realized Fred's moment of clarity had passed.

As I drove home, it was dark and raining. I gripped the steering wheel so tightly my hands hurt. "Oh, my God, oh, my God," I chanted.

I pictured the tube sticking out of him; it seemed barbaric, invading his body this way, cutting into the sweet vulnerable spot just above his pubic hair.

At home, Annie needed a walk. It was still raining, but I had to do something.

Close to home, we met a male yellow Lab. He and Annie started checking each other out, darting around me. I got tangled in the leashes and tripped as the dogs ran away.

"God damn it!" I screamed as I hit the rough pavement, skinning my knees and re-spraining my wrist.

Annie stopped to eat some stray substance, God knows what, and I grabbed her. A kid who saw me crash asked if I was all right. I said yes, but I doubt that I sounded convincing as I dragged my dog back toward home.

I wanted to crawl into bed and stay there.

The mailbox held an $1,100 invoice for Fred's first ambulance trip to the hospital in Albany.

Could we both check into hospice and quietly fade away?

The next day at my monthly therapy appointment, Reatha gave me tea, and I settled back in the big recliner.

We talked about The Decision: Put in the suprapubic catheter or let Fred die of urine retention? She said he wouldn't suffer because nitrogen builds up in the brain, the same as when one's kidneys fail, and patients gradually become less aware.

Putting in the suprapubic catheter was not much different from inserting a feeding tube, something Fred had specifically declined in his legal forms. Was this going too far, going against his will?

Reatha said I could tell the doctor I didn't want to make those life-and-death decisions. But if I did that, wasn't I deciding, especially since I knew what Dr. G. wanted to do?

45 Sunrise Northwest

The day after Fred's surgery, he looked half dead. His hands kept wandering toward his new catheter. A rolled-up bedspread blocked the way. An Ace bandage around his left arm kept him from getting at the IV dripping saline solution into his veins.

The doctor had said he could go "home," but he couldn't go back to Timberwood, at least not yet. The staff there was not equipped to care for post-surgical patients, so the hospital social worker had arranged to send him to Sunrise Northwest, a nearby skilled nursing facility. If the staff at Sunrise could get his catheter and his behavior under control, he could go back to Timberwood.

They transported him, still asleep, on a gurney in a black van. It was like taking him out in a hearse. I tried to follow in my car, but the van moved out of sight, and I took a wrong turn, so they were already unloading Fred when I got to Sunrise Northwest.

A long one-story stucco building, Sunrise sat next to low-rent apartments and down the street from an elementary school. It was hot and noisy inside, with TVs blasting the Super Bowl from many of the hospital-style rooms. I followed as the driver put Fred in a double room with a man who screamed about strangers invading his territory. "You people think you can come in and take over! I'm calling the police!"

"Are you Fred's daughter?" the nurse on duty asked.

"No, I'm his wife." I struggled to control my voice.

The room seemed clean, but the bathroom smelled like an outhouse. I used it in the dark because I couldn't find the light switch.

There wasn't any space for Fred's things, not even a chair for me to sit. At Timberwood, he had a private room with two easy chairs, a dresser and nightstand, a full-size closet, and a double bed. Now Fred was in a hospital bed crammed between a curtain and a wall, with a scarred-up, two-drawer nightstand and half a closet. The only decoration was a black cork board on which someone had made a smiley face out of push pins.

This is where you wind up when you're old and poor, I thought.

The nurse lifted Fred's hospital gown and checked his body for bruises and cuts. With existing wounds documented, they would know if new ones appeared while Fred was under their care. She issued him a toothbrush and attached an alarm to his gown. It was like being processed into jail.

I still hadn't seen the new catheter or talked to a doctor, only the hospital social worker, who had told me that he was not eating, his behavior was a problem, and he might slip away from an infection or other complication.

Fred lay on his back, oblivious to everything. The aides put a foam rubber pad beside the bed in case he fell. I wondered if he was purposely taking himself away like my mother had done toward the end.

A week earlier, he had been walking around. Maybe he would again. Maybe not.

As the afternoon passed, there was nothing more I could do. I couldn't seem to clear my throat. It was getting dark outside. I needed to go home before I made myself sick again.

Fred was going to wake up in a place where he had never been with people he had never seen before. He wouldn't have a clue what was going on, and I wouldn't be there. I ached with guilt.

I didn't see Fred awake for almost a week after his surgery, although the aides claimed he got up for breakfast. On the third day, a nurse called to report that he had fallen and was fighting everyone who tried to help him, so they had given him Ativan, a tranquilizer, and moved him to a quieter room with no roommate.

He was unconscious again when I arrived that afternoon. The administrator grabbed me on the way in to sign papers allowing them to give him Prozac, Seroquel, and Ativan, a powerful cocktail of anti-depressants and sedatives. She assured me it was safe.

When I got to Fred's room, he opened one eye.

"I see you looking at me," I said.

No response. I pulled a chair in from the small dining area across the hall and sat watching my husband sleep.

Once in a while, he raised his hand as if he wanted me to hold it. Sometimes he muttered something, but I couldn't hear or understand what he was saying.

I had hours with nothing to do but watch him. His hair was long, his beard overgrown. His hands would crawl toward his catheter. I'd move them away. Urine trickled down the tube and into the bag at the foot of the bed.

People talked loudly in the hall. Once he yelled, "What?"

"It's okay," I said.

I thought about how I would comfort my dog when she was having a bad dream. "It's okay," I whispered. She would sigh and relax. This seemed like the same thing.

I kept hoping for a flash of recognition from Fred. Nothing.

Before I left, I kissed him. He made kissing motions with his lips, perhaps an automatic response. At least he seemed peaceful, which gave me hope. Maybe in some way he knew I was there.

I hated the seventy-five miles between home and Sunrise Northwest. I was always watching the clock, trying to beat the darkness. Maybe I should have just stayed in Albany, but I still had work and Annie.

On Feb. 11, eight days after the surgery, I found Fred sitting in a wheelchair, gripping the electrical cord for the heater. I tried to talk to him, but before I could get a response, Camille, the facility's social worker, interrupted. She needed me to sign more papers.

When I came back to his room, Fred was in bed, asleep, fully dressed, with his shoes on, food particles in the treads, and his plaid jacket spread over him like a blanket. I lay down with my head on his chest, feeling like a young dog trying to get an old, sick dog to respond. *Wake up, play with me, be with me, be normal.* The old dog thinks, *Leave me alone, I'm dying.*

When I complained that I hadn't seen Fred awake in over a week, an aide said, "We walked him around earlier, and he was tired."

She woke him and put him in the wheelchair for lunch, brought in on a tray. Fred's shaking had subsided, but he no longer knew how to use a fork. On my first attempt to give him a bite of fish, I stabbed his lip.

"Ow!" His voice sounded pinched and high, as if he had something caught in his throat.

"I'm sorry, honey." I loaded his fork and gave it to him. He waved it all over, poking his beard, his cheek, and his lips, sending bits of fish flying.

Every bite was a victory. He didn't want any potatoes or spinach. He accepted a piece of peach. He picked up a lemon wedge, squeezed it, and it squirted onto my vest. He spilled his milk all over himself, the wheelchair, and me. I mopped him up and asked the nurse to bring him a straw.

He looked thin. I asked an aide what he weighed. 195. Fifteen pounds down since he left Timberwood.

Lunch abandoned, he wanted to get out of his chair. An alarm squealed. Just like at Newport Rehab, the folks at Sunrise Northwest wouldn't let him walk on his own. A tall skinny tattooed aide named Ty pushed him back into his chair.

"Damn it," Fred said in his squeaky voice as he fought to stand up.

"He wants to walk," I said.

Ty got a helper. They cinched Fred up with a thick elastic belt and shoved a walker in front of him. The other aide, a young woman, followed with a wheelchair. Fred stood bent over and hesitant, but he put one foot in front of the other. I followed along.

"He was walking on his own last week," I insisted. "He doesn't need to be in a wheelchair."

They weren't listening. Ty was busy coaching Fred. "One more step. That's right."

We walked to the end of the hall, turned around, and walked back. They put him in the wheelchair.

After the aides left, Fred muttered a bit, then turned away, resting his head on his hand. His eyes were closing, sleepy. I wanted that "Oh, you're here" recognition, but it wasn't going to happen. I kissed him on the head, told him I loved him, and left.

I already hated this place. Camille, the social service person, admitted Sunrise Northwest didn't give a good first impression. "If only people could just get through the door and see what we do here," she said.

I was still waiting to see it.

Friends kept asking if there was anything I needed. I didn't know. My life was all variations on horrible.

The liquid flowing into Fred's urine bag was orange. Was there blood in it, or was that how it was supposed to look when it came straight from the bladder?

I caught myself clenching my teeth and picking the skin off my lower lip. Soon I had an ugly scab, yet I kept picking. There was always another ragged edge. Anxiety kept me awake at night. When I turned off the TV and put away my books, all the thoughts I'd been barely holding off bombarded my conscious mind.

On Valentine's Day, I met Fred at the urologist's office. He came via wheelchair transport. His hair and beard looked ratty, and he smelled like sweat, but he lit up when he saw me. "This is my wife, Sue," he told the driver. It had been almost two months since he'd recognized me.

In the examining room, the nurse struggled to remove Fred's onesie.

A wide blood-stained elastic band around his waist constricted his belly but didn't cover the surgery site. When Dr. O. took it off, he said, "Oh!" and let out a big breath.

The suprapubic catheter looked like a thick yellow electrical cord coming out of his body. The stitched skin was red and raw around it. As the doctor examined him, I rubbed his chest and belly, trying to comfort him.

"Has he showered?" she asked.

"I don't know."

"Has he been pulling at his tube?"

"I don't know. Not when I've been with him."

"What meds is he on?"

"I don't know."

I felt like an idiot, but someone else was taking care of him.

She put a giant bandage over the site and taped up the tube so it wasn't pulling so much. She said it looked good. Come back in six weeks.

At Sunrise Northwest, we wheeled around the building, then settled in the front lobby. I played the piano, a beat-up cabinet grand, wishing I remembered something besides church songs. Unhooking the alarm, I helped Fred out of the wheelchair. He walked around the room, then sat on the sofa with me, watching people come and go.

A woman came in to visit her husband, a nicely dressed man in a wheelchair. She brought a big stuffed bear from the grandkids, a box of candy, and a card in a red envelope for Valentine's Day.

"I didn't get you anything," the man said.

"Yes, you did."

My heart broke a little more.

When they rolled away together, they were both eating chocolate.

Getting Fred back in the wheelchair took ten minutes of "Sit, come on, bend your legs, the chair is right here. . . ." I said a prayer of thanks when he finally landed in the seat. If he lost his balance and fell, it would be my fault.

It was late. I had to go. As I walked out to the parking lot, the sun came out, but I could hear Fred banging his wheelchair against the door. The concept of "I go, you stay" didn't work anymore.

I had told an aide that Fred needed to be helped back into bed, but the aide didn't move, so he sat there with nothing to distract him from watching me leave.

At Timberwood, as soon as the door closed, the hallway door blended into a solid beige wall. Here, the door opened into the world. He could see people coming and going in the parking lot. He wanted out.

46 Fighting

On a Monday morning, the phone rang. On Thursday night, Fred's suprapubic catheter had been partially ripped out, despite the stitches. The staff at Sunrise Northwest had waited all weekend to tell me or the urologist. They had sent him to the ER, had the Foley catheter reinserted into his penis, and let it go.

When I came in about eleven on Monday morning, he was sitting in his wheelchair, boxed in by the tray table and the curtain.

He looked straight at me and said, "I don't want to be here."

"I know you don't." I held his hand, noticing the hospital bracelet still on his wrist. He was wearing the same red polo shirt and blue sweats he'd had on when I visited a few days earlier. They were filthy.

We sat, so quiet I could hear my watch ticking.

Aides brought his lunch a little before noon: breaded pieces of nasty-tasting meat, potatoes, mixed vegetables, and a tiny wedge of cantaloupe. He drank his milk without spilling it but didn't want any of the food on his plate.

After lunch, I followed the wheelchair van transporting Fred to Dr. O.'s office in Corvallis.

"It's probably too late to fix it," she said pointing to the catheter hanging to Fred's bloody skin by a few stitches. "If they had called me when it happened, but . . . now we might have to do the surgery again."

"Oh, God. Really?"

"I know. This is so frustrating." She took a deep breath. "Let's wait a week and see if the wound heals enough to keep this catheter in." She typed something into her computer. "I'm writing an order that they need to hook the urine bag to his leg, not to the wheelchair. That's probably why it got pulled out."

No one at Sunrise Northwest was saying exactly what had happened, and Fred couldn't provide any answers, but it made sense.

As Dr. O. and Lisa, her assistant, cleaned and bandaged the surgery site, he kept crying out, "No, no, please!"

I wondered if we should tell him that without his catheter he would die and ask him if that's what he wanted. I didn't know whether he would understand, but nobody asked him.

Outside in the rain, my head hurt, and my sinuses were clogged. I needed a catheter to drain out the tears that needed to be released.

As I drove back to the coast, rain streaked the windshield. The sky got darker by the mile.

At Milepost 35, halfway home, my cell phone rang. Rosa from Sunrise Northwest said they were taking Fred back to the hospital. He had already pulled out the Foley catheter in his penis.

I smacked the steering wheel and cursed, but I kept driving west. It was supposed to snow that night, and I needed to get home. I couldn't help Fred.

Urinary retention was a stupid-ass thing to die of.

Six days later, I drove through a snow-covered landscape to meet Fred's older son, Ted, at Sunrise Northwest. I had been surprised when he called to say he was coming but was looking forward to some family support. On the phone, I had updated him on the catheter situation.

"God, I'm sorry you guys are going through all this."

"Thanks."

"So, he's in a different place?"

"Yeah." I gave him directions and agreed to meet at three o'clock.

I arrived first. Fred sat in his wheelchair, holding the curtain, working it with his fingers. He had lost almost thirty pounds in three weeks. His head looked indented. His arms and legs were sticks, and his back looked knobby.

When I complained about Fred's weight, the nurse said they needed a doctor's orders to give him the nutrition supplement shakes they called TwoCal.

"Just do it," I said.

When Ted got there, Fred gripped his hand. Ted said he thought he heard him say, "I'm ready to go." He took that for the greater meaning of ready to die. I don't know. Maybe he was just ready to go back to bed or to go home.

His lips were crusty. Ted wiped them with a wet paper towel and got him some water. Fred drank as if he was dying of thirst.

He still had the catheter bag attached to his wheelchair instead of his leg, despite the doctor's orders.

Ted kept saying he was grateful to me for sticking by his dad and taking care of him.

What else could I do? I was glad he got a clear look at how things were. I hoped he would share that information with the rest of the family and get someone to help me. I knew the kids were all busy with their lives, and they had issues with their father that started before I met him, but he was in bad shape.

Taking a break in the unoccupied dining room while an aide checked Fred's catheter, Ted asked, "Have you made plans for a funeral?"

"No. He's still here."

"Sue, you need a plan."

Leave me alone, I thought. "Okay, I know Fred wants to be cremated and that we will probably place his ashes in the mausoleum in Newport with your grandparents and your Uncle Don. As for a funeral, I don't know whether we should do it in Newport or go back to San Jose, where it would be easier for family and friends who live there."

Ted shrugged. "In the end, it's up to you."

"But what do you think?"

"It doesn't matter to me. Do what's best for you."

The aide interrupted. "You can go back in."

Back in Fred's room, Ted held his father's hand, talking louder than usual. "Well, Dad, I hope you feel better soon. It's time for me to take off. You're in good hands here. I love you."

Fred just stared at him.

I walked him to the door. Ted cleared his throat, "I know it's rough, Sue. Thank you for everything you're doing."

"I'm his wife."

We hugged, and he walked across the parking lot to his car while I went back to sit with Fred. "More water?" I offered.

He shook his head.

When we returned to Dr. O.'s office on March 2, she checked Fred's incision; the suprapubic hole had sealed up. "It's just too late. Do you want to try again? I can schedule him for surgery on March 15. He could wind up back in the hospital before then."

"I know." The catheter in his penis was at risk every second. "I guess we should do it."

"Okay. I'll set it up."

"He's not eating. He has lost a lot of weight."

"It's the Seroquel," she said. One of the "harmless" drugs from the nursing home. At this rate, the damned pee problem was going to kill him. That and the nursing home. They were taking away the last bits of his life. He wasn't eating or drinking enough to keep a mouse alive. He turned down food, but he was thirsty. He drank two cups of water from the cooler in the waiting room and would have drunk more if I had given it to him.

When we were finished with the doctor, I called the wheelchair ride service hired by the nursing home. The driver said she couldn't come back for about twenty-five minutes. I took Fred outside, parked him a couple yards beyond the door, and set the brake.

Suddenly Fred stood up. Wobbly, he started to walk by shoving his left foot ahead and catching his right foot up. Afraid he would fall, I dropped my purse and put my arms around him. We hugged. He was so thin and weak he didn't feel like Fred anymore.

"I love you," he whispered. He wanted to kiss me. His beard was so full of food and snot I just gave him a quick peck on the lips then kissed his cheek.

He kept inching toward the parking lot as I held him up. The farther we got from the building, the colder it was. When we got about twenty feet from the chair, he started shaking. There was no one around. I couldn't reach the wheelchair or my phone. Should I holler for help?

Fred started working at my clothes with his hand, pulling at my sweater. I moved his hand, and it went down to my butt. He probably didn't know he was touching my clothes, not his.

We stood there like that until the driver showed up. She waved, probably thinking it was sweet that we were hugging. I yelled, "We need the wheelchair *now*!"

I wanted so badly for Fred to be able to stand and walk, but he couldn't hold himself up anymore.

It took forever to get him seated and into the van. As I explained about his Alzheimer's, the driver's eyes filled with tears. "I'm so sorry."

"Thank you." I squeezed Fred's shoulder. "Bye, honey."

No response.

Before I returned to Sunrise Northwest, I stopped at Elmer's in Corvallis and ordered the crab Benedict. I sat in a pretty booth with flowered curtains and lots of light. I couldn't afford it, but I needed a few minutes of normality before facing the nursing home again.

I pictured an aide at Sunrise Northwest offering Fred breaded meat, mushy vegetables, soggy fruit and a milk drink from a carton.

He would seal his lips up tight and refuse all but the drink, which he would dribble into his beard and down his shirt.

I couldn't do a thing about it.

When I got back to the nursing home, I complained about Fred's weight, now down to 174, and told Camille that Fred was having the suprapubic surgery again. Dr. O. was pissed, and so was I. The catheter had been pulled out on their watch and now Fred had to start over with another surgery because of their negligence in reporting it. I stood in front of her desk, waiting for her response.

"I guess we screwed up. I'm sorry. If it helps any, the nurse who was on duty that night doesn't work here anymore. Do you want to file a grievance?"

"No. What good would it do at this point? It wouldn't help Fred. What about the Seroquel?" I asked. "Dr. O. said that's why he's not eating." I remembered Elena from Su Casa back in the early days telling me nursing homes drugged their patients until they died. That wasn't true at Timberwood, but it seemed to be happening at Sunrise Northwest.

"I'll have the nurse talk to the doctor." Rubbing her forehead, she said, "I'm having a bad day."

My temper flashed. "You want to trade lives with me? Your husband isn't dying of Alzheimer's, and you have a job!" I walked out, trying to ignore the hurt on her face.

I wouldn't want her job. Multiply me times however many residents Sunrise Northwest housed, and I could understand how she'd have a headache.

47 Tsunami!

On March 11, a few days after Fred's catheter fiasco, my phone woke me a little before six thirty. I was sure the nursing home was calling, but it was not. My Aunt Suzanne, whom I was supposed to meet in Albany that afternoon, wanted to let me know that my cousin in Hawaii was safe and to tell me that Annie and I could share her hotel room if we needed a place to stay. Why would we?

I had stayed up until midnight watching horrifying scenes of an earthquake and tsunami in Japan. Helicopter video showed the ocean chewing up bridges, houses, hotels, cars, and boats as if they were toys. Two women stood waving white cloths from the second story of a blue-roofed building that was surrounded by water. Hundreds, perhaps thousands of people died. Fires burned, untended.

Tsunami warnings had been issued for Hawaii and all of western North and South America, but nothing was expected to hit Oregon until one o'clock the next day, and my house was not in the danger zone.

I turned on the radio and found my oldies station in nonstop news mode. We had been upgraded from a tsunami watch to a warning. Now the surge was supposed to come at seven fifteen that morning. Schools had been closed and low-lying areas evacuated. The roads were crowded with people trying to get to higher ground or to park where they could watch the waves.

I looked out my window at the trees standing perfectly still against the powder blue sky. Nothing had changed at my house. It was hard to believe things were so different elsewhere.

I carried the portable radio around with me, stubbornly pursuing my routine: bathe, feed the dog, eat my breakfast, put on my clothes. I worried about my friends who lived in the pink house overlooking the ocean. What about the Bayfront, the Performing Arts Center, the aquarium, and the shops in Nye Beach? Would they all be turned into kindling and floating bodies? What about our brick church on the ocean side of the highway? Was it safe?

TV news broadcast pictures from beaches far north of us. The waves went out, the waves came in. One commentator said it was like watching somebody mow the lawn. Around seven thirty, the tide pulled back farther than usual and rolled in a little closer but well within the bounds of the beach. Was that it? My oldies station started playing rock and roll again. The TV station repeated the pictures from Japan. It was over. My trees were still standing, calmly stretching into the sky.

I turned on my computer. Back to work.

That afternoon, I met my aunt at Sunrise Northwest. She was only a couple years older than I was, and I usually just called her Suzanne. She was considerably younger than my Uncle Bob, who was eleven years younger than my mother and a year younger than Fred.

Uncle Bob, who had died three years earlier, had been a quadriplegic for forty years. Suzanne had met him in the spinal cord unit at Stanford Hospital, where she was working as a nurse. She knew her way around hospitals and nursing homes. When I explained the suprapubic situation, she nodded. "I've heard of some quads and paraplegics going that route. Bob and I never really considered it. For Fred, I don't know. They're redoing it later this week?

"Yes."

"I hope it turns out better this time."

I led her to Room 109, where Fred was sleeping.

She stroked his face. "Hey, Fred."

No response.

"Suzanne is here," I said.

Nothing.

I pulled in a chair from the dining room for her while I sat in Fred's wheelchair. We watched tsunami news on the TV, made and received calls on our cell phones, and took turns holding Fred's hands.

Lunchtime came and went.

"You say he's not eating. What if we bring him something special, something that's not hospital food?" Suzanne suggested.

"Maybe."

But what? We settled on a vanilla milkshake from the Burgerville two blocks away.

When we came back, two aides transferred him to his wheelchair. He stared into space, not responding to anyone.

The staff had told me he had been "perkier" since they reduced the Seroquel. Really?

Suzanne offered him the milkshake. He pushed it away, but she insisted he at least taste it. He did. He liked it. We rolled down the halls with Fred while he chugged most of the drink.

When we returned to his room, Fred rolled up close to the TV and stared at the nonstop tsunami pictures. "Park," he said. "Park." I didn't know what he meant. The TV showed fires, explosions, people running, waves washing away houses and cars. I clicked through the channels, stopping at *Little House on the Prairie*.

I hugged him and told him I loved him.

Suzanne and I ate a late lunch at Elmer's. Then I went home, and she went back to La Quinta. She left in the morning to visit friends who lived elsewhere in Oregon.

On March 15, four days after the tsunami, my phone rang at six forty-five in the morning. A nurse wanted to know when I would get to the hospital. "Later," I croaked and went back to bed. The phone rang two more times. The hospital needed my written permission before they could begin Fred's surgery to insert the new suprapubic catheter. I got up, dressed, and drove to Albany.

Hours later, I was sitting in the waiting room when a nurse came looking for me. After the surgery, Dr. O. had found that the bladder was not draining. The tube was too close to the enlarged prostate. She wanted to redo the surgery. I signed another permission form.

Fred had a double dose of general anesthetic that day. I sat with him in the recovery room for hours, staring at the fish picture taped over the fluorescent light, watching the heart monitor, and listening to the conversations outside our curtained area. Occasionally Fred twitched or moaned, but he was clearly not going to wake up for a long time. When an orderly arrived to wheel him to a room upstairs, I headed back to South Beach. Please God, I prayed, let it stay in this time.

Over the next couple weeks, there were no more problems with Fred's catheter. In addition to the one in his bladder, he still had a catheter in his penis, with urine draining into two plastic bags. If all went well, Dr. O. would remove the Foley at his next appointment, and we could look forward to getting Fred back to Timberwood.

Or so we thought. On March 31, the phone jolted me out of the story I was working on.

"I'm very sorry," said Tina, the director at Timberwood, "but I need you to take Fred's belongings out of his room."

"What? Why?"

"He won't be able to come back. He's progressing in a negative direction. He's mostly unresponsive, and he needs full-time nursing. We can't hold his room any longer."

Fred had been at Sunrise Northwest for almost two months. If someone had said a few weeks earlier, "You need to get his stuff out by the end of the month," I could have made plans, but now it was just me with a sore back and no truck.

For weeks, Camille had talked about calling Timberwood, about people not calling back, while I tried to keep my schedule open to move Fred "home" to his pretty room, his friends, better food, and better care. No one told me that a Timberwood nurse had evaluated Fred and decided he couldn't come back.

At home, my pellet stove wasn't working, and the house was freezing. I didn't have the time or money to get it serviced. I had screwed up my taxes, and now I owed $761, due in two weeks, but I didn't have time to deal with that either. I had to go to Timberwood and remove all of Fred's clothes, pictures, knickknacks and personal items.

After a quick, angry drive to Albany, I walked into the familiar lobby, told Kim at the front desk what was happening, and got to work piling pictures and clothing on the bed in Fred's room. I held onto my tears until I remembered the locked box in his closet. There, I found Fred's shaving kit, which had been with us on so many trips.

I felt like Fred was dead. I knew he was never going to use most of this stuff again. I sat in his mother's old mauve chair and cried.

The bedroom set we had bought at Roby's was still there. When I pulled the sheets off the bed, the cream-colored mattress, not quite two years old, was stained with shit and blood. No one was ever going to want that mattress. I covered it with a sheet and left it.

On my fourth trip to the car, one of the administrators asked if I needed help. At that point, no. It was too late.

An aide asked, "Is Fred coming back? We miss him so much."

I shook my head and hurried out to the car.

As I returned for one last load, staff and residents called, "Hi, Sue." I was part of the family there. But I had been exiled along with Fred.

I passed Sam's room. Just turned ninety, he sat in his easy chair with his afghans, pictures, and memorabilia.

It seemed like I had just been there for the Halloween party. The trees outside had been full of gold, orange, and rust-colored leaves. Now it was raining. Outside Fred's window, the trees were bare.

In the car, shaking, I looked through Fred's old black wallet: library card, picture of Fred and me, another of his parents, Golden Age passport for the parks, aquarium membership card, Blue Shield card, Medic Alert Safe Return card, and his driver's license, which was good for two more years. It was all useless to him now.

At Sunrise Northwest, Fred slept. He was naked, except for his diaper and a pair of studded white socks with "Salvation Army" printed on them. Occasionally he wiggled his toes and stretched. Sometimes his hand wandered down, pulling at the elastic band around his waist.

I sang softly with the radio, hoping he would know I was there. His blinds were closed, and his room felt like a little spot of calm in a crazy world.

Camille said Fred could stay at Sunrise Northwest as long as I wanted him to. She didn't think it mattered to him where he was. She talked about the "progression." I kept hearing that word now, "progression."

There was no place at Sunrise Northwest to put all the things I had taken from Fred's room at Timberwood. He didn't need them anyway. I took them to the house and piled them on his bed, where nobody slept anymore.

48 Yes

A week later, the sky turned blue-black and broke open with thunder, lightning, and hail. It rained hard all the way from South Beach to Highway 20, turned to sleet on the hill, and stopped when I got to Corvallis. Now as I waited for Fred at the neurologist's office, it was raining again.

I was shocked when the driver from the wheelchair transportation service rolled him in. Fred's lips were swollen, the skin on his hands flaky, his legs like sticks. He was wearing someone else's clothes, blue sweatpants and a print top. His beard was freshly trimmed, but his eyes were bloodshot, and he looked terrified.

Dr. L. bustled in, shaking our hands as usual. He tried to check Fred's eyes but had trouble getting Fred to look at him. He ordered a blood test to determine the level of drugs that Fred was taking. Fred kept moving his arm, making it difficult for the nurse to insert the needle.

"Is it the drugs making him so out of it?"

Dr. L. shook his head. "The disease is progressing. His brain is deteriorating."

"How much longer do you think it will be?"

"Not too long." He pointed to Fred's catheter tube trailing from his pants to the bag attached to the wheelchair. "He's got some blood in there."

Red and orange globules floated in the urine. "An infection?"

"Maybe. But at this point I wouldn't recommend treating it with antibiotics."

"No?"

"He would quickly become resistant to the drugs, so ultimately it wouldn't help much." Dr. L stood and reached across Fred to shake my hand. "Hang in there."

"Thank you for everything."

He rested his hand on Fred's shoulder. "Take care, my friend."

On the way out, we scheduled an appointment for six months later, just in case.

While Fred rode back to Sunrise Northwest in the van, I drove to Timberwood to get my mother-in-law's chairs, which I hadn't been able to fit in the car before. I told Tina to give the rest of the furniture to charity.

At Sunrise Northwest, I found Fred sitting up in bed. I sat in his wheelchair and rolled it up close. I held his hand and stroked his face, his chopped beard, and his bony shoulders and chest. I sang along with the radio and looked out the window, watching children walking down the street on their way home from school.

When someone shouted down the hall, Fred startled. "What's happening?" he whispered.

"Not much."

He raised his hand and clasped mine. On the radio, Rod Stewart sang "Sunny Side of the Street." We tapped the beat with our hands.

I wanted to talk, play music, do something, but maybe he got tired of people talking at him. Maybe I was the only person who touched him gently with no purpose other than to connect.

The rain had stopped. Sun shone through the window. Little kids ran around in the street outside.

I wanted to stay because he seemed to know me, but he was falling asleep. I kissed his forehead, told him I loved him, and left.

* * *

That night I slept badly, with nightmares. In the morning, I couldn't write. I didn't want to do anything. I dressed in one of Fred's flannel shirts and my old jeans. In the mirror, with my hair cut short because I didn't have the energy to deal with it, I looked like a tired old man. Earrings and a necklace didn't help much.

I took the chairs still in my car to the storage locker we had rented for Fred's mother's things and never gotten around to cleaning out. It was raining, and the lock was rusted shut. I went home and got a can of WD40, came back, and sprayed it on. Still no go. I was so tired of trying to handle everything myself, tired of being almost-widowed, horrified by Fred's decline, discouraged about work, money, and all the things falling apart in the house.

I drove to the jetty. Now the sun was shining again, that fickle orb that kept hiding behind clouds. A white-breasted gull stood on its rock and stared evenly at me as I sobbed, gasping and wailing until the gentle blue surf gradually took my attention away from my woes. Was that a sea lion moving on the rocks? Damn these glasses that didn't quite work with only one of my cataracts fixed. Yes, there were several sea lions lying on the rocks.

Another gull soared nearby, put down his yellow feet, and landed neatly on the rock to my left. It occurred to me that I had had that experience of landing, placing my feet on solid ground. But I had never flown. Was it in my dreams? Gradually it came to me. In swimming, I sometimes put my feet down just like that. Swimming was like flying in water. I remembered laughing with Fred at the aquarium birds. Even when he wasn't on duty as a docent, he loved to tell people about the auklets, oystercatchers, puffins, and gulls.

I returned to the storage lockers again. The WD40 had sunk in, and the lock opened. I wrestled the massive chairs out of the car and into the locker, slammed the door shut, and clicked the lock. Victory.

* * *

Fred was leaning over in his wheelchair in his blue sweats and blue aquarium shirt, both dirty.

"Hi," I said."

Nothing.

I tried to touch his face.

He ducked away.

I stretched my foot out to touch his and he pulled his foot back.

My guitar was still in the car from church choir practice the night before. In desperation, I brought it in and started singing Fred's favorite songs. Every time I stopped, he looked at me or put out his hand like he wanted more. Sometimes he moved his lips a little. He might have tapped his foot to the beat so slightly it was hard to tell.

I had asked the staff about his weight. They hadn't weighed him since April 2, when it was 174. He weighed less than that now. His bottom was so small.

The aide brought in his lunch: beef stroganoff, peas, a roll, and angel food cake with chocolate frosting, plus three cartons of protein shake. He wouldn't touch any of it. When she tried to feed him, he ducked away, saying, "No." He drank one of the shakes, then refused more. He burped and whispered, "Excuse me."

It's strange how some things stick with people.

When I offered him his drink again, he sighed.

"Oh, babe," I said.

It was time for me to go. I kissed him on the forehead, told him I loved him and that I'd be back.

I left to a chorus of staff saying, "You have a beautiful voice."

Singing felt like the only thing I knew how to do at that point.

Driving west under dark clouds backlit with sunlight, daffodils blooming alongside the road, I felt more thoughtful than sad. Not long ago, we could hold hands. Now we didn't even have that connection.

Fred was not eating. Did he want to check out, or were the drugs making everything taste bad? Was it time to let him go?

I don't know why I didn't stay in Albany, close to Fred. I could have gotten a dog-sitter. Someone else could have played for me at church. I guess I felt like this could go on forever, and I needed my routine. Probably I couldn't face the fact that Fred was truly dying, that it was time to call everyone and go into crisis mode.

When I met Fred at the urologist's office the following week, I could see he was more tuned in. His eyes looked brighter. He seemed to be aware of his surroundings. He locked eyes with me several times.

Red streaks and clots floated in his catheter tubes. As I held his hand, Dr. O's assistant, Lisa, pulled the Foley out of Fred's penis and replaced the tube for the suprapubic as Fred said, "No. No."

While we waited for the doctor, he stared at me and said, very clearly, "Mer." He said it twice. There seemed to be recognition, a "Hey, it's you." But Mer?

Dr. O. bustled in. She checked his incision and his catheter tube.

"It looks fine," she said. "The people at Sunrise Northwest should be able to manage it—unless it gets pulled out again. If it does, they need to get him back here within twenty-four hours."

"I will remind them."

Once more, I followed the van back to Sunrise Northwest. It was a gorgeous day, the fields deep green, the sky blue with puffy clouds, the air smelling of mowed grass. I hated to go inside, but I went in and sat on Fred's narrow bed while he remained in the wheelchair.

This was our first good visit in ages. Fred looked around, seeming to actually see things. He talked quite a bit, although his words were almost impossible to understand. He smiled at me now and then, almost laughed once. He tried to sing along with the music on the radio.

We made silly noises and winked at each other. When it was time to go, I kissed him, hugged him, and told him I loved him. As I started to walk away, Fred said something. I turned back. "What?"

"Yes."

That was the last word he ever said to me.

49 The Call

The first call came while I was singing during the Good Friday Mass. The nurse's message said Fred had fallen and "taken a turn." When I called back, she thought he was doing a little better. I went to bed with the phone next to me.

The phone rang at two thirty in the morning. The night nurse said it looked like Fred was dying. I got up, put on my clothes, and waited for daylight so I could see to drive. At five thirty, I couldn't stand it anymore and called Sunrise Northwest.

"Mr. Lick expired a few minutes ago," the nurse said.

"He died?"

She repeated the same words again.

Dear God. He died, and I wasn't there.

I woke Fred's kids to tell them the news.

Michael already knew. The nursing home had called him. Apparently, it was their policy to alert the nearest child, based on the assumption the wife would be old and unable to handle the news. If I weren't in shock, I would have been furious. I was the wife, the one who was always there. Why didn't they call me?

Gretchen was crying when she picked up the phone.

"Honey, I'm so sorry. Your dad just passed away."

"I knew what you were going to say," she said, sobbing. When her grandfather died, she had had a vision of him saying goodbye and knew he was gone. Now she had known about her father without being told.

Ted took the news calmly. He had been expecting it. "He was ready to go."

"I know."

"Let me know what your plans are. I probably won't be able to come up, but I'm there in spirit."

It was still dark, and I needed to get to Albany. I called my friend Pat. "I'll be right there," she said.

I hugged Annie, soaking her fur with my tears. "Our Fred is gone."

The sun had just come out when Pat arrived. A robin sang in a tree beside the garage. As we drove east into the rising sun, Pat talked about her mother, who had died of Alzheimer's at a facility not far from Timberwood.

When we got to Sunrise Northwest, I grabbed Pat's hand. "I feel like I'm twelve years old. I'm not nearly old enough for this."

A curtain hid Fred's bed. Pulling it back, I saw him and became hysterical. His mouth was open, he had blood in his beard, and his skin was cold. My friend held me as I sobbed and shrieked and said goodbye to my husband for the last time. I knew his body was just a shell for his spirit, that Fred wasn't in it anymore, but I had made love to it, slept with it, and taken care of it. I would never see it again.

At the same time, I was grateful he had escaped to a world where Alzheimer's disease did not exist.

The sun was shining bright that morning as we loaded Fred's clothing and his wheelchair into Pat's car and called the mortuary to arrange to take Fred's body back to Newport. I began making phone calls to my family and friends on our way to breakfast at Elmer's, where I had often stopped for lunch before visiting Fred.

After each call, I'd cry a little, then dial the next number.

It felt so strange sitting in a restaurant, ordering breakfast as if it were an ordinary day. What would we say if the waitress asked us how we were?

At home hours later, before my father and brother and Fred's kids arrived, I lay on the deck and marveled at a big rainbow around the sun. Maybe Fred was giving me a sign. He was okay now. I could rest.

I mourned, but I also felt my recovery beginning. Fred had been dying for years, and I had been grieving all that time. I had already cried so hard I thought a person could not survive such convulsions. Sometimes I saw nothing ahead but darkness. But now, I felt something positive, a coming out the other side of the tunnel into the sunlight, and something else: satisfaction. Our marriage was complete. We had loved deeply, vowed to stay together to the end, and we had done it, supporting each other, helping each other, never cheating, never doubting our love. It had been a good marriage, a successful marriage. Now we were both free to move on.

I brought Fred's radio home. Anytime I wanted, I could push the button and hear "Music of Your Life," feel his arms around me, and hear him singing in my ear. It would never be the same, but he was there.

At his funeral in Newport, we played big band music as his friends and family gathered to honor his life. My father and brother were at my side, along with Michael and Gretchen and Fred's ex-wife Annette. Ted was unable to come. On a table at the front of the funeral home chapel sat a glass of wine, Fred's aquarium cap, and a big picture of Fred as we all remembered him.

My church choir sang, the barber shoppers sang, and if my father hadn't been sitting next to me, I would probably have jumped up and sung along. I'm sure Fred was singing the bass part in heaven.

50 Bubbles

Fred's death felt more like an emptiness than a shock. After nine years living with Alzheimer's disease, I could move on.

I was already used to living alone. It had been two years and three months since Fred had fallen and gone into full-time care. I still couldn't sleep in the bed we had shared. Too many memories. But I could handle cooking for myself, doing the household chores, and paying the bills. I knew widows who had never written a check or filled their own cars with gas. When their husbands died, they didn't know how to take care of themselves. But I had never been that kind of woman. My parents had always pushed my brother and me to figure things out for ourselves. Fred was not my first husband. After my first marriage ended in divorce, I lived alone for three years in Pacifica, a beach town just south of San Francisco. I had traveled for my work and spent a great deal of time on my own. It wasn't what I wanted, but I could live without a man.

Fred died on Holy Saturday, the day before Easter. The following Wednesday, I was back at church singing with the kids in religious education. A month later, I traveled to Washington to research articles on an outdoor art gallery and a wolf sanctuary. I cried when I needed to, but I kept going.

Oddly, I missed my trips to Albany. Without them, some days felt so incredibly long. I had work and Annie and countless people and agencies to notify about Fred's death, but that still left empty hours on evenings and weekends. I used some of that time to go through Fred's things. I sorted photographs and sent them to his brother and the kids. I hung the big photo from his funeral on the wall above his side of the bed. I kept his blue suit, his red Hawaiian shirt, and his aquarium jacket jingling with badges. I shifted his flannel shirts to my side of the closet and started wearing them. The rest I donated to Goodwill. His sons were too tall to fit in Fred's clothes, although I did send them some of his neckties.

The first holidays and anniversaries were difficult, but other unexpected moments hit harder. When I saw couples holding hands or kissing, it gutted me. When I didn't hear from my stepchildren after the funeral, it hurt. I flinched when people who hadn't seen me for a while asked, "How's your husband?" or when callers on the phone asked to speak to Fred. My heart ached when the barber shoppers insisted I come to their fall concert, and I didn't see Fred in the bass section, when I attended a party alone and found myself with no one to talk to, when I had to carry all of my music equipment up a steep flight of stairs to play for a garden tour with no one to help or cheer me on, when I thought about how I might never have sex again . . .

I frequently fell into the swamp of depression and grief, but I was always able to climb out. I continued my therapy sessions with Reatha and took my antidepressants. I still battled anxiety and restless legs, but I had the tools to keep going. I had faith in God and was grateful for the talents he had given me. Fred had shared his optimism, his lifelong "yes."

I had Annie. I had the friends who had filled the chapel at Bateman's Funeral Home for Fred's service. We had arrived in Oregon knowing only our realtor, but now my life was full of wonderful people. Many widows relocate after their husbands die. I knew it seemed odd to live alone in a four-bedroom house in the middle of nowhere, but I planned to stay. It was my home.

Of course, there were moments of frustration. I'd stand in the garage looking at all the tools I had no idea how to use and shout, "Why did you die before showing me how to use this stuff?"

The summer day I figured out how to change a spark plug on the lawn mower was a triumph. "Hey, Fred, I did it!" I shouted.

Money was tight, but with careful planning and the frugality I inherited from my father, I got by. When I turned sixty in March 2012, eleven months after Fred died, I qualified for survivor benefits based on his Social Security. I waited on hold on the phone for over an hour to speak to a representative. When she told me how much money I would receive, I screamed in her ear, "Oh, thank God! Thank you so much!" And yes, I cried again. It wasn't a fortune, but it was enough to make a difference.

A month after the funeral, Pat and I went shopping at the outlet stores in Lincoln City. I had been wearing subdued colors, not all black like my Portuguese ancestors would have, but nothing flashy. Then I found the most beautiful red shoes.

"Pat, would it be okay if I wore red shoes?"

"Of course. Get 'em."

Exactly what Fred would have said.

I wore them to church the following Sunday. I was going to be all right.

As the first anniversary of Fred's death approached, I knew I had to commemorate the day.

In 2002, after my mother and mother-in-law had died, I had started the ritual of the bubbles. Fred and I went to a cliff overlooking Nye Beach, and we blew soap bubbles, watching them float out over the sand toward the ocean. Some popped on the fence or the grass nearby, but others soared until they disappeared into the sky. With these bubbles, we set our mothers' spirits free.

"Go, bubbles," I said. "Take our mothers' spirits places they couldn't go before. Carry away, too, all our grief and pain. Let us keep only the love, the memories, and the lessons they taught us."

It was time to do the same with Fred.

Where should I go to blow bubbles? Nye Beach? Yaquina Head Lighthouse where Fred loved to watch the sea birds? The aquarium? On this sunny afternoon with a light breeze, I was drawn to our own vast backyard surrounded by trees.

I used the deck for a stage, singing to Fred as I had so many times when we were together. Fred was my biggest fan, always in the audience clapping harder than anyone else. For years, I used to end each performance with "Wind Beneath My Wings," dedicated to him. I sang it that day. I followed it with "Shoes Full of Sand," a song I wrote for him when we first fell in love.

Then I got out the ninety-nine-cent bottle of Mr. Bubble. As Annie chased the bubbles, they caught on the breeze, flew up over the house and into the sky. I thanked God for giving me Fred and thanked Fred for everything he had given me. I wished him well on his journey and told him I hoped to see him again someday.

In that moment, I knew we were meant to be together just for a while. Before he left, Fred gave me everything I needed to go on. He gave me a house, a car, and so many other material things that I never would have been able to afford on my own. He took me on trips to wonderful places I might never have seen. He also gave me the kind of love most people never know. He made me feel special, worthy, and strong. Fred loved life; he didn't wear himself out worrying about the small stuff. He taught me that. In making me Fred's caregiver through his illness, God gave me new wisdom, a kinder heart, and an understanding that our time here is temporary.

Every time I see a rainbow-tinted bubble floating in the air, I will think of Fred, raise a glass of cabernet sauvignon, and smile.

Epilogue

Thirteen years later, I still live in the house in South Beach that Fred and I bought together. I still write and play music. I struggle to take care of everything on my own, but I manage. I still take a low dose of antidepressant. I'll always have problems with depression and anxiety, but I'm getting better at riding the waves.

I had my second cataract surgery, and my vision is good.

Annie lived a very long life for a dog. Her muzzle turned white with age, she went deaf, and we were both plagued with arthritis. We took care of each other for fifteen years, still walking through the forest until she couldn't anymore.

Fred's children are in their forties and fifties now. Gretchen is a grandmother. Ted is married and living in Idaho. Michael, a quiet wanderer, enjoys going on wilderness adventures in Oregon and beyond.

I'm not sure what my role is with them now that their father is gone, but I will always welcome them as an important part of my life.

I wrote this book to share our story, to let people know what it's really like in the world of Alzheimer's. This disease can happen to any of us. It's not always old people who get it. It's not necessarily people who neglect their health. Fred was strong, intelligent, upbeat, and active.

I pray that a cure for Alzheimer's can be found soon. Millions of people suffer with this disease and other types of dementia. Please offer support however you can. Visit the Alzheimer's Association website, https://www.alz.org, for information.

Resources

A Place for Mom—**https://www.aplaceformom.com**. This nonprofit organization helps families find appropriate care facilities for their loved ones. They helped me find Timberwood, the memory care center where Fred spent almost two years.

Alzheimer's Association—**https://www.alz.org**. This is the main clearing house for information about Alzheimer's disease and other forms of dementia.

Dementia and Seizures—**https://www.alzheimers.org.uk/blog/what-link-between-seizures-and-dementia**. This site offers information on the link between Alzheimer's and seizures.

Driving Assessment—**https://www.alz.org/help-support/caregiving/safety/dementia-driving**. This site provides general information about driving and dementia. The procedures in each state are different, so check with your local Department of Motor Vehicles.

In-Home Care—**https://www.alz.org/help-support/caregiving/care-options/in-home-care**. Finding trustworthy caregivers to come to your house is challenging. This site offers some help.

Medicaid, the federal program that helps low-income families pay for nursing home care—**https://www.medicaid.gov/medicaid/eligibility/index.html**. Medicaid—not the same as Medicare—can be confusing and frustrating, but here's a place to start.

Mini-Mental Status Exam—**https://www.dementiacarecentral.com/mini-mental-state-exam.** Find general information here on the tool used most often to assess cognitive ability.

Music for Alzheimer's Patients—**https://www.mayoclinic.org/diseases-conditions/alzheimers-disease/expert-answers/music-and-alzheimers/faq-20058173** Music can work magic with Alzheimer's patients. Read about it here.

National Institute on Aging: Getting Help with Alzheimer's Caregiving. **https://www.nia.nih.gov/health/getting-help-alzheimers-caregiving**. This site is loaded with information and links to valuable resources.

Nursing Home ombudsman program—**https://www.nursinghomeabuse.org/nursing-home-abuse/ombudsman.** If things don't seem okay at the facility caring for your loved one, you have every right to complain. Find information here.

Safe Return Program—**https://www.dshs.texas.gov/alzheimers/return.shtm**. Wandering is common for dementia patients. With a Safe Return medallion identifying their name, condition and contact information, odds of getting them home unscathed greatly increase.

Therapy Dogs—**https://petpartners.org.** Animals can work wonders with patients who can no longer communicate with people. Find out here how it works.

Books and Magazines:

ALZ magazine—**https://www.alzmagazine@alz.org.** It's all about Alzheimer's, and subscriptions are free.

AlzAuthors book club—**https://alzauthors.com.** There are more books about Alzheimer's than can possibly be listed here. Visit this website for books about Alzheimer's, including advice for patients and caregivers, memoirs, and ways to explain the disease to children.

Brain & Life magazine—**https://www.brainandlife.org.** This free magazine is full of fascinating information about dementia and other neurological disorders.

Kuhn, Daniel. *Alzheimer's Early Stages: First Steps for Family, Friends and Caregivers.* Hunter House, 2013.

Lick, Sue Fagalde. *Gravel Road Ahead.* Finishing Line Press, 2020. This is my poetry chapbook about our family's Alzheimer's experience.

Mollier, Mary, MSW, CAS. *Alzheimer's Through the Stages.* Althea Press, 2019.

Mace, Nancy L. *The 36-Hour Day.* Johns Hopkins University Press, 2017.

Weatherill, Gail, RN, CAEd. *The Caregiver's Guide to Dementia.* Rockridge Press, 2020.

Acknowledgments

No Way Out of This started as more than a thousand pages of tearful journal entries, which, with lots of help, I was able to turn into this book.

I am grateful to the following publications for publishing pieces of the story: *Creative Nonfiction*; *Hippocampus* in its anthology *Dine*; Chatter House Press in its anthology *Biting the Bullet: Essays on the Courage of Women*; *Full Grown People*; *Persimmon Tree*; *The Sun* Readers Write, and *Oregon Quarterly*.

Thank you to Willamette Writers and Writers on the Edge for education, inspiration, and support. I thank Clare Hall, Teresa Wisner, and Dorothy Blackcrow for their tough-love critiques in the early stages, Jennifer Lauck for the workshop that showed me how to structure this book, and Jessica Jarlvi for her skilled editing and her ability to build my confidence while insisting that certain passages absolutely must be revised.

I thank AlzAuthors, the Newport Alzheimer's support group, and the Alzheimer's Association for all they do for families dealing with dementia.

Thank you, Brooke Warner, Shannon Green, and all the She Writes Press staff for your help producing this book.

I thank my church family at Sacred Heart Church in Newport, especially Pat and John Stern, Tim and Teresa Grady, Georgia York, Mary Lee Scoville, Roy Robertson, and Father Brian Allbright, my neighbors Pat and Paula Walsh, the Tuesday afternoon docents crew at the Oregon Coast Aquarium, the Coastal-Aires barbershop chorus, the outstanding staff at Timberwood Court, and the caregiving staff at Aging Wisely with Heartfelt Hands.

Thank you, Reatha Ryan, psychiatric nurse practitioner, and Dr. Richard LaFrance for your kindness and wisdom.

Thank you to my late father, Ed Fagalde, who knew exactly what I was going through because he had lived it with his own father. Dad, your voice on the phone was my lifeline.

Thank you to Fred's children, Gretchen, Michael, and Ted Lick, and my brother, Mike Fagalde, for putting up with having a writer in the family.

My biggest thanks go to Frederick Allan Lick, whose most difficult years and most intimate problems are shared here. Fred, I hope it's okay to talk about this now that you are free of Alzheimer's and enjoying your reward in heaven.

Thank God for making me a writer so I had a place to put everything I experienced in our nine-year Alzheimer's journey. I don't know how I would have survived otherwise.

About the Author

photo credit: Kristin Cole

Sue Fagalde Lick escaped life as a journalist in Silicon Valley to write prose and poetry and play music on the Oregon coast. Author of the chapbooks *Gravel Road Ahead* and *The Widow at the Piano: Poems by a Distracted Catholic*, she has published poems in many journals, most recently in *Cirque, American Literary Review*, and the anthology *Into the Azorean Sea*. Her previous prose books include *Stories Grandma Never Told: Portuguese Women in California, Childless by Marriage, Love or Children: When You Can't Have Both*, and the novels *Up Beaver Creek* and *Seal Rock Sound*. When not writing, she sings and plays piano, guitar, and mandolin at St. Anthony's Catholic Church and wherever people will listen. Visit her website at https://www.suelick.com.

SELECTED TITLES FROM SHE WRITES PRESS

She Writes Press is an independent publishing company founded to serve women writers everywhere. Visit us at www.shewritespress.com.

Crash: How I Became a Reluctant Caregiver by Rachel Michelberg $16.95, 978-1-64742-032-1
When Rachel's husband, David, survives a plane crash and is left with severe brain damage, she is faced with a life-shaking dilemma: will she be the dutiful Jewish girl she's always thought of herself as and dedicate her life to caring for him—despite the fact that she stopped loving him long before the accident?

Don't Leave Yet: How My Mother's Alzheimer's Opened My Heart by Constance Hanstedt. $16.95, 978-1-63152-952-8
The chronicle of Hanstedt's journey toward independence, self-assurance, and connectedness as she cares for her mother, who is rapidly losing her own identity to the early stage of Alzheimer's.

Her Beautiful Brain: A Memoir by Ann Hedreen. $16.95, 978-1-93831-492-6
The heartbreaking story of a daughter's experiences as her beautiful, brainy mother begins to lose her mind to an unforgiving disease: Alzheimer's.

The Memory of All That: A Love Story about Alzheimer's by Mary MacCracken. $16.95, 978-1-64742-417-6\
Deeply in love, Cal and Mary brave divorce, marry, and help each other succeed in their work—Cal becomes a renowned inventor, Mary a best-selling author—only to be faced, years later, with their biggest challenge of all: Alzheimer's. It's a battle they can't win— but Alzheimer's doesn't win either, because Cal and Mary's love persists throughout and beyond their battle.

Sandwiched: A Memoir of Holding on and Letting Go by Laurie James $16.95, 978-1-63152-785-2
After her mother has a heart attack and her husband's lawyer delivers some shocking news, James finds herself sandwiched between caring for her parents, managing caregivers, raising four daughters, and trying to understand her husband's choices—so, to keep herself afloat, she seeks therapy, practices yoga, rediscovers nature, and begins to write. Will it be enough to keep her family together?